THE GAY 90s

THE GAY 90s

What the Empirical Evidence Reveals About Homosexuality

PAUL CAMERON

ADROIT PRESS
FRANKLIN, TENNESSEE

Adroit Press
P.O. Box 680365
Franklin, Tennessee 37068-0365

ISBN: 1-884067-01-8

CONTENTS

FOREWORD

William L. Playfair

T he *Gay 90s* is a solid research effort that examines the science and politics that underpin the Gay rights movement. Dr. Cameron traces the assembling and ordering of the scientific community's assault on traditional values to the National Research Council just after WWI. While many have rightly attacked the Kinsey report for having begun the process of 'homosexualizing" our culture, few realize that the National Research Council (NRC) prepared the way for and funded Kinsey. Fewer still appreciate the extent to which the NRC defended and promoted Kinsey against the scientists of his day who identified and denounced his excesses.

Cameron stands alone in having examined, line by line and claim by claim, the 1950s' Evelyn Hooker studies that "proved" homosexuals were normal. He shows that, as so often happens in science, people read the abstracts and the conclusions, but failed to examine the actual details of her work. A generation of psychiatrists and psychologists have been reared on the notion that the Hooker studies proved, in a controlled test, that homosexuals were no different from heterosexuals. Cameron reveals that this interpretation was only made possible by ignoring two thirds of the results. Yet, one can review the encyclopedias and court cases and find this erroneous interpretation presented as scientific truth.

His extensively cited review of the relevant scientific evidence concerning the etiology of homosexuality, as well as his expose of homosexual practices and the violence and child molestation which result from this lifestyle, is more complete and comprehensive than one can find anywhere else. His insights into the development of the dropping of the military ban on homosexuals come from the "inside" so the reader is able to observe how this transformation of policy came to be. As one D. C. politician noted, "this will be the activists' Bible on homosexuality."

Fifty years ago Pitrim Sorokin studied the life spans of rulers and potentates and found that they averaged only 54 years. Yet Christian saints living at the same time, eating inferior food, living in poorer housing, and often working under incredible privation, averaged 69 years of life. The detailing of the life span of another group given to sexual excess—the homosexuals—reveals the same kind of pattern. I am honored to have been part of the research team that nailed down the life span of homosexuals. I believe that the relative brevity of homosexual life should end the twin calls for gay rights and the promotion in our schools of the homosexual lifestyle. *The Gay 90s* tells the reader how the data was collected and what it all means.

This work demonstrates the importance of empirical research in current social policy formulation and adoption. "Published science" now has a canonical place in our society. As a wise man once noted, "the race is not always to the swift, nor the victory always to the strong." Oftentimes the marketing of a scientific finding is far more important than the finding itself.

The extent to which Big Business and Big Government have promoted the homosexual agenda is extensively documented. Especially troubling are the many concrete examples of the federal government, utilizing our tax dollars, to attack religion in general and Christianity in particular.

The elite of our society seems determined to alter the nature of society itself. Contemptuous of history, devoid of principle, this elite seems determined to destroy the only value system that has actually worked in the past and still works—the one practiced by a majority of my fellow Americans—the Judeo-Christian ethic. What Pitrim Sorokin warned about in 1956, that Western Civilization was unleashing sexual forces that would topple us from our position of world leadership, is happening before our eyes. *The Gay 90s* has the credibility and clarity to help America come to its senses.

1

SCIENCE, RELIGION, AND MYTH

T he controversy over homosexuals in the military did not occur in a cultural vacuum. It is one crucial battle in an ongoing sexual revolution that has escalated in intensity since the 1950s. The current assault on our armed forces is simply the latest and boldest strategy of the gay rights brigades, an operation like MacArthur's Inchon Landing, in which a force has struck behind an enemy's lines, cutting off his supply route, leaving him trapped between hostile forces.

If you wanted to pinpoint the beginnings of the U.S. sexual revolution, you might well choose 1921. That was the year the National Research Council [NRC], flush with its success in WWI, organized *The Committee for Research in Problems of Sex*. In a highly partisan account of this historic occasion, Sophie De Aberle[1] of the NRC writes:

> [A] group of responsible American philanthropists, physicians, and scientists felt an urgent demand for study of human sex behavior with all the resources of modern science. Faced with growing national concern about sex problems in the community, they realized that the need for social, educational, and medical information was greater than current science could supply. They believed that sexual behavior, like other problems of human con-

1

duct, depends basically upon biological and psychological factors in human personality. (p. 1)

The physicians and scientists were lesser known figures of the day, but among the philanthropists they numbered the Rockefellers, a family that would play a key role in the sexual revolution for the better part of the twentieth century. And they began early: Shortly after the "white slavery" scandal broke in 1910, John D. Rockefeller, Jr. helped to organize the *Bureau of Social Hygiene* and, according to De Aberle, "In the nearly thirty years of the existence of the Bureau, Mr. Rockefeller gave it more than $5,800,000 for the 'study, amelioration, and prevention of those social conditions, crimes, and diseases which adversely affect the well-being of society'" (p.4).

Within decades, his descendants, through the Rockefeller Foundation, would be pouring even larger sums into promoting activities that virtually guaranteed the spread of those very same social conditions, crimes, and diseases. Indeed, by the last decade of the twentieth century, many of the crimes would be "decriminalized" and the diseases would be protected by special laws and an entirely new public health policy, designed to shield the sexually promiscuous, while exposing the general public. Once the Committee for Research in Problem of Sex had been formed and began its activities, the decline of sexual probity was rapid. This decline grew in some measure from the narrow and unimaginative view of life these scientists held and from their stubbornness in desiring to impose that view on society at large. De Aberle defines this attitude as it were somehow broadening and visionary: "These men, like the psychologists and anthropologists, were mentally prepared to look upon human sex behavior as the result of chemical, physical, and mental factors, all of which demanded investigation by the methods and in the spirit of unfettered scientific inquiry" (p. 7).

It obviously never occurred to any of these people, De Aberle included, that according to their lights, "scientific inquiry" was inherently "fettered" or restricted, since, by definition, it brushed aside some of the most important dimensions of human experience: religion, morals, emotions, sensibilities, and esthetics—all of which are probably more important to a complete understanding of human sexuality than all the measurements that scientists could possibly record. (That is why the Bible, while saying nothing prescriptive about chemistry or physics, has much to say about sex.) In their intellectual narrowness, these "sex scientists" weren't even neutral in their treatment of other dimensions of human behavior. In some instances they were quite hostile. For example, very early in its life, the Sex Committee took aim at the underpinnings of traditional morality—the church. They proclaimed that "puritanism" (which they ignorantly equated with Christianity) had inhibited the objective, scientific examination of human sexual behavior. Again their official historian, Sophie De Aberle:

All through the history of Christian Europe, down to the present century, education and research have largely been carried on within the churches or close to them. The path of scholarship and science has therefore run very close to that of theology—the theology of a fundamentally ascetic religion that in principle pitted the spirit against the body and subordinated the latter's claims; that elevated continence to a high rank among the virtues, and recognized celibacy and mortification of the flesh as attributes of religious service. This is not to say that the church neglected the implications of sex, in which it saw both the necessary means of propagating the faithful and also a means of falling from grace; not that the clerics aimed at restraining the physician and the jurist from studying its aberrations from the standpoint of health and law. Nor does it mean that science when emancipated from dogma will necessarily speak in favor of self-indulgence and libertinism; self-denial and moderation are as characteristic of scientists as of any other group of men. It does mean that down to the present century the scientists, sharing the outlook of learned professions that inherited the attitudes of religious conformity, were simply not in a position to think of human sex behavior, scarcely indeed that of other animals, as an honorable subject for disinterested study. (p. 2)

This passage—a good example of the superstitions entertained by a large segment of the modern scientific community—turns the history of the Christian West into a morality play, with religion twisting its black mustaches and blonde, blue-eyed science tied to the railroad track. At the very least, this view is flawed in the following ways:

- As most well-educated people know, the separation of science and religious dogma began in the renaissance, was well on its way by the 18th century, and was virtually achieved by the latter half of the 19th. Indeed, a main theme of 19th-century English literature is the war between faith and science, as reflected in the works of major writers like Tennyson, Browning, Matthew Arnold, Thomas Huxley, and others. The second half of the 19th century was an age in which scientists at every intellectual level had declared their independence from theology. So the history of the question hardly supports De Aberle's statement that "it required a good deal of courage" (p. 30) to organize the *Committee for Research in Problems of Sex.* As a matter of fact, just a few pages later (p. 9) she cites an objective, scientific sex survey of college men by Dr. Max J. Exner, published in 1915, six years prior to the formation of the NRC sex committee. Dr. Exner was employed by the *Young Men's Christian Association.*

- The description of Christianity as "pitt[ing] the spirit against the body" displays a radical ignorance of Christian dogma. The passage comes closer to describing Hinduism than the only great religion that rests on the ideas of the Incarnation and the Resurrection of the Body.

According to orthodox Christians, God created our bodies as well as our sexuality, so they are both, by definition, "good" until mankind begins to misuse them as a consequence of The Fall. Jesus performed His first miracle at a wedding, a Jewish religious ceremony that blessed the sexual union of a man and a woman. And, like the Jews before them, Christians have taken sex into the church by making marriage one of its most important rituals. "Whom God hath joined together" is a phrase that refers to physical union as well as to spiritual and legal union, and that is why the church is so hard on adultery—not only because the marriage partner is betrayed, but also because God, a party to the physical aspects of marriage, is betrayed as well.

The vast majority of Christians don't practice celibacy. They follow a couple of basic rules regarding sexuality: don't have sex with anyone but your wife or husband; don't commit perverse acts. These restrictions, commended by all the world's great religions, should not seem "ascetic" to anyone but members of wife-swapping clubs and the National Gay and Lesbian Task Force. Whether deliberate lies or the products of ignorant superstition, "scientific" distortions of history and religion are self-serving fairy tales devised to justify a mean-spirited and cramped view of human behavior.

In creating these fairy tales, scientists like De Aberle hoped to "capture" the study of humanity and say to others who take a broader view of human behavior: "Henceforth, we will be the only ones to make pronouncements on such matters as human sexual behavior, because the rest of you are tainted by morbid religious preoccupations." They knew such a capture had previously taken place in Germany, where a "Scientific-Humanitarian Committee" had been formed shortly before the turn of the century and had already funded several studies based on the premise that the sexual behavior of human beings could be studied in a philosophical and moral vacuum, like the behavior of rats. So following the lead of the Germans, the National Research Council through its Committee for Research in Problems of Sex, began to fund studies, using money from the federal government as well as from the Rockefeller Foundation—projects that laid the groundwork for a completely "scientific" view of sexual behavior. Then, all of a sudden, the activities of the NRC were thrust into the spotlight with the funding of the Kinsey studies. Alfred Kinsey, in his famous "report" *Sexual Behavior in the Human Male* (1948)

for the first time stated unequivocally that man was more inhibited in sexual activity than other primates and that such
inhibitions proceeded from religious "taboos." These he
treated as no more than foolish superstitions, whether they
were patterns of behavior followed in primitive societies or
Judeo-Christian rules governing marriage.

Forty years ago, Kinsey was a voice crying in the wilder-
ness, supported by the NRC but dismissed or severely criti-
cized by most scientists, who saw grave defects in his methodology. The general public also distrusted the Kinsey
message, and understandably so. He was characterizing as su-
perstitious nonsense the most important institutions in society—the church and the family. (Marriage, he suggested, was
like prostitution—no more than an exchange of sex for
money.) However, out of Kinsey's pioneer studies grew a
new scientific "discipline"—sexology, the study of sexual behavior. This "discipline" was slow in developing, and its initial practitioners were either Kinsey's disciples or others of
the NRC committee. Today most sexologists can trace their
lineage to the Kinsey Institute at the University of Indiana or
to programs that were founded by Kinsey alumni. As a consequence, a strong bias against religious prescription has become an essential part of the lore of sexology. Kinsey would
not hire assistants who did not look with equanimity on all
sexual behaviors, including adultery, homosexuality, and bestiality. Religion, then, has been the enemy of sexologists and
sexology from the very beginning.

With the acceptance of sexology as a legitimate science, and
with the strong influence of sexologists on the practice of psychology, the scientific community in general has now come to
accept the idea that religion imposes unnatural restraints on human sexual behavior, that these restraints are "unhealthy" and
even destructive to individuals and to society, and that the only
people with license to talk about human sexuality are the social
scientists, who deal in facts and predictable patterns of behavior.

On what evidence does such a view rest? Do human beings behave in perfectly predictable ways?

Never have.

Never will.

Indeed, many of the best social scientists admit the limitations of their discipline and acknowledge the modest role that scientific data can play in solving the mystery of human existence. Those who argue to the contrary bear watching. They are either deceiving themselves or trying to deceive the rest of us. If a purely "scientific" view of human behavior is unproven and unprovable, then what can we say about a belief in its absolute validity? Is this "science" in the traditional sense or is it something else? There is much that is unscientific about contemporary science, particularly when it is used to influence public policy. Indeed, those most likely to speak for the scientific establishment in the current debate over sexuality are among the least trustworthy experts.

- The Kinsey studies, as I will demonstrate, have been exposed as ill-conceived and improperly executed, yet scientists and educators nationwide continue to cite Kinsey statistics as authoritative and to use them in influencing public policy.

- Studies have clearly indicated that sex education programs emphasizing explicit information and contraception have no significant positive effect on student attitudes or behavior. Health warnings often have a modest dampening effect upon the sexual activities of adults, yet the same warnings, because they broach issues that excite the young, often increase teenage sexual activity and risk. Yet the health-care and education communities spend hundreds of millions of dollars annually to promote such programs, while often attacking abstinence programs, which, according to well-documented research, are actually effective.

- Despite the high failure rate of condoms in preventing unwanted pregnancy (around 16–18 percent among teenage girls), the scientific community continues to recommend these devices as a reliable contraceptive and means of avoiding AIDS.

- Dr. Louis Girard of Dallas compiled case histories of over 2,500 sex offenders who had been castrated. He determined that the repeat offenses were reduced from approximately 50 percent to 3.5 percent. Yet a scientist at respected Georgetown University, citing no data of his own, announced that rather than decrease sexual attacks, castration might well increase them.

This obsessive rejection of legitimate research suggests that the people involved have abandoned any pretense of objectivity and indeed are moved by basically irrational forces. Though they pretend to be scientists, they are vehemently anti-scientific, rejecting or perverting all evidence, however convincing, that does not support their narrow point of view. They hide or distort reasoned dissent. They shout down all opposition at scientific gatherings. While they decry those who live "by faith," they too "live by faith." But it is a faith that can ignore, distort, or invent "facts" as they are required to maintain their belief-system.

They falsify data to gain ideological advantage. They use coercion and physical intimidation to further their agenda. They utilize outdated or discredited science to subvert legitimate institutions for their own ends, and they employ invective and public humiliation as tools to silence their opponents.

So the National Research Council and its followers have not merely managed to discredit traditional religion in the eyes of the scientific community. They have destroyed objective science and succeeded in establishing a dogma of their own, one that demands unreasoning belief and obedience. On the other hand, orthodox Christians and Jews now find themselves in the enviable position of holding most of the scientific cards. The legitimate studies support a traditional view of sexuality, and the best social scientists are arguing that we must maintain the old-style family if we are to save our society from chaos. Slowly, inch-by-inch, scientists who support sexual orthodoxy are beginning to make an impact on public opinion, not by appeals to faith, but by the use of legitimate scientific evidence.

With this background in mind, it is much easier to understand the current scientific debate on such matters as teenage pregnancy, sex education, and gay rights. All of these matters are of particular interest to the secular zealots in our midst because such issues are crucial to the sexual revolution and the new creed that proposes a society virtually free of all sexual restrictions. It is for this reason, among others, that sexual revolutionaries either ignore science or distort its findings in order to maintain their opposition to traditional morality and their commitment to a "quasi-scientific" view of the world, one that cannot be submitted to the rigors of genuine scientific scrutiny.

In order to understand better the mind of these new zealots, we must ask ourselves several questions. How accurate and authoritative are their studies of sexual behavior? How much do they really tell us about the way people behave, and how can we know when they are useful or when they are worthless? In short, how can we distinguish between genuine science and quasi-science? Here are some guidelines to follow.

No studies on human sexuality can be regarded as beyond question or argument.

Every conclusion of every study is subject to challenge. When you read that "social scientists have proven" this or that proposition about sexual behavior, you can be certain that such a statement is false. "Proof" in the sense that physicists use the term is impossible in sexology or psychology or any other social science. There are no laws in these fields—only well-documented or highly tenuous theories that other reputable social scientists can and will challenge.

No study is "the last word on the subject."

The infant study of human sexuality is always "ongoing," and all we really receive are "progress reports" subject to future revision.

For example, studies that investigate the incidence of homosexuality among twins have been conducted for the past 40 years, and every time one supports the idea of genetic transmission, you will hear people say: "This is it. We have finally proven our point." One of these studies appeared in 1991, and homosexual activists and apologists have hailed it as the final proof they had been waiting for. We saw the same response at the publication of the Kallman twin study in 1952.[2] Yet scientists soon found egregious flaws in Kallman's methodology, and within the next few years several more reliable studies appeared that came to different conclusions. The same thing will happen again.

Beware of studies that focus on a small, select group rather than a broad random sampling.

Recent studies on the origins of homosexuality involve fewer than twenty subjects, yet their admirers draw conclusions that are deemed applicable to all human beings in every age and society. These studies may be limited in scope because those who conduct them are anxious to publish results that will further the "gay rights" agenda. A sense of urgency impels them to take short cuts and to draw hasty conclusions. They are encouraged in this behavior by the immediate attention that such studies receive from the media and because the results are seldom challenged by anyone of stature. The recent LeVay study of 19 brains is a good example. As I will demonstrate later in this chapter, this research is so flawed as to prove virtually useless in determining anything about sexual orientation and brain configuration. Yet the study is currently being touted as a finding of major significance by the scientific establishment.

*Studies that treat primitive societies
as models worthy of analysis and emulation are
notoriously untrustworthy, particularly when they are
used to further the idea of cultural relativism.*
American and European scholars are perennially dimwitted
when they deal with primitive cultures. Among other things,
they tend to romanticize people who don't have automobiles
and washing machines and to attribute to them an innate good-
ness unspoiled by Western civilization, the modern equivalent
of Rousseau's "noble savage." In many cases, these tribes are
vicious and mean-spirited trolls, by no means the unspoiled
paragons of virtue they are made out to be. Like modern industrial societies, they vary in sensibility and virtue. Also, in
the study of primitive tribes, language has been a barrier to
understanding and so has culture and temperament.

When white Europeans landed in Tahiti, they were told that
certain areas, certain people were "taboo." They immediately
concluded that "taboo" meant forbidden, and to social scientists
the word has held that restrictive meaning ever since. Only after
greater familiarity with these people did Westerners realize that
"taboo" meant "holy" or "belonging to God" and hence forbidden. The difference in meaning was more than incidental. It shed
an entirely different light on the beliefs and practices of the Tahi-
tians, even though anthropologists persisted in translating the
word to mean something much narrower. Today you will hear
them speak of prohibitions against homosexuality as a "taboo,"
thereby distorting the original meaning of the word.

But that is by no means the only example of the misuse or
misunderstanding of primitive cultures. The study by Margaret
Mead, *The Coming of Age in Samoa,* was regarded as a classic
for decades, and many social scientists appealed to its authority. Then, after many years of enthronement, it was exposed
for what it was: hopelessly wrong-headed and perhaps even
fraudulent. Currently, some social scientists are using what on
the surface appear to be sexual practices among primitive
tribes to "prove" that Americans should change their laws and

alter their sex practices. In general I would make this point: just because some primitive tribe or foreign nation condones sexual practices condemned in our own society doesn't mean that there is no universal morality, no right or wrong. In the first place, *some societies are better than others.* Anyone who doubts that statement must contend with the argument that Nazi Germany was no more reprehensible than any other modern nation. And in the second place, while societies may differ as to sexual practices, *no society in the history of the world has believed that anyone can have sex with anyone else at any time.* If primitive tribes want to restrict the practice of sex to certain phases of the moon or practice polygamy, social scientists tell us we are not to be judgmental. Yet when presented with the prohibition of sex outside of monogamous marriage in Western societies, these same people sniff contemptuously at such patent superstition. Surely the majority of people in our society have the same rights as the aborigines of New Guinea.

Such devices as statistics and graphs should be examined carefully to make certain they follow prescribed methodology and the rules of fair discourse.
In a recent study on the origins of homosexuality, I found a statistical error of some import. The authors (Bailey and Pillard) claimed a significant difference between groups. However, according to the generally accepted rules of statistics, no significant difference existed. The study relied heavily on this seeming distinction, and the press picked up the study and reported its conclusions without critical examination.

Years ago, a marvelous book appeared called *How to Lie with Statistics* that demonstrated the dishonest use of graphs, tables, and charts to exaggerate differences or to minimize them. Scale is everything, so look carefully at the numbers and determine if your mind is being manipulated by graphics or the creative arrangement of figures.

Many studies are rigged. Examine carefully the methodology of the study to make sure it has not been deliberately structured to reach a certain conclusion.
Several of the most widely quoted studies on sexual conduct were skewed from the start. One researcher chose to sample from groups where a large percentage of respondents were sure to have engaged in perverse behavior. Another openly eliminated anyone who might disprove the thesis; and when a significant number slipped through the net, these were in turn eliminated. Such manipulation is not uncommon among studies that seek to overturn traditional morality and establish sexual license as the norm. The stakes are very high in this cultural Armageddon, and people who will allow any kind of sexual conduct often permit themselves other liberties of conscience as well.

Having defined the limitations of scientific studies, let me hasten to say that science is by no means useless in the debate over the sexual revolution, nor do religious people have anything to fear from an honest and meticulous scientific study of the subject. Indeed, if anyone should shrink from legitimate scientific inquiry, it is those who favor sexual license; and as noted above, they are becoming more and more anti-scientific in their attitudes and practices. The best science, conducted without a methodology designed to serve political or social bias, supports the idea of traditional Christian sexual morality, bolstered by strong religious prescription and a tough legal system, including one that forbids obscenity and pornography, particularly if such materials might influence the young. The worst science falsifies or misuses data to serve a political and social agenda.

In order to illustrate these key points, we will first examine several examples of key research by well-known scientists who have distorted or misrepresented the nature and frequency of sexual behavior. These studies are significant because they have been accepted without serious question, not only by a substantial segment of the news media and general public, but also by the medical and scientific establishment. Their influence on public policy has been incalculable, and they have become a part of legal literature as well as the scientific canon. Yet they are all demonstrably flawed and in some instances suspiciously so.

THE KINSEY STUDIES

As noted above, Kinsey is regarded by many as the first "sexologist," and his performance has set the standard for those who have followed. As a consequence, most of the work in the field has been ill-conceived, careless, and ideological. The errors in Kinsey's methodology and the brash authoritarian tone of his conclusions have been incorporated into later works by his students and spiritual disciples. On the whole they are an arrogant and irresponsible lot, full of grim certitude and high-flown nonsense.

Kinsey came to sex studies accidentally. A professor of biology at the University of Indiana, he had spent most of his career catching and measuring tens of thousands of gall wasps to see if they were undergoing some mutation that might illustrate the theory of evolution. Then something happened to alter his life: the University developed an interdisciplinary sex education course that involved teachers from a variety of disciplines—from biology to theology. Kinsey was the biologist. Soon he had captured the course, stopped measuring wasps, and started recording the sexual histories of his students—a scientific exercise that became an obsession. Before long he was journeying to Chicago and other large cities, frequenting homosexual bars, encouraging the men he met there to answer detailed questions about their most intimate sexual practices. He also broadened his interviews to include civic clubs, professional organizations, hitchhikers—and inmates of penitentiaries.

With backing from the National Research Council and the Rockefeller Foundation, he transformed his haphazard inquiry into a full-blown study that would eventually involve thousands of case histories and culminate in two books that have helped to alter the moral landscape of America and civilized nations throughout the world. Those books were *Sexual Behavior in the Human Male* (1948) and *Sexual Behavior in the Human Female* (1953). The first of the volumes, known popularly as "the Kinsey report," became a best seller, largely because of enthusiastic, if careless, coverage by the popular press. For the most part, the scientific community expressed skepticism, and a number of reputable figures wrote highly critical reviews, pointing out numerous errors in methodology. Yet because of financial support and continued endorsement by the NRC, the Kinsey report outlived its more distinguished detractors and survived to be described as a "classic study," accepted by a later generation of scientists who were less scrupulous in their skepticism, less well-trained in methodology.

To a generation of ardent worshippers at the shrine of quasi-science, Kinsey's studies became Holy Scripture, along with Marx, Freud, Darwin, and Keynes—a set of laws and prescriptions to be accepted without question, the pure dogma of the new secular faith.

The *Male* volume said, among other things, that 4 percent of those interviewed had been homosexuals for their entire lives and 10 percent had been predominantly or exclusively homosexual for at least three years. It is this latter figure that gay activists now use when they say that 25 million Americans are homosexual—10 percent of an estimated 250 million population. This 10 percent figure has been of enormous importance to the homosexual activists and their agenda. If the percentage is accurate, then homosexuals comprise one of the largest minorities in the country, much larger than the Jewish population (at approximately 2.5 percent), only slightly smaller than the black population (at 12 percent). So at 10 percent, the homosexuals would constitute a formidable voter bloc if organized, one that could easily make the difference in elections at every level of government. It is this perceived potential for political power that has cowed most politicians in recent years and contributed to the unprecedented successes of the gay rights agenda (though there is no convincing evidence that they have ever made a difference in any election, except at the local level in areas where they have gathered). We would not be exaggerating to say that without Kinsey there would be no gay rights, since much of their political power rests on the illusion of large numbers. Yet the Kinsey study was poorly designed and executed. Its conclusions are absurd. It has virtually no legitimate utility at all. And the 10 percent figure is among its most outrageous exaggerations. Consider the following facts:

- Of the 4,300 men interviewed in the homosexual section of the survey, perhaps 20–25 percent were prison inmates. Kinsey's assistants warned him that prisoners were much more likely to have engaged in homosexual behavior than men from the population as a whole, but he scoffed at such an idea, arguing it was impossible to say that those outside of prison would not themselves be behind bars in due course. Later Kinsey would admit that he had been wrong, but only after the *Male* volume had been published and its conclusions widely disseminated.

- Kinsey also included in his sample a large number of histories taken in homosexual bars and rooming houses, thereby compromising the sample even more. You can understand fully the significance of this weighting if you imagine that the Gallup organization, polling the electorate in a presidential election year, would conduct a significant number of its interviews with members of the Democratic National Committee.

- Even Kinsey's student interviews were skewed. As in all his research, Kinsey relied on volunteers from among his students. The problem of volunteer bias potentially affects all studies relying on interviews and questionnaires.

- Psychologist Abraham Maslow, one of the most famous figures of his day, had tested his own students extensively and classified them according to personality—from the most self-assertive to the least self-assertive. Maslow challenged Kinsey to solicit volunteers from this pool of already classified students to see if a pattern emerged. Kinsey accepted the Maslow challenge, and Maslow later reported that student volunteers overwhelmingly came from a single category—the one most likely to have been involved in adventurous sexual conduct. When Maslow reported his findings to Kinsey, the latter ignored them and never spoke to Maslow again.

- Kinsey's method of soliciting information was designed to wring confessions out of reluctant interviewees. In many instances it may have led to false data. According to coauthor and biographer Wardell Pomeroy[3] when Kinsey questioned prisoners—and they constituted a significant percentage of his sample—he offered them soft drinks, candy, and tobacco. (At the time, bottled soft drinks were not permitted in Indiana prisons.) When prisoners refused to admit to certain behaviors, Kinsey would throw up his hands in disgust and tell them that if they persisted in lying, he would terminate the interview and send them back to their cells. According to Pomeroy, they usually told Kinsey what he wanted to hear. Pomeroy fails to note any connection between the treats the prisoners received, Kinsey's threats, and the fact that recalcitrant interviewees ended up admitting to the sexual behavior in question. It seems likely, however, that prisoners might have considered a false admission of sexual deviancy a small price to pay for a few hours away from their cells with free cold drinks, snacks, and cigarettes.

- And even if Kinsey's studies were beyond challenge, they still did not say what the gay activists maintain. Kinsey never said that 10 percent of the population was homosexual. He said that 10 percent of adult white males had been predominantly homosexual for a period of 3 years. Kinsey's *Female* volume concluded that about 2–6 percent of women had engaged in homosexual conduct comparable to the 10 percent referred to in the *Male* volume. If you combine the two, you get a figure of approximately 6–8 percent of adults. Not 10 percent.

But gay activists are not the only ones to cite the 10 percent figure:

- Testifying before the American Bar Association House of Delegates in 1989, Bryant Welch, Executive Director of the American Psychological Association, proclaimed: "[A]ll the research support[s] the conclusion" that homosexual orientation "is found consistently in about 10 percent of the male population. . . ." Welch went on to say that "research show[s] that across different historical eras and in totally different cultures the incidence of homosexuality remained the same irrespective of public attitudes and prohibitions."[4]

- In 1991, Richard Simon, editor of *The Family Therapy Networker,* wrote that from "Kinsey's historic study in the 1940's to the present, surveys consistently show that 10 percent of the population is either gay or lesbian—that's 25 million people."[5]

- *Fortune* has stated: "Kinsey's classic 1948 studies suggest that about 10 percent of American adults are homosexual, a figure that more recent surveys support."[6]

- *USA Today* has referred to "USA's 25 million gay men and lesbians."[7]

- Even a more conservative newspaper such as the *Washington Times* has blandly asserted: "10 percent of American men are homosexual and 5 percent of women are lesbian,"[8] offering no authority, assuming the figure is universally accepted.

But what is the truth about other sex surveys? Do they all, as Bryant Welsh unequivocally stated, come to the conclusion that about 10 percent of males and 5 percent of females are homosexual? Is the 10 percent figure not only constant throughout history but also from nation to nation, culture to culture? In fact, no scientific studies have come to the conclusion that 10 percent of males are homosexual, and not one has said that 10 percent of the population is homosexual. If we examine the reputable studies on the subject, we find that few even approach Kinsey's high of ten percent for males. Indeed, most range somewhere between one percent and three percent, with a sizeable number of people refusing to participate in such surveys. Here is a summary of the most reputable scientific studies in the field, those that are reasonably objective, random or likely to be unbiased, and involve a sizeable number of subjects.[9]

- In 1966, Schofield[10] conducted a random study among 1,873 English youth 15–19 years of age and reported that 7 percent of males and 3 percent of females had reported any homosexual contact at all. (Kinsey's figure for American males in the same category was 37 percent!) Since few sexologists suggest that one contact or even several contacts prove sexual orientation, Schofield's study indicates a figure for exclusive homosexuality considerably below 10 percent for males.

- In an unpublished 1966 Kinsey Institute study, cited by Paul Gebhard in a 1972 article,[11] only 8 percent of the males and 1 percent of the females reported any postpubertal homosexual activity. According to Gebhard, this study was based on a sample of 593 male and 584 females interviewed by the National Opinion Research Center at the University of Chicago. Again, this must be compared with Kinsey's 37 percent of males and 21 percent of females reporting some homosexual activity.

- In a nationwide random study of 3,018 adults conducted in 1970, 2.4 percent of males and 1.8 percent of females reported having homosexual relations "fairly often."[12]

- In a 1984 study of U.S. adults, Ubell[13] found that 11 percent had "some homosexual experience." Though this figure is higher than other studies, 11 percent by no means approaches the comparable Kinsey figure of 62 percent.

- After a 1984 study of 2,787 13–18-year-old inner city youths attending clinics in 10 cities, Stiffman and Earls[14] reported that 3.1 percent of males and 0.5 percent of females had engaged in some homosexual activity over the past year.

- In a 1987 study of 540 consecutive admissions to a VA hospital,[15] 1.9 percent of the all-male sample reported engaging in homosexuality in the past ten years.

- Johnson *et al* in a 1987 study[16] of 785 British adults aged 16–64 found that 0.6 percent of males and 0.7 percent of females claimed they had ever had sex with a member of their sex.

- In a 1989 English study of 480 men with testicular cancer and 480 matched male patients conducted between 1984–1987, Forman and Chilvers[17] reported that in the group with cancer, 2.9 percent reported they "had ever had homosexual intercourse" as compared with 1.7 percent of the other patients.

- In a nationwide survey conducted in Australia in 1986, Ross[18] reported that 11.2 percent of males had "ever" engaged in homosexual activity, and 6.1 percent had engaged in "the last year." The rate for females was 4.6 percent "ever" and 2.7 percent "in the last year." (Note that these figures do not represent exclusive homosexual behavior.) This report is particularly significant since it seems to negate the argument, made by Bryant Welch of the American Psychological Association, that the 10 percent figure held "in totally different cultures . . . irrespective of public attitudes and prohibitions."

- In 1987, Sundet *et al* queried approximately 6,300 Norwegian adults, aged 18–60, and found that 3.5 percent of males and 3.0 percent of females reported any homosexual experience during their lifetime.[19] They also found that 0.9 percent of males and females reported homosexual experience in the past three years.

- In a 1987 study, Schmidt *et al* found that of 1,155 Danish men aged 16–55, 2.9 percent admitted to "some kind of sex with one or more men."[20]

- In a 1988 study of 1,481 U.S. adults, Michael *et al* reported that 2.7 percent of males and 0.1 percent of females had engaged in relations with homosexual partners over the past 12 months.[21]

- In a statewide random telephone survey conducted in Massachusetts in 1988, Hingson *et al* found that 2 percent of males reported homosexual behavior in the past year.[22]

- In 1989, Kotloff *et al* surveyed 1,017 University of Maryland undergraduates and found that 3.3 percent of males said they had engaged in anal intercourse with another male.[23]

- Upchurch *et al*, in a 1989 survey of 607 consecutive patients of an STD clinic in Baltimore, found that 3.6 percent of males reported homosexual experience.[24]

- In a study on homosexual activity by U.S. adults conducted in 1989 by the National Opinion Research Center (NORC), Smith *et al* stated that only 1.2 percent reported any homosexual partners in the past year.[25] As for sexual activity since the age of 18, 90.9–91.6 percent reported only heterosexual partners, 4.9–5.6 percent reported sex with both males and females, and only 0.6–0.7 percent had been exclusively homosexual in their conduct.

- In a 1989 Dallas survey conducted by the Research Triangle Institute, 7.6 percent of males reported some homosexual activity since 1978 and 4.4 percent in the past twelve months. 2.8 percent[26] of females reported homosexual activity since 1978, and 2.1 percent over the past twelve months.

- In 1989–90, Breakwell and Fife-Shaw queried 2,171 16–20-year-olds in two regions of England and found that 2.4 percent of males and 0.9 percent of females had ever received homosexual oral sex.

- In 1989 Melbye and Biggar interviewed a well-drawn random sample of 3,178 Danish adults aged 18–59. Only 2.7 percent of sexually experienced males admitted to any homosexual experience in their lifetime.

- In a 1990 study of 2,655 Croatians aged 15–30, Ajdukovic reported that 1.7 percent of non-virgin males and 2.3 percent of non-virgin females reported having ever engaged in homosexuality.

- Between 1990 and 1991 Johnson *et al* sampled 18,876 individuals aged 16–59 in Great Britain. Only 6.1 percent of males reported homosexual experience, 3.6 percent reported any homosexual partners in their whole life, 1.4 percent reported any homosexual partners in the past five years, and

1.1 percent reported any homosexual partners in the past year.

- In 1991–1992 Spira *et al* did a nationwide random telephone survey of 20,055 French adults aged 18–69. 4.1 percent of males and 2.6 percent of females reported ever having engaged in "homosexual intercourse." In the past 5 years, 1.4 percent of males and 0.4 percent of females reported homosexual intercourse. In the past year only 1.1 percent of males and 0.3 percent of females reported homosexual intercourse.

- In a 1993 report, John *et al* interviewed 3,321 men aged 20–39 and found that only 2.3 percent of sexually active men had engaged in any same-gender sexual activity during the past ten years, and approximately 1.1 percent had been exclusively homosexual during the same period.

- Perhaps the most significant study in the field is a continuing survey by the Federal government on homosexual activity and drug use. By March of 1991, the number of U.S. adults randomly surveyed reached a staggering 119,347, making it the largest study of its kind ever conducted. This study[27] revealed that only 3 percent of males had reported any homosexual activity or IV drug use since 1977! This ongoing study continued to reveal the same proportion as it moved through 1992.

Consider the significance of this long list of studies—as complete as any ever compiled. First, it is obvious that Bryant Welch, Richard Simon, and others, who baldly state that either 10 percent of males or ten percent of the population are more or less exclusively homosexual, are either uninformed or else are ignoring the published data for their own ends. When Welch states that "all research" supports his 10 percent figure for males, he is ignoring the studies listed immediately above, including several conducted by people openly sympathetic to homosexual rights. When Richard Simon argues that 10 percent of the population is homosexual (i.e. male and female), he is making a statement that no study supports, including the 1948 Kinsey Report itself, which, as noted above, does not state that 10 percent of all people surveyed were mainly homosexual for the previous three years—but only the white men.

Second, a significant segment of the scientific community is clinging to the Kinsey estimate out of mindless reverence for the past. The Kinsey study is the Bible of the fledgling religion of sexology and Kinsey an iconic figure. Remove the Kinsey reports that rise like cathedrals to tower above the landscape, and you stare at a bleak horizon, devoid of spires and flying buttresses. All that remains is a cluster of lesser, newer edifices, without significant authority.

Third, while these studies differ in the nature of the questions asked, they all suggest that the number of confirmed homosexuals stands at something under three percent and probably even lower. The reason I say "probably" is because in all studies that depend on voluntary responses, the researcher must take into consideration the number of people who have refused to answer his questionnaire and must attempt to determine the reasons for their rejection. In some of the studies listed above, the refusal rate is in excess of 50 percent. In only a few cases does this rate drop below 20 percent. So what can we say of those people who refuse to answer sex questionnaires? How do we figure them into our calculations? Homosexuals and their apologists like to argue for a higher proportion of homosexuals among those who refuse to answer than among those who consent. They cite the social stigma attached to homosexuality and maintain that out of fear a high number will decline to admit their homosexual behavior, even when their anonymity is guaranteed. In fact, there are good reasons to believe that the very opposite is true.

Maslow's account of his students' reaction to Kinsey's invitation to volunteer for the study suggests that those who are most likely to engage in sexual adventures are also those most likely to volunteer to talk about them. Also, Wardell Pomeroy in his biography of Kinsey reports that homosexual volunteers were the most eager of all interviewees to recount their sexual histories once assured of a non-judgmental ear. It is significant that those

who assume high refusal rates among homosexuals have made
little or no effort to determine whether or not their assumptions are accurate. It would be easy to do so. All sex studies
that explore the question of belief conclude that strong religious convictions significantly curtail the rate of illicit sexual
activity. Indeed, Kinsey reported that devoutness was the single most important factor in determining whether or not a
male or female would engage in sex outside of marriage. De-
vout Jews, Catholics, and Protestants were most likely to observe prohibitions against illicit sexual relations. It would have
been a simple matter to have polled these groups about their
willingness to volunteer for a sex survey and then poll a group
of known homosexuals for comparison. The fact that no significant study of this sort has been conducted suggests that
scientists like Kinsey have been considerably less "scientific"
than they should have been in compiling their data.

Fourth, remember that in several of the studies above, a single sexual experience counts as much as habitual sexual practice. For example, the 3 percent figure in the last study cited
(which focuses on the behavior of 119,347 adults over a ten-
year period) includes not only IV drug use but also a single
instance of experimentation as a teenager or perhaps even a
case of victimization. In other words, if as a eighteen-year-old
you were sexually assaulted by an adult of the same sex, you
could be included in this 3 percent category, despite the fact
that all your subsequent experience was heterosexual. On the
other hand, Kinsey included in his 10 percent figure for males
only those who had been more or less exclusively homosexual
for a three-year period. The 3 percent figure in the NCHS
study would be roughly comparable to Kinsey's 37 percent, a
percentage that appears to be more and more fanciful as studies continue to multiply.

Finally, sexual activity is in some ways the best indicator of
sexual orientation and in some ways perhaps less reliable. If you
base your estimates on what people have actually done (as opposed to what they would prefer to do) you have concrete phe-

nomena on which to base your conclusions rather than someone's report of his or her subjective feelings. It is easy enough to count sexual experiences, particularly if you define "experience" as those culminating in orgasm, as did Kinsey and most of those who followed him. As long as you are comparing apples and apples (i.e. the sexual behavior of homosexuals and heterosexuals), then you are dealing with what is unambiguously "knowable." On the other hand, some argue that it is better to rely on studies that focus on homosexual "desire" or "orientation." Such a focus, they maintain, tells us more about the percentage of homosexuals in the population, since many who feel strong homosexual urges do not fulfill them because of religious strictures, social taboos, or lack of opportunity.

There is some evidence that those who have homosexual desires are very likely to engage in homosexual behaviors. For example, J. Harry[28] in "Sexual Orientation as Destiny" reported an almost perfect correlation of 0.96 between claimed attraction to people of the same sex and homosexual activity. However, we needn't rely on such evidence to deal with the argument that "desire" or "orientation" as an index of the homosexual population supports the oft-quoted 10 percent figure. We have a good many studies that focus on "orientation." A vigorous examination of this research reveals once again the uselessness of the Kinsey data. It also exposes the absurdity of Bryant Welch's statement that "all the research supported the conclusion that homosexuality . . . is a sexual orientation found consistently in about ten percent of the male population. . . ." Here is a compendium of available studies.

- Bell *et al*, summarizing[29] the results of a 1969 sampling by the Kinsey Institute, reported that in assessing the sexual orientation of siblings, 91 percent said "exclusively heterosexual," 7.5 percent said "mainly heterosexual,".5 percent said "bisexual," and only 1 percent said "mainly or exclusively homosexual."

- In 1970, Klassen *et al* asked the question, "Have you ever thought that you might be a homosexual or lesbian?" 3.1

percent of males and 2 percent of females answered "yes." (Of course, allowing the thought to cross your mind and finally affirming your homosexuality are obviously two different things.)[30]

- From 1975–78, Cameron and Ross[31] reported that in a random (cluster) sample of 2,251 over the age of 12, 92.6 percent of males said their desires were exclusively heterosexual, 3.7 percent said they were mainly heterosexual, 1.2 percent said they were bisexual, and 1.9 percent said they were homosexual. Among the females, 90.8 percent said they were exclusively heterosexual, 4.5 percent said they were mainly heterosexual, 1.9 percent said they were bisexual, and 2.0 percent said they were homosexual.

- In a 1983 random (cluster) sample of 4,340 adults from 5 metropolitan areas, Cameron *et al* reported that 2.1 percent of males said they were "not sexual," 90.4 percent said they were exclusively heterosexual, 2.1 percent said they were mainly heterosexual, 2.6 percent said they were bisexual, and 2.8 percent said they were homosexual. Among females in the same study, 3.9 percent said they were "not sexual," 89.0 percent said they were exclusively heterosexual, 3.0 percent said they were mainly heterosexual, 1.7 percent said they were bisexual, and 1.9 percent said they were homosexual.[32]

- Harry, analyzing a 1990 random telephone sample, reported that 3.7 percent of males said they were attracted to members of the same sex.

- Zuliani, after taking a stratified random sample of 6,580 Canadian military personnel, reported that 96.6 percent of the males said they were exclusively heterosexual, 2.0 percent said they were predominately heterosexual, 1.0 percent said they were bisexual, and 0.4 percent said they were homosexual. Among the females, 93.9 percent said they were exclusively heterosexual, 3.6 percent said they were predominately heterosexual, 0.6 percent said they were bisexual, and 1.8 percent said they were homosexual.

- In 1986–87, Remafedi *et al* conducted a stratified cluster sample of 36,741 Minnesota public school students (grades 7–12) and found that 10.1 percent of males were unsure of sexual orientation, 88.6 percent were heterosexual, 0.7 percent were bisexual, and 0.6 homosexual. Among females, 11.3 percent were unsure, 87.7 percent were heterosexual,.8 percent were bisexual, and 0.2 percent were homosexual.

- Schmidt *et al* interviewed 1,155 Danish men, aged 16–55, and found that 0.3 percent said they were bisexual and 0.3 percent said they were predominantly homosexual.

- Trocki, in a 1987 study, found that out of 968 adults in the San Francisco area, aged 18 or older, 97 percent of the males said they were heterosexual, 2 percent said they were bisexual, and 1 percent said they were homosexual. Among females, 98 percent said they were heterosexual, 1 percent said they were bisexual, and 1 percent said they were homosexual.

- Kotloff, in a 1989 random mail survey of 1,017 University of Maryland undergraduate students, found that 95.3 percent of males said they were heterosexual, and 4.7 percent said they were bisexual or homosexual. Among females, 98.6 percent said they were heterosexual and 1.4 percent said they were bisexual or homosexual.

- MacDonald *et al* conducted a random (cluster) sample of 5,514 Canadian college students and reported that 98 percent said they were heterosexual, 1 percent said they were bisexual, and 1 percent said they were homosexual.

- In 1989, Hatfield conducted a nationwide random telephone sample of 4,148 adults and reported that 93.8 percent said they were heterosexual and 6.2 percent said they were bisexual or homosexual.

- In 1990, Runkel, after analyzing the responses to a questionnaire by 1,500 West German respondents, reported that 92.9 percent of the males said they were heterosexual, 3.4 percent said they were bisexual, and 3.8 percent said they were homosexual. Among the females, 93.9 percent said they were heterosexual, 4.5 percent said they were bisexual, and 1.6 percent said they were homosexual.

In these surveys, the question asked was not, "What you have done?" as in the case of the Kinsey studies, but, "What might you prefer to do?" Yet only one study (which deliberately oversampled from cities known for their large homosexual populations) even approached the 10 percent figure. Again, the extravagant claims of gay activists and the American Psychological Association seem to be contradicted by the extant studies—even those conducted by scholars and media who are sympathetic with the gay rights agenda. To give you some idea of what is really going on in the world of science, several years ago I attended a meeting in the Dirksen Building of the U.S. Senate in order to hear a presentation by advocates of Project 10 ("10" for 10 percent of the population), a homosexual youth program instituted in the Los Angeles Unified School District by Virginia Uribe, an avowed lesbian teacher. The meeting was sponsored by U.S. Senator Edward Kennedy and the national office of the PTA. After the meeting, two of the advocates for this highly controversial program were standing in the hallway, and I asked them to explain why they maintained that 10 percent of the population was homosexual. Thinking we were supporters, one of the spokesman said with a wink: "Because 10 percent commands a lot more respect from politicians than 5 percent." And indeed it does. It also commands a lot more respect than 3 percent or 1 percent or 0.8 percent, all of which—given the high refusal rate of most volunteer studies—are arguably better estimates of the homosexual population in the United States than the discredited 10 percent of Dr. Kinsey and his followers.

It is important to note that the lower the rejection rate on such samples, the lower the homosexual percentage tends to be—a hard fact that suggests homosexuals are among the first to submit to such random questionnaires, despite their highly publicized fear of being exposed. This correlation squares with Maslow's published observations on volunteer bias, which demonstrated that the sexually adventurous are much more apt than conventionally minded people to talk about their sex lives with strangers.

The surprising thing about this bogus 10 percent figure is how long it endured unchallenged in the face of all the existing evidence surveyed above. Up until recently, no one citing the 10 percent estimate—from gay activists to scientists to public educators to government officials—had ever bothered to examine the scholarship to which they boldly alluded, perhaps because no one in a position of authority had seriously called the Kinsey estimates into question, despite the fact that two of Kinsey's coauthors had admitted the *Male* sample was skewed.

Let me say parenthetically that since 1975, after conducting a random survey that included questions about sexual orientation, I had stressed the absurdity of the 10 percent figure at scientific meetings and at press conferences year after year. Occasionally my observations were noted and reported. Most of the time they were ignored—even as some evidence in support of my position was accumulating in the scientific literature. Too many people wanted and needed to believe in the 10 percent proposition. After my son, Kirk, received his doctorate in statistics from Stanford, we collaborated on a full-blown presentation of the case against the 10 percent prevalent estimate. We surveyed the literature, both domestic and international, and spent four years analyzing all the available data. Finally, in late 1992, after numerous rejections, our article was tentatively accepted by *Psychological Reports*. At that point we knew that the 10 percent figure was moribund. It would be dead in a matter of months. Sure enough, *Newsweek* got wind of our study and called, asking for a prepublication copy of our findings. They assured us that they would give us full acknowledgment and build the article around our findings. Unfortunately they published a piece somewhat less generous. However, in an article entitled "How Many Gays Are There?" the magazine did acknowledge the weakness of the 10 percent figure and made this admission: "Policymakers and the press (including *Newsweek*) adopted the [10 percent] estimate—despite protests from skeptical conservatives—citing it time and again."

The *Newsweek* article came out on February 15, 1993. On March 31, the *Wall Street Journal* published "Homosexuals and the 10 percent Fallacy," an op-ed piece by Dr. J. Gordon Muir that credited Kirk and me for our work in finding and assembling the evidence. *The Wall Street Journal* has the largest circulation of any newspaper in the United States, and the Muir article made an indelible impression on the consciousness of the nation.

In the wake of these articles, a new scientific study caught the public eye. It was conducted by a team associated with the Battelle Centers in Seattle and published in April, 1993 by *Family Planning Perspectives*.[33] Out of a sample of 3,321 men aged 20–39, in face-to face interviews, only 1 percent reported exclusive homosexuality in the last ten years and only 2 percent had any same-sex experience during the same period. This study merely provided the last straw. The word was finally out: the ten percent figure was on its last legs; the scientific community was ready to read last rites over this Kinsey-rigged superstition. It had taken almost twenty-five years of attack to come to this moment. Talk shows discussed the Battelle report in conjunction with what Muir had revealed in his article. Suddenly the homosexual population had shrunk to a fraction of its size—and in only a matter of weeks.

At this point gay activists adopted a new line. After boasting for years that they numbered ten percent of the population and were therefore entitled to ten percent of society's goodies, they now said numbers didn't matter, that their agenda did not stand or fall on numbers. What's more, they maintained, such studies are always suspect and therefore nothing on which to base public policy. This constituted nothing less than a complete reversal of previous strategy. Yet they weren't able to shift into reverse as easily as they had hoped—because a newly released U.S. Census Bureau study reminded them of their own mindless devotion to studies. Released on April 12, 1993 in *USA Today,* it was a report on the number of homosexual couples counted in the 1990 census—a count that gay activists themselves had demanded. Some had stated that there were at least 6 million homosexual couples living in long-term stable relationships with children. Needless to say, their total estimate for homosexual couples was much, much higher. But the U.S. Census Bureau figures gave the lie to that estimate. The total: a mere 88,200 gay male couples and 69,200 lesbian couples—less than one fifth of one percent of all the couples in the nation. (Unmarried heterosexual couples totaled 3.1 million—a little over 3 percent of the total.) Again, they had gotten caught in a grand deception, the kind of scientific abracadabra that the press had been dutifully reporting for years. The Census Bureau report was ignored or given a few back-page lines by most newspapers, but legitimate scientists took note of its existence. The cat was not only out of the bag; it was yowling on the back fence of every yard in America.

EVELYN HOOKER AND THE NORMALIZATION OF HOMOSEXUALITY

The Kinsey Report did much to legitimize homosexuality among scientists, because many reasoned that if 10 percent of males were routinely engaging in a behavior, it must be accepted as a part of the social landscape. But everyone wasn't convinced by such statistics. After all, many scientists reasoned, if 10 percent of the population were schizophrenic, it wouldn't mean that the condition was either a "normal variant" of human behavior or socially desirable. Schizophrenics are clearly troubled people, and they also make trouble. Homosexuality, for many, was an equally disturbing phenomenon—and therefore equally unacceptable. Indeed, such had been the position of the American Psychiatric Association for most of the twentieth century, as an examination of their *Diagnostic and Statistical Manual* (DSM) indicates.

In the 1918 DSM, homosexuality was not specifically mentioned as a psychopathology. Instead, it was lumped under a category called Constitutional Psychopathic Inferiority—"e.g., criminal traits, moral deficiency, tramp life, sexual perversions and various temperamental peculiarities." At the time such a listing cut against the grain of public opinion, which tended to regard all deviant sexual behavior as morally deficient rather than pathological, sin rather than disease. By 1952, as modern psychological theory gained wider public acceptance, homosexuality was listed in the DSM under "Sociopathic Personality Disturbance," subheaded "Sexual Deviation"—e.g., "the type of the pathologic behavior, such as homosexuality, transvestism, pedophilia, fetishism and sexual sadism (including rape, sexual assault, mutilation)." It is important to note here that sexual problems expanded from two words in 1918 to seven lines in the 1952 DSM and that for the first half of the twentieth century, homosexuality was scientifically categorized as "psychopathic" and "sociopathic." Kinsey's 1948 study helped to alter that perception in the following years. But perhaps as influential was the frequently cited research by Evelyn Hooker, whose paper was first read at the American Psychological Association in 1956 and then appeared as articles in 1957 and 1958.[34]

When "gay activists" summarize Hooker, they always say that her work proved homosexuals were as normal as anybody else. In fact, the work proves no such thing, nor did she, at the time, draw such a conclusion. Let's take a look at how her study developed and what it really proved—if anything.

As reported in the *Los Angeles Times Magazine* (June 10, 1990), Evelyn Hooker first became interested in homosexuality as the result of her friendship with a young homosexual student named Sam From.

Hooker and her husband spent a great of time with From and a male companion and once even drove 400 miles to San Francisco with the homosexual couple to attend a "drag" show. Knowing that she was a psychologist, From encouraged Hooker to undertake research to prove that homosexuals were normal. Because she had no experience in clinical testing (she had conducted experiments with rats), she at first refused; but

From persisted, and finally she agreed to undertake a study. It is important to note that from the beginning, Evelyn Hooker understood what conclusions she wished to reach. Her own perception of homosexuals had been a positive one, and her friend Sam From had assured her that many of his fellow homosexuals were leading normal, happy lives. So she did not enter the project with the objective and dispassionate curiosity of a pure researcher. And indeed her lack of objectivity was obvious in her methodology.

First, she began with the hypothesis that homosexuals were mentally healthy, as healthy as heterosexuals. As she herself said to the *Los Angeles Times* in 1990, "How could my hypothesis have been anything else? I'd seen these men and saw nothing psychopathological in their behavior" (p. 22). (It is interesting to compare these statements with the neighbors and co-workers of mass murderers, who report: "He was a nice fellow, quiet, but friendly. Who could have thought he would have gone berserk and murdered 14 people?")

Rather than attempt to choose a random sample of homosexuals, Hooker allowed Sam From and other members of the Mattachine Society (a gay rights group) to choose subjects for her from among the homosexual community. Given the purpose and import of her study, they chose the most likely prospects. For a "control group," (a sample to use for comparison), Hooker selected a "matched" group of heterosexuals. The homosexual group initially numbered 40. However, after she had reported on the initial stages of the study in 1956,[35] she subsequently, without explanation, dropped 5 of each group. Then she dropped 5 more. As she put it, "If, in the preliminary screening, evidence of considerable disturbance appeared, the individual was eliminated." Eventually she narrowed her group to 30 "normal" homosexuals" and 30 heterosexuals. Her plan was to administer three psychological tests to the 60 participants and then see if trained judges could pick out the homosexuals and whether there was a significant difference between the responses of the two groups. The three tests were:

the Rorschach Test, the TAT, and the MAPS Test. The Rorschach Test, the most famous of the three, consisted of a series of ink blots which the subjects were asked to interpret. The TAT Test (Thematic Apperception Tests) presented pictures of people in various settings and then asked the subject to make up a story involving the people. The MAPS Test (Make-a-Picture-Story) asked the subject to place paper dolls in various situations and then to tell a story about each situation. These tests had been given so many times that a lore had developed that provided psychologists with a key to normality and abnormality.

As in all such testing devices, there are those who believe the tests are fallible and cite numbers of cases where they have not accurately identified pathological subjects. Indeed, clever people who understand the nature of these tests have been able to provide "normal" answers; and for this reason, the courts do not recognize the tests as sufficient to define legal sanity or insanity. No one is sent to jail solely because of a Rorschach test, nor is anyone released from a mental institution solely because they score well on it.

However, Evelyn Hooker based her conclusions about the pathology of homosexuals exclusively on the outcome of these tests as applied to a highly selective group of homosexuals. In other words, she assumed that even though homosexuals engaged in sexual behavior that was, by DSM definition, pathological, they could be regarded as "normal" if they said that they saw the same kinds of images and told the same kinds of stories that normal heterosexuals told. After administering the tests, Hooker handed the results over to expert judges and asked them to pick out the homosexuals from the heterosexuals. On the Rorschach test, the judges did slightly better than chance. One picked 17 homosexuals correctly. The other picked 18. (Mere chance selection would have resulted in 15 accurate picks.)

On the other two tests, however, the single judge easily identified almost all the homosexuals, because, as Hooker pu it, "few homosexuals failed to give open homosexual stories on at least one picture." In other words, on two of the three tests, an expert judge was able to pick the homosexuals solely on the basis of their test answers. Many scientists might have concluded that she had failed to prove her hypothesis.

After all, on two out of three tests, the homosexuals revealed themselves as "different" from heterosexuals, indeed unable to suppress their sexual fantasies. Note, however, the way in which her results have been reported—by scientists as well as by the popular press.

- In a 1990 article, the *Los Angeles Times* gave the following account: "Next, the judges were presented with pairs of tests and asked to distinguish between heterosexual and homosexual. They were able to do so no more accurately than if they had been flipping a coin. . . . Experts agree that it was the first careful, controlled scientific study of the mental health of gay people. . . . 'It was the reference point we always went back to,' says Dr. Judd Marmor, a former APA president and a leading proponent of 'depathologizing' homosexuality." (p. 25, p. 20)

- In his chapter on homosexuality in the prestigious *Comprehensive Textbook of Psychiatry—II,* Marmor states that "Hooker (1957) conducted a comparative study of 30 male homosexuals and 30 male heterosexuals who were matched for age, I.Q., and education. The homosexuals were all rated 6 and the heterosexuals 0 on the Kinsey scale. None of the subjects was in therapy. Two judges independently, without prior knowledge of which subjects were which, reviewed the Rorschach protocols, Thematic Apperception Tests, and Make-A-Picture-Story responses, and tried to distinguish the homosexuals from the heterosexuals, but they were unable to do so." (p. 1516) (Dr. Marmor misrepresented the study in precisely the same language 15 years later in his affidavit in the court case on which we were on opposite sides, *Morales v. Texas.*)

- Dr. Gregory Herek, testifying in *Morales v. Texas,* said: "The classic study in this area was conducted by Hooker (1957). She administered the Rorschach, Thematic Apperception Test, and Make-A-Picture-Story Test. . . . When asked to assess which protocols were obtained from homosexuals, the experts were unable to distinguish respondents' sexual orientation at a level better than chance."

Let's make certain we understand the significant discrepancy between what these experts said about Hooker's study and what she herself said. In her October report she stated that homosexuals were readily differentiated on the TAT and MAPS test, since "few homosexuals failed to give open homosexual stories on at least one picture." She continued by saying, "The second task given the Rorschach judges, of distinguishing the homosexual from the heterosexual records [of the TAT and MAPS tests] when they were presented in matched pairs, *was therefore omitted*" (Hooker, 1957, p. 25, italics added). So the accounts above are in error, and this error is perpetuated in most of the textbooks—and in major court decisions.

It is an astonishing distortion to those unfamiliar with the lengths to which homosexuals and their advocates will go to justify the "gay rights" agenda. Yet Evelyn Hooker's study is only one of many that have been devised and distorted to improve the image of homosexuals in the scientific community and in the general population. Indeed, like many of these studies, Hooker's research tells more about homosexuals than she intended, and much more than Marmor *et al* have been willing to admit. After all, thirty homosexuals—the cream of the crop, the most "normal" that Sam From could find—were unable to refrain from including some homosexual fantasizing while taking the TAT-MAPS tests, *despite the fact they knew they were the guinea pigs in an experiment that would affect the reputation of the entire homosexual population.*

Would heterosexuals under a similar situation be unable to refrain from introducing their sexual fantasies into their narratives? We have no record of the accounts given by the 30 heterosexuals in this study. But we have Hooker's statement that it was the homosexuals rather than the heterosexuals who tipped their hand, suggesting that the heterosexuals did not produce stories of a sexual nature.

Clearly the difference between the homosexuals and the heterosexuals was more than mere orientation. It was also the difference between a normal sex drive kept in proper perspective and an obsessive preoccupation that is irrepressible, that must assert itself despite every reason to remain silent. (We must remember that at the time of this testing, homosexuality was officially regarded as pathological, and those tested had strong motivation to prove themselves normal.)

To understand fully the true meaning of the Hooker research, we must think of the MAPS and TAT tests as the laboratory equivalent of the life we all lead when we are not directly pursuing sexual satisfaction. The life of ordinary situations is represented by the dolls and pictures: the workplace, recreation, church, family activities, casual conversations between people of the same sex and opposite sex. While normal heterosexuals do not attempt to convert these situations into sexually charged occasions, apparently most normal homosexuals do. Remember Hooker said that "few homosexuals failed to give open homosexual stories on at least one picture." So Hooker's study suggests that sexual fantasies among homosexuals are irrepressible, so much so that such people cannot always see ordinary situations and relations as devoid of sexual content, but must, on occasion, interject sexual significance where it does not exist or, at the very least, need not exist. Following the logical conclusions of this experiment, we are compelled to conclude that there is something substantively different about the way homosexuals and heterosexuals look at the world. Their "orientation" colors the world for them and renders them hypersensitive to sexuality.

It is curious that Evelyn Hooker failed to note the larger significance of her study. Why did she toss aside the MAPS and TAT tests as somehow irrelevant, while treating the Rorschach as infallible? A better scientist would have explored the reasons why two tests exposed differences in sexual orientation and one did not. Perhaps Hooker was too inexperienced in the field of clinical testing to understand the importance of these discrepancies. Perhaps she felt reluctant to question the validity of a well-established tool such as the Rorschach Test. Perhaps she thought she was inadequate to the task of evaluating the relative merit of the tests in the light of her experiment. However, it seems more likely that, given her sympathy with the homosexual community, and her "dozens of gay friends," that she desperately wanted the Rorschach Test to be right and the MAPS and TAT tests to be wrong and consequently assumed without attempting to prove that such was the case. Her own overt commitment to the cause of gay rights, both in her published studies and in her public statements, suggests the degree to which she compromised her scientific acumen in order to further ideological ends. And the same could be said of Marmor, Isay, and the rest. They, too, should have raised these obvious questions, even if Hooker did not. Yet they chose not only to ignore the weaknesses in Hooker's methodology, but even went so far as to cover them up by misrepresenting the true nature of her findings.

Indeed, later advocates and activists would say in the wake of the Hooker study that homosexuals lead as healthy and normal a life as heterosexuals. For example, in a study widely quoted in gay rights publications, physician J. Bancroft concludes[36] that "a homosexual lifestyle is compatible with all the criteria of health except fertility." Sociologist-psychoanalyst Ernst van den Haag proclaims categorically[37] that "homosexuality does not shorten life." And in a statement that defies proof, biologist Peter Dusberg asserts that "[male] homosexuality . . . hasn't become any more dangerous in 1980 than it was in Plato's day."[38]

HOMOSEXUAL ACTIVITY AND ITS CONSEQUENCES

The American Psychological Association and the American Public Health Association assured the U.S. Supreme Court in 1986 that "no significant data show that engaging in . . . oral and anal sex, results in mental or physical dysfunction."[39] Indeed, gays claim that the "prevailing attitude toward homosexuals in the U.S. and many other countries is revulsion and hostility. . . . for acts and desires not harmful to anyone."[40]

These claims are crucial to the case for gay rights. If homosexual behavior is as healthy as heterosexual behavior, then the charges against homosexuality are significantly reduced and what remains is the moral or religious argument—an argument that activists dismiss as subjective and irrational, a matter of private prejudice rather than of public policy. On the other hand, if what homosexuals do results in increased danger to health and life, then the gay rights agenda is fraught with peril, not only for individuals who engage in homosexual practices, but also for society, which will have to share both the risk and the expense of what some call no more than an "alternative lifestyle."

In order to address the claims of homosexuals that they are as healthy as heterosexuals, the Family Research Institute considered four questions central to the issue: (1) "What do homosexuals do?" (2) "What, if any, are the medical consequences of such behavior?" (3) "How violent is the homosexual lifestyle?" and (4) "Is there any difference between the average lifespan of homosexuals and heterosexuals?" After an exhaustive survey of the literature and original investigation, we came to some objective and definitive conclusions. Let's take each question in order.

What Homosexuals Do

The major surveys on homosexual behavior are summarized below. Two things stand out: 1) homosexuals behave similarly the world-over, and 2) no more than modest changes in behavior have accompanied the AIDS epidemic. (For example, a 1993 report by the San Francisco Department of Public Health[41] found that the HIV-infection rate among homosexual men ages 17 to 22 has not changed in three years, in part because they are still frequenting the bathhouses and still engaging in dangerous sex practices.)

- Oral sex: Homosexuals fellate almost all of their sexual contacts (and ingest semen from about half of these[42]). Semen contains many of the germs carried in the blood. Because of this behavior, gays who practice oral sex do the next thing to consuming raw human blood with all its medical risks. Since the penis often has tiny lesions (and often those of homosexuals will have been in unsanitary places such as a rectum), individuals so involved may become infected with hepatitis A or gonorrhea (and even HIV, hepatitis B, and hepatitis C). Since many contacts occur between strangers (70 percent of gays estimated that they had had sex only *once* with *over half* of their partners[43]), and gays average somewhere between 10[44] and 110[45] *different* partners per year, the potential for infection is considerable.

- Rectal sex: Surveys indicate that about 90 percent of gays have engaged in rectal intercourse, and about two-thirds do it regularly. In a 6-month long daily sexual diary study,[46] gays averaged 110 sex partners and 68 rectal encounters a year.

  Rectal sex is dangerous. During rectal intercourse the rectum becomes a mixing bowl for: 1) saliva, with its germs, and/or some artificial lubricant; 2) the recipient's own feces; 3) whatever germs or substances the penis has on it; and 4) the seminal fluid of the inserter. Since tearing or bruising of the anal wall is very common during anal/penile sex, and since sperm will readily penetrate the rectal wall (which is only one cell thick) causing immunologic damage, these substances gain almost direct access to the blood stream. Unlike heterosexual intercourse (in which sperm cannot penetrate the multilayered vagina and no feces are present),[47] rectal intercourse is probably the most sexually efficient way to spread hepatitis B and other forms of hepatitis, HIV, syphilis, and a host of other blood-borne diseases.

  Tearing or ripping of the anal wall during anal/penile sex is especially likely with "fisting," where the hand (and sometimes the arm) is inserted into the rectum. It is also common when 'toys' are employed (homosexual lingo for objects which are inserted into the rectum—bottles, carrots, even small animals[48]). The risk of contamination or serious injury is very real.

- Fecal sex: About 80 percent of gays (see table 1) admit to rimming, "inserting the tongue into the anus of partners," and thus ingest medically significant amounts of feces. Those who eat or wallow in feces are probably at even greater risk. In the diary study,[49] 70 percent of the gays had engaged in fecal activity—half regularly—over 6 months. Result? The "annual incidence of hepatitis A in . . . homosexual men was 22 per cent, whereas no heterosexual men acquired hepatitis A." A 1992 report[50] noted that the proportion of London gays engaged in rimming had not declined since 1984.

Table 1
Percentage of Survey Respondents Engaging in Sex Acts

	Source and Date of Sample							
	US 1940	US 1977	US 1983/ 1984	US 1983	Canada 1990	US 1983	London 1985	Sydney/ London 1991
	Ever			During year	In last 3 months	During the month		In last 6 months
Oral/penile	83	99	100/ 99	99	76	95	67	
Anal/penile	68	91	93/98	95	62	69	100	
Oral/anal	59	83	92/92	63	34		89	55/65
Urine sex	10	23	29/					
Fisting/toys		22	41/47	34			63	
Eating feces		4	8					
Enemas		11	11					
Torture sex	22	37	37					
Public/orgy sex	61	76	88					
Sex with minors	37	23	24/					

- Urine sex: About 10 percent of Kinsey's gays reported having engaged in "golden showers" [drinking or being splashed with urine]. In the largest survey of gays ever conducted,[51] 23 percent admitted to urine-sex. In the largest random survey of gays,[52] 29 percent reported urine-sex. Of 655 gays,[53] only 24 percent claimed to have been monogamous in the past year. Yet even among these monogamous gays, 5 percent *drank* urine, 7 percent practiced "fisting," 33 percent *ingested feces* via anal/oral contact, 53 percent *swallowed* semen, and 59 percent received semen in their rectum in the previous month.
- Other Gay Sex Practices

Sadomasochism: As the Table indicates, a large minority of gays engage in torture for sexual fun. Depending on the study, the percent of gays reporting *sex in public restrooms* ranged from 14 percent[54] to 41 percent[55] to 66 percent;[56] 9 percent,[57] 60 percent,[58] and 67 percent[59] reported *sex in gay baths*; 64 percent[60] and 90 percent[61] said that they used *illegal drugs*.

Fear of AIDS may have reduced the volume of gay sex partners, but the numbers are prodigious by any standard. Morin[62] reported that 824 gays had lowered their sex-rate from 70 different partners/yr in 1982 to 50/yr by 1984. McKusick[63] reported declines from 76/yr to 47/yr in 1985. In Spain[64] the average was 42/yr in 1989.

Medical Consequences Of Homosexual Sex

Death and disease accompany promiscuous and unsanitary sexual activity. While the body has defenses against fecal germs, exposure to the discharge of dozens of strangers each year is extremely unhealthy. About 10 percent of gays have eaten or played with feces. Here are some of the consequences:

- Ingestion of human waste is the major route of contracting hepatitis A and the enteric parasites collectively called the *Gay Bowel Syndrome.*
- Consumption of feces has also been implicated in the transmission of typhoid fever,[65] herpes, and cancer.[66]

- The San Francisco Department of Public Health sees "75,000 patients per year, of whom 70 to 80 per cent are homosexual men. . . . An average of 10 per cent of all patients and asymptomatic contacts reported . . . because of positive fecal samples or cultures for ameba, giardia, and shigella infections were employed as food handlers 'n public establishments; almost 5 per cent of those with hepatitis A were similarly employed."[67]

- In 1976, a rare *airborne* scarlet fever broke out among gays and just missed sweeping through San Francisco.[68]

- The U.S. Centers for Disease Control reported that 29 percent of the hepatitis A cases in Denver, 66 percent in New York, 50 percent in San Francisco, 56 percent in Toronto, 42 percent in Montreal, and 26 percent in Melbourne in the first six months of 1991 were among gays.[69]

- The Stockholm study "suggested that some transmission from the homosexual group to the general population may have occurred."[70]

- 70 percent[71] to 78 percent[72] of gays reported ha ing had a sexually transmitted disease.

- The proportion with intestinal parasites (worms, flukes, ameba) ranged from 25 percent[73] to 39 percent[74] to 59 percent.[75]

- As of 1992, 83 percent of U.S. AIDS in whites had occurred in gays.[76]

- The Seattle sexual diary study[77] reported that gays had, on a yearly average:
  - fellated 108 men and swallowed semen from 48;
  - exchanged saliva with 96;
  - experienced 68 penile penetrations of the anus; and
  - ingested fecal material from 19.

No wonder 10 percent of them came down with hepatitis B and 7 percent contracted hepatitis A during the study.

President Clinton recently attempted to lift the ban against immigrants with AIDS and other sexually transmitted diseases. Every year, about a quarter of homosexuals visit another country.[78] Unfortunately the danger of these exchanges does not merely affect homosexuals. In the past, travelers carried so many tropical diseases to New York City that officials had to institute a tropical disease center. And it was a two-way street. Gays likewise carried HIV from New York City to the rest of the world.[79]

Most of the 6,349 Americans who got AIDS from contaminated blood as of 1992 received it from homosexuals, and most of the women in California who got AIDS through *heterosexual* activity got it from men who had also engaged in homosexual behavior.[80]

How Violent is the Homosexual Lifestyle?

In 1992 two Jeffersonville, Indiana lesbians, aged 17 and 16, abducted a 12-year-old girl whom they accused of trying to "steal a girlfriend." The little girl was pushed into the trunk of a car, stabbed repeatedly, and beaten with a heavy metal bar. While still struggling, they poured gasoline on her and set her ablaze. Later that year a Fort Lauderdale, Florida, 14-year-old was convicted of first-degree murder for helping to kill his 40-year-old father. The father "was stabbed 45 times and beaten so badly with an iron skillet that the skillet shattered." The boy confessed that he helped his father's former homosexual lover and roommate kill him so he and the 31-year-old "could live together."

These murders fit traditional psychiatric opinion: excessive violence is naturally associated with other forms of social pathology. From this perspective, those who rebel against society's norms—homosexuals, prostitutes, alcoholics, etc.—are more apt to be violent also. Gay leaders reply that they are not pathological, rebellious, or sexually deviant. They contend that gays are gentle, loving people and that the violence they experience proves that they need special 'hate crime' laws to protect them from non-homosexual 'gay bashers.'

Who's right? Does the excess of violence naturally well up *from within* a pathological gay subculture or do outsiders direct violence *toward* homosexuals? Keeping in mind that only about 2 percent to 3 percent of adults are homosexual or bisexual, let's examine varieties of violence in society at large to see if homosexuality is by nature violent.

Murder and Mass Murder

Although the total number of victims dispatched by a given killer is often in doubt, (e.g., homosexual Henry Lucas claimed that he killed 350), it appears that the modern world record for serial killing is held by a Russian homosexual, Andrei Chikatilo, who was convicted in 1992 of raping, murdering and eating parts of at least 21 boys, 17 women, and 14 girls. The pathology of eating one's sexual victims also characterized Milwaukee's Jeffrey Dahmer in 1992. He not only killed 17 young men and boys, but cooked and consumed their body parts.

The top six U.S. male serial killers were all gay:

- Donald Harvey claimed 37 victims in Kentucky.

- John Wayne Gacy raped and killed 33 boys in Chicago, burying them under his house and in his yard.

- Patrick Kearney accounted for 32, cutting his victims into small pieces after sex and leaving them in trash bags along the Los Angeles freeways.

- Bruce Davis molested and killed 27 young men and boys in Illinois.

- A gay sex-murder-torture ring (Corll-Henley-Brooks) sent 27 Texas men and boys to their grave.

- Juan Corona was convicted of murdering 25 migrant workers (he "made love" with their corpses).

Lesbian Aileen Wuornos laid claim in 1992 to "worst female killer" with at least 7 middle-aged male victims. She singlehandedly topped the lesbian nurse team of Catherine Wood and Gwen Graham, who had killed 6 convalescent patients in Grand Rapids, Michigan.

The association between serial murder and homosexuality isn't recent. Two gays compete for the spot of "world's worst murderer." During the Nazi rein of terror, Auschwitz executioner Ludwig Tiene strangled, crushed, and gn wed boys and young men to death while he raped them. Though his grand total is uncertain, he often murdered as many as 100 a day. Gilles de Rais (Bluebeard) brutally destroyed the lives of 800 boys. Each lad was lured to his home, bathed and fed. Just as the poor boy thought "this is my lucky day," he was raped, ripped or cut apart, and then either burned or eaten.

A study of 518 sexually-tinged mass murders in the U.S. from 1966 to 1983 determined that 350 (68 percent) of the victims were killed by those who practiced homosexuality and that 19 (44 percent) of the 43 murderers were bisexuals or homosexuals.[81]

Though probably less than a majority of mass murderers are homosexual, given that no more than 1–3 percent of the populace is gay, homosexual murderers show up much more frequently than one would expect.

Along with serial murder, there appears to be a connection between homosexuality and murder. Evidence gathered prior to the gay rights movement is limited. Of 444 homicides in one jurisdiction from 1955–1973, investigators noted 5 clear "sexual motivation" murders. Three of the 5 involved homosexuality and 2 involved heterosexuality.[82]

Probing more deeply into the connection between murder and homosexuality, Jim Warren, who worked as a counselor at the Washington State Corrections Center, did the intake interview for almost all the younger murderers (i.e., under age 36) in the state of Washington from 1971–82 (during the growth of the gay rights movement). He was "probably the only one who examined the entirety of each of their case files." Warren testified[83] that he was struck with how frequently homosexuality turned up in the cases.

Starting with a trickle of 2 or 3 murders per year in 1972 until dozens per year by the 1980s, he noted a recurrent pat-

tern: Although the motive listed in the report was often rob-
bery or theft, "about 50 percent of the time" it was also associated with homosexuality. Typically, a homosexual would
meet someone at a bar or park and invite him to his home.
Before the morning, an argument would ensue and he or his
visitor would be dead.

Violent Sexual Practices

A substantial minority of homosexuals (between 22 percent[84]
to 37 percent[85]) indulge in painful or violent sex (e.g., bondage and discipline [B/D], where the partner is physically re-
strained and mildly tortured, or sadomasochism [S&M], where
partners are tortured or hurt during sex). Even in the 1940s,
ychiatrist David Abrahamsen[86] noted, "It is well known that
homosexual inclinations may be accompanied by sadistic or
masochistic tendencies. . . . These perversions play a great
part in many sexual offenses and in many cases of murder." In
a national survey of random samples of homosexuals and heterosexuals,[87] 32 percent of those males who called themselves
homosexual or bisexual versus 5 percent of heterosexual males
reported having engaged in sadomasochism; 17 percent of lesbians versus 4 percent of heterosexual women also admitted to
S&M. Likewise, gays and lesbians were about four times
more apt to engage in bondage than were heterosexuals.

- Homosexual books and magazines celebrate the "fun" of
  violent sex. For instance, a Denver gay columnist (the
  "leathersex fairy"), told his readers how to strangle and flog
  one's partner during sex. He also extolled the practice of
  "hanging from a tree by meat hooks through the pectoral
  muscles" and described "guys who like to have burning ci-
  gars, cigarettes, or matches held near or pressed into their
  skin."[88] Likewise, national and international gay tour books
  matter-of-factly list places where sadomasochistic sex can
  be obtained.[89]

- In 1993, London gays raised £100,000 to appeal a conviction
  in which the judge ruled that "sex is no excuse for violence.

. . . Pleasure derived from the infliction of pain is an evil thing." The crime? "Nailing a foreskin and scrotum to a board" and "pouring hot wax in a urethra."[90]

- The 1980 CBS-TV documentary, *Gay Power, Gay Politics* reported that about 10 percent of the accidental deaths among young men in San Francisco resulted from sado-masochistic sex gone awry.

Deliberately Infecting Others During Sex

Gay activists often argue that what consenting adults do in private is nobody else's business. However, gays have sex with so many different partners[91] that they increase their risk of getting or transmitting sexually transmitted diseases (STDs). Indeed, homosexuals are considerably more apt to get STDs than are non-homosexuals.[92]

Most who get an STD decide that they will do all in their power not to infect partners. But others—an important minority—decide that they will make their partners suffer as much as they have. As Mirko Grmek[93] noted "every historian of disease knows that such an attitude of vengeance, or at least of recklessness, had contributed in other times to the spread of tuberculosis and syphilis." Limited evidence suggests that, compared to heterosexuals, homosexuals are more apt to harm their sexual partners deliberately. The only comparative study[94] on this issue found that about 1 percent of male and female heterosexuals compared to 7 percent of gays and 3 percent of lesbians admitted to deliberately passing on STDs that they had acquired.

When the disease is AIDS, the personal and social costs of deliberate infection are exceptionally high. Several examples of homosexuals who were deliberate spreaders of AIDS have been documented,[95] but the most notorious is that of "patient zero," the Canadian flight attendant who, until his death at age 32, shared his body and infection with 250 men every year. From the late 1970s through the early 1980s he was personally responsible for at least 40 of the first 248 American cases of

AIDS and told public health officials in San Francisco it "was nobody else's business but his own."

There also appears to be a connection between the practice of violent sex and one's willingness to infect someone else deliberately. Dividing our random national sample[96] into those with no interest in homosexual activity (non-H) and those with at least some homosexual interest (H)—and combining males and females—we found that 4.0 percent of the non-Hs *vs* 21.8 percent of those with at least some homosexual interest said that they had participated in sadomasochism (S/M); 7.8 percent of the non-Hs admitted to bondage (B/D) *vs* 27.5 percent of the Hs. Further, those who had engaged in violent sex of either type were twice as likely to have deliberately attempted to infect a partner than those without such violent experience (see graph B).

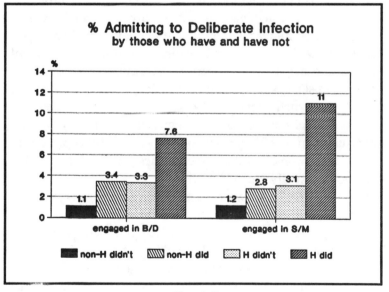

Graph B

In 1992, three London STD clinics reported that almost half of their homosexual patients who *knew* they were infected with HIV had *then contracted* rectal gonorrhoea.[97] These gays were not permitting their deadly infection to spoil their sexual fun. By 1993 over 100,000 U.S. gays had died of AIDS and tens of thousands had died of hepatitis B. Most of these had been infected, deliberately or carelessly, by other homosexuals.

Homosexual Rape

The National Crime Survey[98] reported that about 1 of every 10,000 males over the age of 11 is raped each year (*vs* 13 of every 10,000 females)—that is, about 7 percent of rapes are homosexual. In two jurisdictions, Columbia, SC[99] and Memphis, TN,[100] males accounted for 5.7 percent of the victims of rape reported to authorities—in only one instance was the assailant a woman.

Along with the rise of the gay rights movement, homosexual rape of men appears to have increased in the past few decades.[101] Homosexual rape is twice as common in urban areas where gays congregate than in suburban or rural areas.[102] It may also be more common where the gay subculture is accepted: A 1970 study in San Francisco found that 9 percent of male heterosexuals and 24 percent of gays, 2 percent of female heterosexuals and 11 percent of lesbians reported having been homosexually raped.[103] In our 1983 national urban survey (which did not include San Francisco), 1.3 percent of heterosexual men *vs* 12.5 percent of gay men and 0.6 percent of heterosexual women *vs* 8.6 percent of lesbians reported having been homosexually raped.[104]

More alarmingly, between 15 percent to 40 percent of statutory rape (child molestation) involves homosexuality.[105] In one study, 25 percent of white gays[106]admitted to sex with boys 16 or younger when they were aged 21 or older.

Rape at any age is violent and emotionally devastating. But it can also edge victims toward homosexuality. In our national study, almost half the lesbians said they had been *heterosexually* raped—perhaps gravitating to homosexuality because of the experience. Males often react differently. Thus the Masters and Johnson Institute reported that a "25-year-old man had had his first sexual experience when he was 13 years old. It was arranged by his lesbian mother with an older gay man. After that episode, his imagery and interpersonal sexual experience were exclusively homosexual."[107] Likewise, "Mr. K, age 22, felt that his change in sexual preference was related to his having been raped by two men. . . . After the assault he experienced sexual identity confusion and began engaging voluntarily in homosexual activity. When he was seen for evaluation he labeled himself as openly homosexual."[108]

Of course, homosexual activists habitually argue that they are the victims of violence rather than the perpetrators. Yet even this argument is not born out by the facts. The FBI reported 431 hate crimes against homosexuals for the U.S. in all of 1991. Only one was "confirmed" for Washington, D.C.— yet D.C. gay activists claimed 397 incidents! When pressed, they admitted that at least 366 of these "crimes" consisted of "verbal harassment."[109]

In line with traditional psychiatric opinion, violence goes hand-in-hand with the 'gay' lifestyle. Almost all the exposure by homosexuals to violence and disease is encountered in the gay subculture. Most of the murderers in the lifespan study whose sexual orientation could be determined were also homosexual. While violence toward homosexuals is deplorable, most violence involving gays is self-induced (and the gay subculture probably exports more violence than it absorbs from without).

The Effects of Homosexual Practices on the Lifespan of Homosexuals

Do persistent unhealthy sexual practices and the high incidence of violence in the homosexual community significantly affect the mortality rates among homosexuals? This is the question we asked ourselves after completing our studies of at-risk behaviors among homosexuals. However, in attempting to determine the relative lifespans of homosexuals and heterosexuals, we immediately ran into difficulties. The data available were sketchy and unsatisfactory. No one had addressed the problem in a thorough and exhaustive way.

Obviously we would need to conduct some research of our own.[110] Of course, such a project posed problems. It would be impossible to determine from conventional sources precisely who was and who was not a homosexual. Such information does not appear on death certificates nor in insurance records. There is no biological "marker" as there is with women or Blacks. How, then, to isolate a homosexual sample from the general population and compare it with a control group of heterosexuals?

We concluded that the best possible method was to gather our statistics on homosexual deaths from the many gay newspapers and magazines currently published in cities throughout the United States, then compare them with the obituaries listed in mainline newspapers. This methodology had two obvious defects, or rather two "traits" that would skew the study, if ever so slightly. In the first place, gay publications would record only the obituaries of avowed homosexuals or those of whom they knew, and not those of homosexuals still "in the closet." Would there be a significant difference between homosexuals who "went public" and those closeted so deeply that even other homosexuals didn't know of their existence?

Gay rights advocates maintain that life "in the closet" is a terrible psychological strain, that the necessity to hide one's true identity leads to alcoholism, drug abuse, and even suicide. On the other hand, those who "come out" have claimed that their existence is less stressful, that they achieve a new peace with themselves, that they lead happier and more productive lives. If these generalizations are indeed true, then the avowed homosexuals might be expected to live longer than those in the closet.

On the other hand, it is also possible that "closeted" homosexuals lead a more conventional life, away from gay bars and bathhouses, and therefore are healthier human beings, however frustrating their lives. If such is the case, then the obituaries in homosexual newspapers might well be misleading in the other direction. We concluded that since no one could possibly identify the obituaries of "closeted" homosexuals, we would have to content ourselves with a study that dealt onl with avowed homosexuals, or those known to their own community. Such a sampling might shed light on only the lifespan of one segment of the homosexual community, but it would be the only large cohort that could be studied in this manner.

The second problem we faced was related to the first. Just as "closeted" homosexuals could not be included in the homosexual sampling, so could they not be excluded from the control group. Clearly some of the obituaries carried in mainline newspapers would be those of homosexuals. We could avoid some obvious cases by eliminating AIDS deaths from the control group, unless they were clearly identified as people who contracted the disease by a means other than homosexual conduct. Still, some homosexuals would remain in the so called "heterosexual" sampling. We concluded, however, that with the homosexual population no more than a fraction of the oft quoted 10 percent, our comparison group would still be roughly indicative of what was happening in the heterosexual population, particularly if it coincided with current actuarial charts used by the insurance companies. (In fact, it did, so we put aside our doubts about the validity of the comparison group.)

We collected and analyzed obituaries from 16 homosexual newspapers or journals and 2 mainline newspapers to determine a number of facts. In order to have a sample sufficiently large for valid generalization, we analyzed a total of 6,574 male homosexual obituaries and 140 lesbian obituaries. First, we noted age at the time of death and cause of death (if given). We differentiated between those homosexuals who died of AIDS or AIDS-related diseases and those who died of other causes. Then we catalogued those other causes, if given. Finally, when possible we noted those who were living with a "partner," since married people tend to live longer lives than unmarried people.

Our best source for homosexual obituaries was the *Washington Blade*, a weekly tabloid published for the homosexual community in the nation's capital. The *Blade*, unlike other such newspapers, published obituaries of unknown as well as widely known homosexuals, and hence was the most "democratic." But even though most of the other fifteen publications focused on the well-known or politically active, the data gathered from all sources painted the same picture.

When we had finished our survey and analysis, the results were remarkably consistent from newspaper to newspaper, region to region, city to city—and they were grim, far grimmer than we had expected. The average life span for a male homosexual who died of AIDS was 39. This figure held true regardless of whether or not the deceased had a longtime sexual partner (LTSP). The average lifespan for a male homosexual who died of causes other than AIDS was 42–41 for those with lifetime sexual partners, 43 for those without.

The 140 lesbians in the sample died at a median age of 45. Only 9 percent of homosexual males lived to the age of 65, as opposed to 73 percent in the male population as a whole. Twenty-three percent of the lesbians lived past the age of 64, as opposed to 83 percent of women in the general population (see graph C).

As we began to develop these figures, we asked ourselves: "How is it possible that homosexuals who do not die of AIDS could live only 2 or 3 years longer than those who contract the fatal virus? What else could possibly cause them to die at such a young age?" We knew, of course, that they were much more susceptible to a variety of diseases as a consequence of unhealthy and unsanitary sexual practices. (For example, according to a 1990 American Medical Association report on adolescent health, a homosexual teenager is 23 times more likely to contract a sexually transmitted disease than a heterosexual

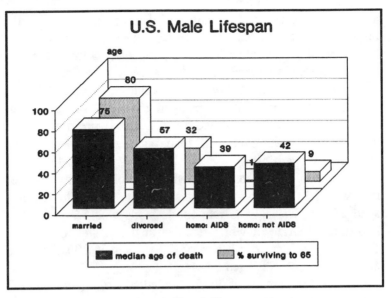

Graph C

teenager.) But it never occurred to us that fatal illnesses would plague them at such an early age.

Unfortunately, the obituaries did not give us a complete picture.

Phrases like "sudden death," "brief illness," and "natural causes" hid many of the facts we would like to have gathered for analysis. However, the information provided in the publications did give us some clues as to why the lifespan was so short. For example, we discovered that even with incomplete data, the murder, suicide, and accident rates were substantially higher than in the general population.

Using our sample, we discovered that 1.4 percent of the homosexual males were victims of murder—21 times higher than black males, 116 times higher than white males aged 25–44. 0.61 percent of homosexual males in our sample were listed as suicides, which is 30 times the rate of black males and 24 times the rate of white males in the general population. The accident rate was also dramatically higher for homosexuals. 0.55 percent died in automobile accidents—18 times higher than white males and 14 times higher than black males. 0.30 percent died in other kinds of accidents, 10 times the rate of white males in general, and 8 times the rate of black males.

Overall, 2.9 percent of homosexual males died violent deaths 17 times the rate of black males aged 25–44, 28 times the rate of white males in the same age bracket. The figure only begins to explain the lower overall lifespan, but the differences in this category are significant.

As for lesbians, almost all of whom were white, the murder rate was 7.1 percent—595 times the rate of white females aged 25–44. The suicide rate for lesbians was 5.7 percent—816 times the rate of white females in the 25–44 age group. The motor accident death rate of 4.3 percent is 306 times the rate of white females aged 25–44.

Overall, 20 percent of lesbians died a violent death—512 times the rate of white females aged 25–44. Incidentally, given the recent publicity accorded the rise in heterosexual AIDS, particularly among women, it is interesting to note that 7.1 percent of lesbians died of AIDS—41,000 times more than heterosexual females 25–44.

The rest of the deaths were from a variety of causes, but mostly from diseases that prove fatal to heterosexuals at a much later median age—heart attack, cancer, hepatitis, liver failure, diabetes.

The heart attacks may be the result of excessive drug and alcohol use. A recent survey conducted in San Francisco revealed that 31 percent of the homosexual population were either addicted to drugs or overused them. Indeed drug overdoses account for a disproportionate number of deaths.

It is also possible that the high incidence of cancer is partially explainable in terms of AIDS. It is difficult if not impossible to determine how many cancers were opportunistic diseases, the by-product of the HIV virus. Undoubtedly some were.

Hepatitis is another disease common among homosexuals since it is easily spread by anal intercourse or oral-anal contact, and is often fatal. Gay Bowel Syndrome is usually spread by anal/oral contact and anal intercourse. This disease is a combination of several protozoa, viruses, and bacteria that often congregate in the digestive/eliminative systems of homosexuals. Though not generally fatal, Gay Bowel Syndrome is extremely debilitating and, under certain circumstances, highly contagious.

In comparing married and unmarried, our research found the same pattern established by other studies. Married men lived, on average, considerably longer than unmarried men, 75 years as opposed to 57 years. But no such discrepancy existed between homosexuals with lifetime sexual partners and those without. In fact, our study indicates that those without permanent homosexual attachments may live slightly longer than those with lifetime partners.

It will be easy for homosexual critics to suggest that this study is methodologically unsound, particularly since we identify gaps in our knowledge. Certainly our conclusions contradict those of Bancroft ("Homosexuality: Compatible with Full Health" in *The British Medical Journal*), who posited no significant differences between the health of homosexuals and heterosexuals, exclusive of AIDS.

However, there are other studies that suggest we are correct in our assessment.

- In 1858, long before the health effects of homosexuality were debated, G. Tardieu reported on the age distribution of males imprisoned in France for sodomy. Of the 216 who ages were given, the age range was from under 15 to 69, with a median age of under 25. Eliminating all under 18, the median age rises to almost 40.

- In 1914, M. Hirschfeld reported on German males convicted of involvement in sodomy. The age distribution ranged from under 15 to over 50, with a median of 24 years. Since "over 50" was the last category, we cannot determine just how many, if any, attained the age of 65. But only 9 percent were over 50.

- In the late 1930s and 1940s, Kinsey and his investigators spent more than 12 years seeking out and interviewing homosexuals at bars, bathhouses, homosexual boarding houses, and their private clubs. He also interviewed a large number of prisoners as well as college students. Indeed, because Kinsey and his colleagues were regarded as sexual liberators, homosexuals were eager to volunteer for his study. There is no reason to believe that his sample was not representative of all age groups available. Yet fewer than 1 percent of his homosexuals, male as well as female, were over the age of 65.

- The Mattachine Society, the earliest of the "gay rights" organizations, gathered together a representative group of homosexuals for Evelyn Hooker [see above] to study in her highly influential 1950's study. The oldest of the 30 subjects was 50 [her Table 1 incorrectly lists a 57], the next oldest was 44, and the median age was 33.

- In the early 1960s, Berger attempted to draw a sampling of elderly homosexuals, but he had to begin his scale at 40 years and only 34 of 112 were over the age of 59.

- From 1969 through 1970, the Kinsey Institute surveyed homosexuals in San Francisco. The researchers devised samplings to cover the full range of homosexuals living in the city. Although they recruited respondents in eight different ways, only 23 percent of male homosexuals and only 18 percent of lesbians were over the age of 45, despite the fact that the investigators tried for 25 percent from this age group. Their initial decision to draw only a quarter of their sampling from homosexuals over 45 indicates they already knew the problem existed, and they ended up omitting figures on age distribution from their report.

- In 1977, the largest survey of homosexuals reported 0.2 percent of its lesbians and 0.8 percent of its homosexual males were aged 65 or older.

- In 1978, the openly homosexual J. Spada polled 1,022 homosexuals by mail and published his findings (*The Spada Report: The Newest Survey of Gay Male Sexuality*) The median age was 30, but only 2.5 percent were over age 65.

- In 1979, the openly lesbian M. Mendola (in *The Mendola Report: A New Look at Gay Couples*) polled 405 homosexuals by mail. The median age of those polled was 34, and only 10 percent were 50 or over.

- In the same year a sample of 101 homosexuals who belonged to a group restricted to those over 40 was reported, and only 21 were over age 65.

- From the mid 1970s to the early 1980s, interest in Gay Bowel Syndrome, sexually transmitted diseases, and hepatitis B generated a number of samples of the homosexual population.
  - In 1982, only one of 103 homosexuals examined in San Francisco was over the age of 65.
  - From 1977 through 1979, 102 homosexuals' case histories were collected in Seattle and the oldest was 58.
  - In 1979, 5,324 homosexual visitors to Denver's STD clinic had a median age of 27, a mean age of 28.5, and the oldest was 67.

Despite a formidable body of evidence to suggest that homosexuality is unhealthy and self-destructive, the scientific community continues to propagate its own fragile fairy tales of a gay community that constitutes 10 percent of the general population, dwells in harmony with its neighbors, never comes down with more than a bad cold, and lives to the fine old Biblical age of three score and ten. Court cases are decided and gay rights laws are passed on the basis of such ill-founded scientific testimony.

OTHER FAIRY TALES

Two additional fairy tales plague the debate over gay rights. Both have been told and retold, like "Cinderella" and "Goldilocks"—so much so that they now constitute "fact" to the scientific community and define immutable truths upon which National Research Council pronouncements and federal policies rest. The first of these tales exonerates homosexuals from the charge that they are more likely to molest children than are heterosexuals. Today the received wisdom says that homosexual molestation is minimal when compa   to heterosexual molestation. Indeed, according to this tale, the most dangerous beast in the woods is the traditional father. The second of these tales is more recent and more relevant to current debate. It goes this way: Homosexuals neither choose their lifestyle nor are they the product of environmental anomalies that have resulted in aberrant sexual tendencies. Homosexuals don't like to think of themselves as either morally deficient or "ill." They prefer to say they are as normal as Ozzie and Harriet, as natural in their behavior as the Cleavers.

Let's take a look at both of these fairy tales and see how well they frame reality.

Child Molestation: A Fairy Tale with Flaws

The American Psychological Association funded a report that asserts: "Recognized researchers in the field on child abuse, . . . almost unanimously concur that homosexual people are actually *less* likely to approach children sexually."[111] Other sci n-tists have echoed this opinion, and even a figure as scientifically authoritative as Ann Landers[112] has repeatedly stated that it is false to assume that "Homosexuals are more inclined to molest children sexually than heterosexuals."

Why then, do we read about homosexual molestation of boys in every newspaper? Why is it such a problem among the Catholic clergy? We know that heterosexual molestation also occurs. But since there are so many more heterosexuals than homosexuals, which kind of child molestation—homosexual or heterosexual—is *proportionately* more common? Or to put the question another way: is a homosexual or a heterosexual statistically more likely to engage in sex with children?

Three kinds of scientific evidence are relevant to this issue: 1) survey reports of molestation in the general population, 2) surveys of those caught and convicted of molestation, and 3) what homosexuals themselves have reported. These three lines of evidence suggest that the 1 percent-to-3 percent of adults who practice homosexuality[113] account for between a fifth and a third of all child molestation.

Reports of Molestation by the General Population. In 1983, a probability survey of the sexual experiences of 4,340 adults in 5 U.S. cities found that about 3 percent of men and 7 percent of women reported sexual involvement with a man before the age of 13[114] (i.e., 30 percent were homosexual).

In 1983-4, a random survey of 3,132 adults in Los Angeles found that 3.8 percent of men and 6.8 percent of women said that they had been sexually assaulted in childhood. Since 93 percent of the assailants were male, and only 1 percent of girls had been assaulted by females, about 35 percent of the assaults were homosexual.[115] The *Los Angeles Times*[116] surveyed 2,628 adults across the U.S. in 1985. Twenty-seven percent of the women and 16 percent of the men claimed to have been sexually molested. Since 7 percent of the molestations of girls and 93 percent of the molestations of boys were by adults of the same sex, about 4 of every 10 molestations in this survey were homosexual.

In a random survey of British 15-to-19 year olds, 35 percent of the boys and 9 percent of the girls claimed to have been approached for sex by adult homosexuals and 2 percent of the boys and 1 percent of the girls admitted to succumbing.[117]

In science, a review of the professional literature published in a refereed scientific journal is considered to be an accurate summary of the current state of knowledge. The latest such review was published in 1985.[118] It concluded that homosexual acts were involved in 25 percent to 40 percent of the cases of child molestation recorded in the scientific and forensic literature.

Surveys of Those Convicted. Drs. Freund and Heasman[119] of the Clarke Institute of Psychiatry in Toronto reviewed two sizeable studies and calculated that 34 percent and 32 percent of the offenders against children were homosexual. In cases they had personally handled, homosexuals accounted for 36 percent of their 457 pedophiles.

Dr. Adrian Copeland, a psychiatrist who works with sexual offenders at the Peters Institute in Philadelphia, said[120] that, from his experience, pedophiles tend to be homosexual and "40 percent to 45 percent" of child molesters have had "significant homosexual experiences."

Dr. C. H. McGaghy[121] estimated that "homosexual offenders probably constitute about half of molesters who work with children." Other studies are similar:

- Of the approximately 100 child molesters in 1991 at the *Massachusetts Treatment Center for Sexually Dangerous Persons,* a third were heterosexual, a third bisexual, and a third homosexual in orientation.[122]

- A state-wide survey of 161 Vermont adolescents who committed sex offenses in 1984 found that 35 (22 percent) were homosexual.[123]

- Of the 91 molesters of non-related children at Canada's *Kingston Sexual Behaviour Clinic* from 1978–1984, 38 (42 percent) engaged in homosexuality.[124]

- Of 52 child molesters in Ottawa from 1983 to 1985, 31 (60 percent) were homosexual.[125]

In England for 1973, 802 persons (8 females) were convicted of indecent assault on a male, and 3,006 (6 of them female) were convicted of indecent assault on a female (i.e., 21 percent were homosexual). Eighty-eight percent of male and about 70 percent of female victims were under age sixteen.[126]

Because of this pattern, Judge J. T. Rees concluded that "the male homosexual naturally seeks the company of the male adolescent, or of the young male adult, in preference to that of the fully-grown man. [In 1947] 986 persons were convicted of homosexual and unnatural offences. Of those, 257 were indictable offences involving 402 male victims. . . . The great majority of [whom] . . . were under the age of 16. Only 11 percent . . . were over 21."

[T]he problem of male homosexuality is in essence the problem of the corruption of youth by itself [i.e., by other boys] and by its elders. [And thereby] . . . the creation . . . of new addicts ready to corrupt a still further generation of young men and boys in the future.[127]

What Homosexuals Admit. The 1948 Kinsey survey found that 37 percent of the gays and 2 percent of the lesbians admitted to sexual relations with under-17-yr-olds, and 28 percent of the gays and 1 percent of the lesbians admitted to sexual relations with under-16-year-olds while they themselves were aged 18 or older.[128]

In 1970 the Kinsey Institute interviewed 565 white gays in San Francisco: 25 percent of them admitted to having had sex with boys aged 16 or younger while they themselves were at least 21.[129]

In the *Gay Report,* 23 percent of the gays and 6 percent of the lesbians admitted to sexual interaction with youth less than 16 years of age.[130]

In France, 129 convicted gays[131] (average age 34 years) said they had had sexual contact with a total of 11,007 boys (an average of 85 different boys per man). Abel *et al* reported similarly that men who molested girls outside their family had averaged 20 victims each; those who molested boys averaged 150 victims each.[132]

Summary. About a third of the reports of molestation by the populace have involved homosexuality. Likewise, between a fifth and a third of those who have been caught and/or convicted practiced homosexuality. Finally, a fifth to a third of surveyed gays admitted to child molestation. All-in-all, a rather consistent story.

Teacher-Pupil Sexual Interaction. Nowadays parents are labeled bigots for fearing that homosexual teachers might molest their children. But if homosexuals are more apt to molest children and are in a position to take advantage of them, this fear makes sense. Indeed, accounts of disproportionate homosexual teacher molestation appear throughout the scientific literature.

In England, Schofield reported that at least 2 of his 150 homosexuals had their *first* homosexual experience with a teacher and an additional 2 reported that their first homosexual contact with an adult was with a teacher. One of the 50 men in his comparison group had also been seduced by a homosexual teacher, while none of the men interviewed claimed involvement with a heterosexual teacher.[133]

The original U.S. Kinsey study reported that 4 percent of the non-criminal white gays and 7 percent of the non-criminal white lesbians reported that they had their *first* homosexual experience with a 'teacher or other caretaker.' *None* of the heterosexuals were recorded as having a teacher as their first sex partner.[134]

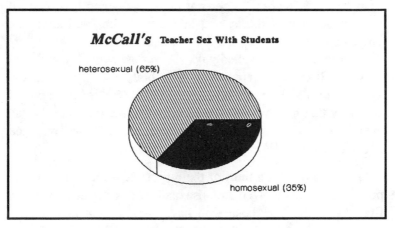

Graph D

Of 400 consecutive Australian[135] cases of molestation, 7 boys and 4 girls were assaulted by male teachers. Thus 64 percent of those assaults were homosexual.

In the 1978 *McCall's* magazine study of 1,400 principals,[136] 7 percent reported complaints about homosexual contact between teachers and pupils and 13 percent reported complaints about heterosexual contact between teachers and pupils (i.e., 35 percent of complaints were homosexual). 2 percent "knew of instances in which teachers discussed their homosexuality in class" (see graph D).

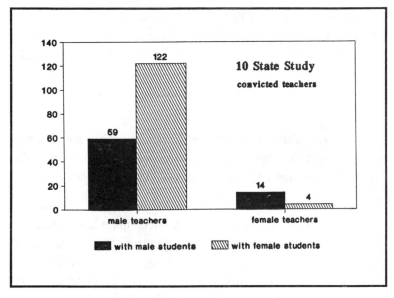

Graph E

In 1987, Dr. Stephen Rubin, associate professor of psychology at Whitman College, conducted a 10 state survey[137] and found 199 sexual abuse cases involving teachers. One hundred and twenty-two male teachers had abused female pupils and 14 female teachers had abused male students. In 59 cases, however, male teachers had abused male pupils and in 4 cases female teachers had abused female students (overall 32 percent were homosexual). (see graph E).

A 1983 survey asked 4,340 adults to report on *any* sexual advances and *any* physical sexual contact by elementary and secondary teachers (4 percent of those who were teachers in the survey claimed to be bisexual or homosexual).[138] Twenty-nine percent of the advances by elementary and 16 percent of the advances by secondary school teachers were homosexual. In addition, 1 of 4 (25 percent) reports of actual sexual contact with an elementary school teacher were homosexual. In high school, 8 (22 percent) of 37 contacts between teacher and pupil were homosexual. Eighteen percent reported having had a homosexual teacher (8 percent of those over the age of 55 *vs* 25 percent of those under 26). Of those reporting a homosexual teacher, 6 percent said that the teacher influenced them to *try* homosexuality and 13 percent of the men and 4 percent of the women said that the teacher *made sexual advances toward them.*

Summary. Whether examining surveys of the general populace or counts of those caught, homosexual teachers are disproportionately apt to become sexually involved with children.

Proportionality: The Key. As noted above, study after nationwide study[139] has yielded estimates of male homosexuality that range between 1 percent and 3 percent. The proportion of lesbians in these studies is almost always lower, usually about half that of gays. So, overall, perhaps 2 percent of adults regularly indulge in homosexuality. Yet they account for between 20 percent to 40 percent of all molestations of children.

Child molestation is not to be taken lightly. Officials at a facility which serves about 1,500 runaway youngsters each year estimate that about half of the boys have been homosexually abused and 90 percent of the girls heterosexually assaulted.[140] Investigation of those suffering severe chronic mental illness implicates child molestation as a primary cause (45 percent of Bigras *et al'*s[141] patients were homosexually abused).

If 2 percent of the population is responsible for 20 percent to 40 percent of something as socially and personally troubling as child molestation, something must be desperately wrong with that 2 percent. Not every homosexual is a child molester. But enough gays do molest children so that the risk of a homosexual molesting a child is 10 to 20 times greater than that of a heterosexual.

Goals of the Gay Movement. The gay movement is forthright about seeking to legitimize child-adult homosexual sex. In 1987, *The Journal of Homosexuality,* the scholarly organ of the gay rights movement, published "Pedophilia and the Gay Movement."[142] Author Theo Sandfort detailed homosexual efforts to end "oppression towards pedophilia." In 1980 the largest Dutch gay organization (the COC) "adop   the position that the liberation of pedophilia must be viewed as a gay issue . . . [and that] ages of consent should therefore be abolished . . . by acknowledging the affinity between homosexuality and pedophilia, the COC has quite possibly made i   asier for homosexual adults to become more sensitive to ero   desires of younger members of their sex, thereby broadening gay identity." In 1990 COC achieved a significant victory: lowering of the age of consent for homosexual sex in Holland to 12 (unless the parents object, in which case it goes up to 15).[143] In the U.S. and Canada, the North American Man-Boy Love Association marches proudly in gay pride parades with the stated goal of removing the barriers to man-boy sex. Note the phrases "*oppression* towards pedophilia" and "*liberation* of pedophilia." It is clear that those who advocate the legalization of sex between adults and children intend to argue that such conduct is a "civil right," deserving of the same legal protections afforded to other minorities. A large proportion of Americans regard that argument as a mere pretext to give "sexual predators" free reign to take advantage of vulnerable children.

Conclusion. Not only is the gay rights movement up front in its desire to legitimize sex with children, but whether indexed by population reports of molestation, pedophile convictions, or teacher-pupil assaults, there is a strong, disproportionate association between child molestation and homosexuality. Ann Landers' claim that homosexuals molest children at no higher a rate than heterosexuals do is untrue. The assertion by gay leaders and the American Psychological Association that a homosexual is less likely than a heterosexual to molest children is patently false.

Heredity: A Fairy Tale with a Purpose

Gay activists regularly claim that they are "born that way" and consequently cannot change their desires or mitigate their activities. In the past, a majority of homosexuals believed otherwise. In recent years, a few scientific studies—highly tentative, yet widely publicized—have made all the difference. But in the final analysis, does it really matter how homosexuals came to engage in their deviant practices?

As a matter of fact, it matters a great deal. The political stakes are high. Indeed, the future of American public policy may turn on this "scientific" question. The March 3, 1993 *New York Times/CBS News Poll* reported that a majority of those who believe that gays "cannot change" favored permitting homosexuals to serve in the military. Only a third of those who believed it is a choice felt the same way. Just about every other opinion about gay rights also hinged on the question of whether gays are "born that way" and "can't change." If homosexuality is a "given" like eye-color or left-handedness, then many are willing to find some way to accommodate gays. On the other hand, if homosexual desire is no more inevitable or unchangeable than drunkenness or drug use, then most folk are willing to insist that homosexuals abandon or contain their behavior.

Two prominent "homosexual" psychiatrists, examining the evidence of their own lives as well as those of others, came to different conclusions in this historic and ever-changing debate. The first of these, Sigmund Freud, saw his homosexual urges as pathological. Through self-analysis, he overcame them and eventually rejoiced in the "greater independence that results from having overcome my homosexuality."[144] The second of these, Richard Isay, confronted his desires, pronounced them "natural," divorced his wife, and joined the gay subculture.[145]

In 1992, Isay admitted that the "conviction among most, though not all, dynamically oriented psychiatrists in general and psychoanalysts in particular [is] that homosexuality can and should be changed to heterosexuality."[146] Yet, while admitting this consensus among his colleagues, he called attempts to change homosexual desire "the greatest abuse of psychiatry in America today. . . . [because t]he attempt to change is extremely harmful."[147] Instead, he demanded that *society* change to accommodate homosexuality.

Dr. Isay, who chairs the American Psychiatric Association's committee on Gay, Lesbian, and Bisexual Issues, argues that "homosexuality is probably constitutional."[148] To support this position, he cited as proof the 1991 "gay brains" research of Simon LeVay, published in *Science,* and the "gay twins" study of Bailey and Pillard, published in the prestigious *Archives of General Psychiatry.*

His recognition of these studies was widely echoed by the media, who interviewed the researchers on television and prominently featured their pictures in the biggest and best newspapers and magazines. They also gave wide coverage to the second half of the twin study when it came out 15 months later. At the very moment when the debate was raging over the military policy toward gays, it seemed as if Science had come riding over the hill, blowing its clear bugle, ready to rout the enemy.

What the media failed to note, either out of ignorance or design, was another article in the issue of *Archives of General Psychiatry* that carried the second part of the twin study. Had they actually read the second Bailey-Pillard study and bothered to turn five pages, they would have found an authoritative survey of all the "born that way" scholarship by Drs. William Byne and Bruce Parsons, researchers at the New York State Psychiatric Institute. These scholars critically reviewed "the evidence favoring a biologic theory" presented by LeVay, and Bailey and Pillard.[149] They concluded that "[t]here is *no evidence at present to substantiate a biologic theory*" of sexual orientation!

How could disinterested researchers dismiss as inadequate the very studies that were fundamental to Dr. Isay's and the mass media's argument? Byne and Parsons remembered that in the 1940s through the 1970s it was widely argued and *believed* in the scientific community that male homosexuals had a deficiency of male hormones. Yet only 3 "studies had indicated lower testosterone levels in male homosexuals, while 20 studies found no differences based on sexual orientation, and two reported elevated testosterone levels in male homosexuals." Textbooks alluded to the supposed "fact" of hormonal differences for *three decades*.

But this "scientific" belief was false.

Byne and Parsons observed that the LeVay study was based upon a supposed correlation between the SDN-POA brain center in male rats and a brain center called INAH3 in humans. LeVay reasoned that since the SDN-POA had an effect on male rat behavior, then a corresponding difference in the same part of the brain would make men homosexual. He assumed that the INAH3 in men was essentially the same as the SND-POA in rats. But, as it turns out, there was a hitch: the "effective lesion site within the anterior hypothalamus for disrupting mounting behavior [in male rats] lies *above, not within,* the SDN-POA. Thus, the SDN-POA *does not* play a critical role in male-typical behavior in male rats, and the correlation between its size and mounting frequencies clearly does not reflect a causal relationship." LeVay's numerous technical errors (e.g., small sample size and the uncertain sexual orientations of subjects) were only a part of his study's problems: much more important was the fact that he compared human brains with rat brains *and failed to locate the analogous region!* Instead of the "bullseye" that Isay and the mass media celebrated, it was an embarrassing *miss!*

Then, the *very next* 'sexual orientation of twins' study reported in the scientific literature[150] found homosexual concordance rates of 25 percent in identical twins. Drs. Byne and Parsons noted the large proportions of identical twins in both studies "who were discordant for homosexuality despite sharing not only their genes but also their prenatal and familial environments . . . [which] underscores our ignorance of the factors that are involved, and the manner in which they interact, in the emergence of sexual orientation."

The evidence supporting the "born that way" claim of Isay and other gay activists is tenuous. It has been uncritically accepted and frantically hyped by the media and some slovenly scientists. But it hasn't been duplicated by other researchers and it is *full* of technical problems.

On the other side of the debate is a body of scientific evidence that suggests that *homosexuality is adopted by people who are confused, exploratory, and/or rebellious.* This evidence suggests that sexual desire can be *flexible, rather than immutable.* These are not small studies that cannot be replicated. They include the largest investigations on the subject, conducted by institutes and researchers on both sides of the gay rights debate.

Sexual Preference Shifts. That sexual desire and behavior are flexible was first demonstrated by the Kinsey Institute, whose later research, though not impeccable, is better conceived and therefore more useful. Their 1970 study reported[152] that *84 percent of 665 gays* and *29 percent of 335 heterosexual men shifted or changed their sexual orientation* at least once; 60 percent of the homosexuals *vs* 10 percent of the heterosexuals reported a *second* sexual orientation shift; 32 percent of the gays *vs* 4 percent of heterosexuals reported a *third* shift; and 13 percent of gays *vs* 1 percent of heterosexuals reported *at least five changes.* The findings for lesbians and heterosexual women were similar: 97 percent of the 277 lesbians *vs* 15 percent of 136 heterosexual women reported one shift; 81 percent of the lesbians *vs* 2 percent of the heterosexuals reported a second shift in sexual orientation; 52 percent of the lesbians *vs* 1 percent of the heterosexuals reported another shift; and 29 percent of the lesbians *vs* none of the heterosexual women reported *at least five changes* of sexual orientation. Immutable traits like eye or skin color don't change once, much less two, three, four, or five times!

Unlike the biological changes that come with maturation, the second shift in sexual orientation began, on average, at age 18 in both gay men and lesbians. Sexual changes, five or more years after puberty, are *exceptionally* late and without precedent in biologic development. But changes in *tastes* (e.g., food or entertainment) often take place around age 18.

The Kinsey Institute also produced evidence that could not be explained in terms of biological determinism, but would readily support the idea that choice was involved in sexual orientation:

- 74 percent of gays (*vs* 6 percent of heterosexual women) admitted to having been *sexually aroused* by a female and 80 percent of lesbians (*vs* 33 percent of the heterosexual males) said that they had been *sexually aroused* by a male.
- 19 percent of gays, 70 percent of heterosexual men, 38 percent of lesbians, and 72 percent of heterosexual women had been *heterosexually* married.
- 20 percent of gays, 5 percent of heterosexual men, 7 percent of lesbians, and no heterosexual women had *sex with animals*.

The Family Research Institute (FRI)[153] conducted a nationwide random survey of 4,340 adults drawn from 5 U.S. cities in 1983 and found results confirming those reported by the Kinsey Institute:

- 82 percent of those currently lesbian and 66 percent of those currently gay said that they *had been in love* with someone of the *opposite* sex.
- 88 percent of lesbians and 73 percent of gays *had been sexually aroused* by someone of the *opposite* sex.

- 67 percent of lesbians and 54 percent of gays reported *current sexual attraction* to the *opposite* sex.

- 85 percent of lesbians and 54 percent of gays, *as adults,* had sexual relations with someone of the *opposite* sex.

- 32 percent of gays, 73 percent of heterosexual men, 47 percent of lesbians and 81 percent of heterosexual women had been *heterosexually* married.

- 17 percent of gays, 3 percent of heterosexual men, 10 percent of lesbians and 1 percent of heterosexual women reported *sex with animals.*

These are the kinds of sexual behaviors and choices one would expect from those who were sexually exploratory or confused. Unless Dr. Isay and his supporters are willing to believe that people are genetically predisposed to marry or to have sex with animals, some measure of *choice,* rather than mere biologic inevitability, *must* have been involved.

Like the 1970 Kinsey study, the FRI results demonstrate that people are not compelled to act on their sexual temptations.

- Of those *heterosexually aroused* (98 percent of both sexes reported arousal), 96 percent had at least one heterosexual partner, and 97 percent of the women and 92 percent of the men said they'd *fallen in heterosexual love;* while

- Of those *homosexually aroused,* 78 percent of the males and 65 percent of the females reported homosexual sex, and 48 percent of the males and 52 percent of the females fell in homosexual love.

Findings in regard to those with homosexual desires and experiences also revealed the ability to change:

- Overall, 7.8 percent of women and 12 percent of men claimed to have been homosexually aroused at some point in their life. Yet 59 percent of the homosexually aroused women and 51 percent of aroused men were currently *heterosexual.*

- 5.1 percent of the women and 9.4 percent of the men admitted to at least one homosexual partner. Of these, only 58 percent of the women and 61 percent of the men were currently gay.

- 4.1 percent of women and 5.8 percent of men reported that they had, at least once, been "in homosexual love."
- 66 percent of those who had fallen in love with a member of their sex were currently gay.
- almost a third of those who admitted to homosexual relations in adulthood *were now heterosexual.*

Where is the "biologic inevitability" or "immutability" in these findings? Even more troubling for the "born that way" argument, the FRI survey in Dallas[154] found that 1 percent of heterosexual females and 3 percent of heterosexual males at one time considered themselves homosexual (i.e., were ex-gay when interviewed).

These are among the findings that seriously challenge the claim that sexual orientation is predetermined before or after birth, or even that it is permanently fixed in adulthood.

CONCLUSION

In examining the uses and abuses of scientific data to justify homosexuality, I have traced in this chapter an unmistakable pattern: On the basis of scant evidence, and with little or no regard for opposing opinion, heralds in white coats state unequivocally that homosexuality is a normal and healthy condition, that it poses no threat to the public at large, and that opinions to the contrary are the products of ignorance and bigotry; the press, always credulous and eager to be of service, reports such statements as incontrovertible fact; the gay rights movement picks up the cry and uses it to further its political agenda; and finally, professional organizations like the American Psychological Association send representatives to affirm this new immutable truth before Congress and the highest courts of the land. The end result has been the legalization of sodomy in 26 states, the AIDS epidemic, the pandemic spread of other sexually transmitted diseases, the celebration of sodomy on the airways, the corruption of our youth, and a growing division among Americans concerning a behavior that once was almost universally condemned.

There are those who say that this pattern suggests a grand conspiracy among scientists to use distortions and misrepresentations to alter the way Americans feel about homosexuals. The truth may be even more depressing: that many of the most noted scientists in the fields of sexology and psychology are so narrowly ideological and so lax in the exercise of their discipline that they instinctively react with one mind when confronted by facts that contradict their own deep-rooted assumptions. Whatever the explanation, people who place their faith in science are in the same situation as many contemporary Christians: their belief is shaken because their spiritual leaders—those who claim to have dedicated their lives to the Faith—no longer believe in the Old Truths, but have sold their souls in the great American marketplace. Indeed, for those who believe the fairy tales of science, the experience may be infinitely more disillusioning.

2

CORPORATE
AMERICA COMES
ABOARD

When Americans over 40 think of the captains of industry, in our mind's eye we see a baldheaded man in a dark suit wearing a diamond stickpin, his eyes two large zeroes in his pleasant face. He is someone we can count on, a tycoon who has always used his enormous power in defense of traditional American values.

He may be a shark in financial waters, but at heart he's a family man, a defender of faith and social order and morality. He has proven his commitment to these principles by adopting a little redheaded orphan girl.

Though Harold Gray is dead, and though Annie sleeps in a hundred morgues of old newspapers, "Daddy" Warbucks still haunts the memory of the nation: "Daddy" the flag waver; "Daddy" the philanthropist; "Daddy" the enemy of foreign entanglements; "Daddy" the believer in a just God; "Daddy" the foster father of us all.

During the years that "Daddy" walked the squares of "Little Orphan Annie," we all felt a little better about ourselves and the kind of country we had created. "Daddy" reminded us that a good man could also be rich—and a rich man could use his wealth for the benefit of mankind, even if he flew around the world in his corporate jet and surrounded himself with servants who could kill with the efficiency of a poisonous snake or spirit enemies off to a terrifying world of demons.

"Daddy," like the President of the United States, symbolized the nation to itself and to the rest of the world. The Leftists could say that capitalism was cruel and exploitative. "Daddy" proved otherwise. So what has happened to "Daddy" since he made his encore appearances on Broadway and in the movies? Where has he been hiding for the past decade? What new worlds has he conquered? To an anxious and quizzical public, I offer the following answer: "Daddy" has been up to no good. As a matter of fact, he has undergone a remarkable change in personality for a man his age. He has altered his views on a number of subjects. He no longer wears his diamond stickpin. He dresses more casually—often in Levis. He is worried about the environment, and his various companies stress this concern in carefully crafted TV commercials. He no longer gives little speeches about the greatness of America. He says now that the United States has many flaws.

He has become Politically Correct.

Oh, he still makes lots of money, billions now instead of millions.

He still wields enormous power. And he still uses that power to further his own private political agenda. But the agenda is substantially altered. He supports gun control and increased social services. He opposes restrictions on immigration. He is also a firm believer in the New World Order, and Punjab and the Asp have become good soldiers in the UN Peacekeeping Force.

Perhaps the strangest transformation off all is "Daddy's" new and passionate commitment to the sexual revolution. Back in the old days, he never thought about sex, or else believed it to be an appetite properly controlled by the institution

of marriage. Today he recognizes all sorts of sexual arrangements, and sees no great danger in widespread promiscuity,
either to his business interests or to the health of the nation at
large.

He believes women have the "right to choose," and he
thinks that homosexuality is just another acceptable "orientation," an alternative lifestyle that must be acknowledged and
even celebrated in a pluralistic society. "Daddy" knows he's
right about these things, just as surely as he knows the Dow
Jones average. "We must break down the barriers that separate
us in the work place and throughout the world," he tells his
fellow members of the Council on Foreign Relations.

"On economic issues Oliver Warbucks may be conservative," the *Wall Street Journal* writes. "but he is a progressive
on social issues." At Warbucks International, he has instituted
a program of sensitivity training to make certain that his employees understand and respect diversity in the work place.
Last June, during Gay Pride Week, all Warbucks employees
were urged to attend a series of lectures and films designed to
educate heterosexuals about gays and their sexual orientation.
Gay activists discussed their life style and answered questions
posed by other employees.

"We've come a long way," said Warbucks, staring out the
window, "but we have a long way to go."

Warbucks International also hands out free condoms to its
employees on holiday weekends and has helped to fund condom distribution in five major school districts. The Warbucks
Foundation is a major contributor to Planned Parenthood and
SIECUS, and has funded pilot programs in sex education in 20
sites nationwide.

"Kids are going to have sex," Warbucks says philosophi-
cally. "We might as well teach them how to avoid the more
serious consequences. That's what this great country is all
about."

He strokes Sandy, a white-muzzled mongrel dog who has
"been in the family forever. The trouble with parents is that

they are basically ignorant about sex. Their kids know more than they do about the subject. We're living in the last decade of the 20th century, and most of these parents are still living in the 1950's. Ozzie and Harriet, the Cleavers—these families are gone forever. We have all sorts of alternate families in this brand new world—single-parent families, families with two gay fathers or two gay mothers. Kids have to adjust to these facts, because they're not going to change."

Asked why his company sponsors shows that the Rev. Donald Wildmon says are pornographic and obscene, Warbucks smiles: "Because that's what people everywhere want to watch, and we're a company that believes in people."

What made "Daddy" change in less than two decades? Or to put the question in more direct, confrontational terms: Why are major American corporations among the chief promoters and funders of the sexual revolution? Why do they promote programs and behaviors that result in major social problems, such as teenage pregnancy, out-of-wedlock births, sexually transmitted diseases, and AIDS? What does American business have to gain from the breakdown of the American family? In a time when corporations are trying to emphasize social responsibility, why are so many encouraging their employees and customers to behave so irresponsibly?

Critics offer several possible answers to these questions, none of them satisfying:

1. Corporate executives are unaware of the dire consequences of the policies they have adopted. This explanation suggests that—far from planning on the basis of long-range social trends—the management of many of the nation's largest corporations are interested only in short-term profits. According to this argument, corporate planners don't understand that if current trends prevail and traditional moral values continue to deteriorate, American society will collapse and with it the affluent marketplace that has supported what some have called "the longest period of uninterrupted prosperity in the history of the world." Ignoring the fate of Rome, Imperial Germany, and other failed societies, they believe that current patterns of behavior can't possibly have long-term effects on the economic strength of the nation.

Such a point of view is puzzling to anyone who knows how a major international corporation operates. Critics of this explanation reply that corporate planners are constantly asking cultural critics, social historians, physicists, psychologists, environmentalists, and other modern soothsayers to tell them what the future will be like. They must have weighed all the evidence, balanced opinion against opinion, computed the pluses and minuses, and made a reasonable projection of a world in which promiscuity, homosexuality, incest, and even "intergenerational sex" are looked upon with relative equanimity. They must have envisioned such a future—and liked it.

2. The destruction of traditional family loyalties would result in the emergence of a new loyalty, a loyalty to company rather than to blood kin, and hence a greater sense of dedication and productivity. This explanation seems slightly more credible than the first one, if only because this kind of thinking has characterized some American corporations for the past 30–40 years. Many multinational companies, taking their lead from the armed services, have systematically rotated their executives from plant to plant, city to city, country to country. Their reasoning: Anyone who puts down roots too deeply in one community inevitably has divided loyalties. Such people tend to establish close friendships, become involved with local institutions, and their hierarchy of commitments is consequently so confused that they may someday come to value their local church or their circle of friends or their civic responsibilities more highly than they do their jobs. Better to keep them on the road, like good soldiers, so that their ultimate loyalty is to the company for whom they work.

The damage that such policies have inflicted on American society is incalculable. It is not too farfetched to suggest that a significant portion of the disorder and violence of the 1960s was the result of an uprooted younger generation, dragged around from city to city, school to school, neighborhood to neighborhood—"corporate brats" to rival a slightly earlier generation of "Army brats." (It is perhaps significant that this generation of rebels saw Big Business as the chief villain in American society.)

Some argue this same kind of thinking prevails in the new corporate contempt for the American family and the traditional religious assumptions that have always justified family life. Are corporations simply attacking one more loyalty that threatens absolute commitment to Warbucks International?

Despite a history of contempt for stable family relations on the part of many major companies, it seems unlikely that such an oblique explanation of current policy can account for everything that has happened over the past 5–10 years. American business is neither so circuitous in its thinking nor so Machiavellian. At best a casual contempt for traditional family values has allowed corporate executives to adopt these new, radical policies towards sexuality.

3. Corporate America believes so strongly in the free market that logic compels the extension of free market principles into the realm of moral behavior. This is an even more viable theory than the other two, in part because corporate executives often voice such a creed themselves in justification for these new company policies. "We allow freedom of choice in the marketplace," they say, "so why not freedom of choice in morality? Americans once dined almost exclusively on hamburgers, steak, and fried chicken. Today we can choose from literally scores of ethnic menus in our restaurants and supermarkets. Why not the same thing in codes of sexual conduct?"

The proper role of corporate America, they say, is either to remain completely aloof in the current cultural war, or else to enter on the side of those who want a freer, more permissive society. If people want to hold religious views that prevent them from engaging in extramarital sex or homosexual activities, then they have a perfect right to do so. But they have no right to impose their views on their fellow members of the work place—or on society at large.

Indeed, Warbucks International has a responsibility to make certain that every idea about morality has an equal chance to compete with every other idea. That's the way it works in free-market economics. That's the way it ought to work in ethics and morality.

For anyone who believes that human behavior can be explained exclusively in terms of economic theory—whether communist or capitalist—this kind of thinking makes good sense, which may be why sexual permissiveness has characterized both Marxist social arrangements from the beginning and why it is increasingly characteristic of a materialistic America. We are becoming a people committed to the dogma of Freedom Unlimited, and corporate America has become the chief advocate of such dogmatism.

One or more of these three explanations for "Daddy's" change in attitude seems satisfactory to most observers, but the remaining few still raise questions. For example, given the long-range planning constantly in progress by the Research and Development arms of multinational corporations, how can top management believe a widening sexual revolution will favorably affect the future of business? Why do they not conclude that such a policy, far from enriching us all and making the world more tolerant, will lead to greater social problems and hence a more unmanageable society?

And even more important: Recognizing that the destabilizing of a social order is a very dangerous experiment to undertake, what are the potential long-term benefits that make such a course desirable, despite the risks? Or to put it another way, why are corporate executives willing to gamble with the future of their own families, their companies, and their communities—unless the ultimate reward is more than worth the gamble?

And finally: What is the reward they anticipate, if not for themselves then for future generations?

The answer to that question is not easy, particularly since all business leaders would not agree with the manner in which the question is formulated. Corporate America is by no means monolithic. To the contrary, these people are at economic war with one another—conducting their strategy sessions in secret, plotting marketing tactics with the imagination and precision of military field commanders, engaging in high-tech espionage.

We are talking here about a social arena full of arch enemies, each out to bankrupt the other like tokens on a Monopoly board. How could such people get together to support a sexual revolution?

Yet despite the highly competitive nature of American business, the planning of many multinational companies is surprisingly well-coordinated. In the holy name of business itself, they get together in thoughtful "round tables" and "councils" and "committees" to map out national and global strategies. They presume to plot the future, albeit for the benefit of all mankind. Since, to such people, the facts of life are ultimately economic, who is better qualified? Small wonder that their response to the sexual revolution is often well-coordinated and all but unanimous.

This is true in large measure because sexuality is just another factor to be considered in an overarching economic plan that anticipates a future so full of promise and prosperity that some businessmen can hardly wait to arrive there. In very general terms, the scenario goes something like this:

Act 1: Following the end of the Cold War, the world enters a period of rapid economic expansion during which the Third World Countries are developed. This is accomplished through massive influxes of capital from the International Monetary Fund and the World Bank. During this same period, the industrial nations of the world surrender enormous chunks of wealth and sovereignty in order to provide the framework for international peace—a prerequisite to Third World Development, since international trade is disrupted by regional wars.

Act II: Once the Third World Countries have been developed, they will become the largest consumers of goods in the world because of their population advantage. In order to do business in a culturally diverse global marketplace, multinational corporations will use their influence to overcome old barriers of nationality, religion, race, sex, and custom (including customs governing sexual behavior). Because their role is to take the lead in such a period of necessary change, the industrial nations cultivate tolerance and love of diversity as paramount virtues during this period. These virtues are promoted in advertising, in entertainment, and in education.

Act III: After several decades of difficult adjustment, the world gradually becomes more uniform, more tolerant, more benign. By now the United Nations has eliminated all threat of war. Nationalism has died out and has been replaced by a New World Order. The religions of the world, after some resistance, have melded into one Great Faith, composed of a few ethical principles common to all world religions and directed toward the betterment of humanity. No one is worried about doctrinal differences because there are none, and all prophets (Jesus, Moses, Mohammed, Buddha, Confucius, Ron Hubbard) are treated with equal respect, insofar as anyone thinks about them at all. Any strong sense of sexual morality has vanished with the changing times, and everyone respects everyone else's bedroom habits, provided no one is forced into any act against his or her will. At this point, international trade is humming along at peak efficiency, God's in His heaven, all's right with the world.

This three-act comedy is, according to some, the future as scripted by multinational corporations in conference with one another. Of course, they don't put it in precisely these terms. Their version is full of facts, figures, computer graphics, statistical projections, and high-tech rhetoric. Nor would they admit, even to themselves, that the elimination of all cultural differences is possible or even desirable. These are matters that must be taken up case-by-case. However, they will point out that, at present, many of these differences (or barriers) prevent the easy expansion of world trade and threaten development of Third World countries. For this reason, we must nurture a more "global" point of view, one that accepts alternative views readily and with equanimity. We can begin this acceptance, they say, by learning more of the world around us and by being more tolerant of other people in our own country—people of different races, different religions, different ethnic backgrounds . . . different sexual orientations.

All corporations have not chosen to push this new tolerance for "diversity." Some are content merely to expand their world markets and to make certain they do not run afoul of the various pressure groups that currently stalk the marketplace, prepared to punish companies that trade with South Africa, threaten the environment, discriminate against racial minorities, or mistreat animals. Others, however, have begun to promote the kinds of attitudes and behaviors that will help usher in the New World Order. Some programs are very tentative and moderate. Others are aggressive and avant garde. Some simply seek to eliminate bias and provincialism. Others attempt to indoctrinate their employees with an entirely new social and political philosophy.

I do not presume to quarrel with all such programs. Some are beneficial. Others are harmless. Still others may go beyond the bounds of propriety in their attempt to mandate political correctness.

However, when these programs take up the question of sexual propriety, they are highly suspect—in part because this kind of preoccupation goes beyond the proper purview of Daddy Warbucks and his Total Quality Management team, in part because they are invariably based on poor information and faulty science. Indeed, if we had only Daddy's understanding of sexual matters to judge him by, we would tremble for the economic future of Warbucks International and the United States of America.

In fact, "Daddy"—in the habit of relying on statistical charts and computer projections—is easy prey for any sexual revolutionary who comes along with a "study" or "report" that supports the agenda. The "free market of ideas" is glutted with falsified evidence, bogus data, and fraudulent figures that support the dogmas of Planned Parenthood, the Gay and Lesbian Task Force, and SIECUS—and "Daddy" has been perfectly willing to accept these "scientific" assertions at face value, without bothering to check their validity or to see if alternative positions exist.

A researcher for the Federal government told me in near despair: "I can give these people [business executives] all the evidence they need to support educational programs that teach conventional sexual morality, but they would prefer to believe the newspapers and television sets."

And indeed corporate policies adopted over the past decade seem to follow the dictates of an increasingly permissive popular culture. Of course, the change has been gradual—a step-by-step abandonment of earlier practice. The first step in promoting "sexual freedom" was to abandon older corporate policies that prescribed a close scrutiny of the private lives of employees, particularly those at the executive level. For generations, major American businesses insisted that management-level employees be married and that their family arrangements be acceptable to the community at large. Flagrant infidelities, messy divorces, even the social ineptitude of a wife or husband, could cost a rising executive the chance for further advancement and in extreme cases resulted in dismissal.

As for homosexuality, it was not tolerated. Regarded as beyond the pale of respectable company, overt homosexuals had no future in the corporate hierarchy—at least not above the level of technician. After all, studies showed that conventionally married employees lived longer, had fewer health problems, and were therefore more productive workers.

The first deviation from this widespread approach was a policy of non-intervention. With the 1960s and the sexual revolution came two problems that made a new approach attractive to many corporations. First, an increasing number of employees were leading "unconventional" sex lives, living with men or women rather than marrying them, enjoying an increasing number of available partners in short-term sexual activities. Second, the Left, and particularly the militant feminists, were more and more insistent that policies concerning sexual arrangements had profound political implications. Not only was the private life of an employee none of the company's business, but any corporate commitment to marriage, "an inherently repressive institution," was "sexist" and "fascist." So many major companies began to abandon previous policies and officially adopt a hands-off approach to the private lives of employees. For example, IBM now tells its executives that the company is informed by three basic principles: service for the customer, peace through international trade, and respect for the individual (i.e., a non-interventionist policy regarding the private lives of their employees).

The second step in advancing sexual freedom was to promote actively the adoption of laissez faire sexuality among the corporation's employees. It was one thing for Warbucks International to stop monitoring the sexual activities of its top executives. It was quite another to promote "sexual tolerance" among all its employees. Not only did such a policy put the company on record in this all-too-sensitive area, but the advocacy of sexual freedom also set a corporate policy that stood in direct opposition to the religious and social values of many of its employees.

Most orthodox religious people were probably willing to grant that they had no right to control the sex lives of fellow employees. But few were willing to assent to the abstract principle that one code of conduct was equal to another. If Fred tells you that he is living with his girl friend (or his male lover), you can easily shrug your shoulders and say, "Well, that's Fred's business, I suppose. Certainly I won't let it affect the way I handle his company paperwork. On the other hand, I believe what he's doing is morally wrong, and I don't intend to ask him and his live-in lover to have dinner with my family."

That particular attitude distinguishes between Fred the Fellow Worker and Fred the Fornicator or Fred the Sodomite, and is perfectly consistent with the old adage "Bad companions corrupt good morals." It is an attitude that also recognizes the need for some sense of sexual propriety in society—a general recognition of rules that have informed Western civilization for thousands of years.

Unfortunately, many corporations, in their zeal to instill a company-wide tolerance toward fellow workers, have concluded that in order to accomplish this end they will have to alter the moral and religious attitudes of huge segments of the work force. In other words, in the same spirit in which they declared war on their competitors, both here and abroad, they also declared war on Judeo-Christian beliefs about human sexuality.

Adopting a new paternalistic stance toward their workers, they began to offer literature, lectures, and videotapes that promoted the idea that sexual behaviors previously regarded as immoral were in fact healthy and normal and positively uplifting. These "educational" materials were usually quasi-scientific in nature and featured the observations of an impartial and omniscient voice that spoke in behalf of absolute reason and unchallenged truth.

In fact, much of what the voice offered was a dose of anti-religious bigotry sugar-coated with the usual popular sex myths—that the idea consensual sex outside of marriage is immoral is the product of puritanism; that most normal people have a variety of sex experiences with both sexes during their lifetime; that intercourse is no longer dangerous if you use a condom; that abortion is an inalienable right; that homosexuality is as natural and rewarding as heterosexuality; that anyone who disagrees with any of these propositions is a bigot and an enemy of democracy.

Much of this sexual revisionism in corporate America was instituted in response to the gay rights movement, whose leaders not only convinced the general public that homosexuals constituted ten percent of the population, but also began to threaten major corporations with massive boycotts if they didn't swing in behind the agenda.

Perhaps the most important statement of how the homosexuals bullied, cajoled, seduced, and captured big business can be found in a discussion of gay rights media strategy coauthored by Marshall K. Kirk and Erastes Pill. Kirk has emerged as one of the most influential spokesmen for the movement; and his book, *After the Ball* is regarded as a major statement on the subject. This outline of strategy for the propagation of the movement, as recommended by Kirk and Pill, was published in at least two gay rights journals—*Christopher Street* and *Guide Magazine*—and later appeared in the longer book.

It has been a matter of public record for five years now. Yet no one seems to have grasped its significance, to say nothing of the enormity of its presumption. Consider, for example, the following passages, which deal with the way in which Americans must be manipulated into support for the gay rights movement. Kirk and Pill begin by defining the limits of what homosexuals can hope to accomplish.

> The first order of business is desensitization of the American public concerning gays and gay rights. To desensitize the public is to help it view homosexuality with indifference instead of with keen emotion. . . . At least in the beginning we are seeking desensitization and nothing more. We do not need and cannot expect a full "appreciation" or "understanding" of homosexuality from the average American. You can forget about trying to persuade the masses that homosexuality is a good thing. But if only you can get them to think that it is just another thing, with a shrug of their shoulders, then your battle for legal and social rights is virtually won.

This is an extraordinarily shrewd observation, one that the gay rights movement has taken to heart and its opponents have ignored. If people can be persuaded to pass over the true nature of homosexuals and merely accept their existence as a natural and inevitable part of the social scene, then it is one small step to granting them the same special treatment under the law afforded to other "minorities."

And how do the authors propose to go about this process of desensitization? They offer a six-point plan.

(1) Talk about gays and gayness as loudly and as often as possible. The principle behind this advice is simple: almost any behavior begins to look normal if you are exposed to enough of it at close quarters and among your acquaintances. The acceptability of the new behavior will ultimately hinge on the number of one's fellows doing or accepting it. . . . The way to benumb raw sensitivities about homosexuality is to have a lot of people talk a great deal about the subject in a neutral and supportive way. . . . In the early stages of any campaign to reach straight America, the masses should not be shocked and repelled by premature exposure to homosexual behavior itself. Instead the imagery of sex should be downplayed and gay rights should be reduced to an abstract social question as much as possible. First let the camel get his nose inside the tent—and only later his unsightly derriere!

And who is best qualified to carry this soft-sell message to the American people as a whole?

The visual media, film and television, are plainly the most powerful image-makers in Western civilization. So far, gay Hollywood has provided the best covert weapon in the battle to desensitize the mainstream.

Bit by bit over the past ten years, gay characters and gay themes have been introduced into TV programs and films (though often this has been done to achieve comedic and ridiculous effects). On the whole, the impact has been encouraging. The prime-time presentation of *Consenting Adult* on a major network in 1985 is but one high-water mark in favorable media exposure of gay issues. But this should be just the beginning of a major publicity blitz by gay America.

And what about religious objects? Again, knowing they can speak out with impunity, Kirk and Pill are very explicit:

When conservative churches condemn gays, there are only two things we can do to confound the homophobia of true believers.

First, we can use talk to muddy the moral waters. This means publicizing support for gays by more moderate churches, raising theological objections of our own about conservative interpretations of biblical teachings, and exposing hatred and inconsistencies. Second, we can undermine homophobic churches by portraying them as antiquated backwaters, badly out of step with the times and with the latest findings of psychology. Against the mighty pull of institutional Religion one must set the mightier draw of Science and Public Opinion (the shield and sword of that accursed "secular humanism.") Such an unholy alliance has worked well against churches before, on such topics as divorce and abortion. With enough open talk about the prevalence and acceptance of homosexuality, that alliance can work here again.

The second strategy is even bolder than the first, and one we see increasingly employed in the political arena.

(2) Portray gays as victims, not as aggressive challengers. In any campaign to win over the public, gays must be cast as victims in need of protection so that straights will be inclined by reflex to assume the role of protector . . . we must forego the temptation to strut our "gay pride" publicly when it conflicts with the Gay Victim image. . . .

By the way, we realize many gays will question an advertising technique which might threaten to make homosexuality look like a disease which strikes fatal "victims." But the plain fact is that the gay community is weak and must manipulate the powers of the weak, including the play for sympathy. . . . The second message would portray gays as victims of society. The straight majority does not recognize the suffering it brings to the lives of gays and must be shown: graphic pictures of brutalized gays; dramatizations of job and 'housing insecurity, loss of child custody, and public humiliation; and the dismal list goes on.

The third tactic is again a manipulation of public opinion by turning the debate away from the practices of homosexuals to questions of equity and justice.

(3) Give protectors a just cause. . . . Our campaign should not demand direct support for homosexual practices, but should instead take anti-discrimination as its theme. The homophobes

clothe their emotional revulsion in the daunting robes of religious dogma, so defenders of gay rights must be ready to counter dogma with principles.

The fourth tactic:

(4) Make gays look good. In order to make a Gay Victim sympathetic to straights you have to portray him as Everyman. But an additional theme of the campaign should be more aggressive and upbeat: to offset the increasingly bad press that these times have brought to homosexual men and women, the campaign should paint gays as superior pillars of society.

The fifth tactic explains much of the current rhetoric in the press and on the airways, the kinds of invective characteristic of a Phil Donohue or Geraldo Rivera show. Remember, however, that Kirk and Pill are here talking about advertising campaigns rather than genuine news. It is interesting to note that in this passage the authors are not only willing but eager to use regional and religious stereotypes to generate their own bigotry.

(5) Make the victimizers look bad. At a later stage of the media campaign for gay rights—long after other gay ads have become commonplace—it will be time to get tough. To be blunt, they must be vilified . . . the public should be shown images of ranting homophobes whose secondary traits and beliefs disgust middle America. These images might include: the Ku Klux Klan demanding that gays be burned alive or castrated; bigoted southern ministers drooling with hysterical hatred to a degree that looks both comical and deranged; menacing punks, thugs and convicts speaking coolly about the "fags" they have killed or would like to kill; a tour of Nazi concentration camps where homosexuals were tortured and gassed.

Finally, these authors know what will make the whole contrived rhetorical circus viable:

(6) Solicit funds: the bucks stop here. Any massive campaign of this kind would require unprecedented expenditures for months or even years—an unprecedented fundraising drive.

Admitting the difficulty of raising money for such a massive propaganda campaign, the authors complain about the necessity to use friendly media contacts to get free publicity of the sort they seek.

Because the most straightforward appeals are impossible, the National Gay Task Force has had to cultivate quiet backroom liaisons with broadcast companies and newsrooms in order to make sure that issues important to the gay community receive some coverage; but such an arrangement is hardly ideal, of course, because it means that the gay community's image is controlled by the latest news event instead of careful design—and recently most of the news about gays has been negative.

As for media, Kirk and Pill suggest that rather than place ads in standard Left-wing journals, where they will be preaching to the choir, gay rights organizations should seek to advertise in such major news publications as *Time, People,* and the *National Enquirer.* For other media, they suggest the following strategies:

As for television and radio, a more elaborate plan may be needed to break the ice. For openers, naturally, we must continue to encourage the appearance of favorable gay characters in films and TV shows. Daytime shows also make a useful avenue for exposure.

They also suggest that homosexuals run for "high political office," just to introduce gay rights themes into the debate. However, Kirk and Pill know better than to put gay rights issues on the ballot:

It is essential not to ask people actually to vote Yea or Nay on the Gay issue at this early stage: such action would end up committing most to the Nay position and would only tally huge and visible defeats for our cause.

Indeed, when gay rights issues have been put to a popular referendum rather than passed by a city council or state legislature, they have nearly always been voted down. Even in San Francisco, gay right measures have actually been defeated in a general election, though not always. In the rest of the country

there are few instances where they have passed the muster of
the ordinary voter. Kirk and Pill also propose a subtle campaign of ads to include "squeaky clean skits on the importance
of family harmony and understanding"—all very quiet and
subdued. Remember: exposure is everything, and the medium
is the message.

In addition they suggest:

> The gay community should join forces with other civil liberties
> groups of respectable cast to promote bland messages about
> America the Melting Pot, always ending with an explicit reference
> to the Task Force or some other gay organization.

After these "bland" messages have gained acceptance, they
propose to "bring gay ads out of the closet." They offer the
following examples:

> To make gays seem less mysterious, present a series of short spots
> featuring the boy-or girl-next-door, fresh and appealing, or warm
> and lovable grandma and grandpa types. Seated in homey sur-
> roundings, they respond to an off-camera interviewer with assur-
> ance, good nature, and charm. Their comments bring out three
> social facts: (1) There is someone special in their life, a long-term
> relationship (to stress gay stability, monogamy, commitment); (2)
> Their families are very important to them, and are supportive of
> them (to stress that gays are not "anti-family," and that families
> need not be anti-gay); (3) As far as they can remember, they have
> always been gay and were probably born gay; they certainly never
> decided on a preference one way or the other (stressing that gays
> are doing what is natural for them, and are not being wilfully
> contrary).

One need only examine these proposed ads carefully to recognize what is now commonplace in television portrayals of
homosexuals: A new stereotype, carefully contrived to present
homosexuals in precisely the way they want to be seen by the
community at large—as normal, family-loving people who are
behaving in a "natural" fashion. While these idealized portraits
have not as yet been presented in television ads (at least, none
that I have seen), because of gay rights pressure on all three

networks, such self-serving stereotypes are standard fare now in comic and dramatic shows. In addition, one can see the same technique followed almost to the letter in propaganda being funded and distributed by major corporations like AT&T. Indeed, one of Kirk and Pill's ideas has been adapted for use by Brian McNaught, Daddy's Favorite Gay Rights Apologist. Curiously, another idea they present is also incorporated into a McNaught video, albeit in slightly altered form:

> The camera approaches the mighty oak door of the boss's office, and the camera (which represents you, the viewer) enters the room. Behind the oversized desk sits a fat and scowling old curmudgeon chomping on a cigar. He looks up at the camera (i.e. at the viewer) and snarls, "So it's you, Smithers. Well, you're fired!" The voice of a younger man is heard to reply, with astonishment, "But—but—Mr. Thornburg, I've been with your company for ten years. I thought you liked my work." The boss responds, with a tone of disgust, "Yes, yes, Smithers, your work is quite adequate. But I've heard rumors that you've been seen around town with some kind of girlfriend. A girlfriend! Frankly, I'm shocked. We're not about to start hiring heterosexuals in this company. Now get out." The younger an speaks once more: "But boss, that's not fair! What if it were you?" The boss glowers back as the camera pulls quickly out of the room and the big door slams shut. Printed on the door: "A Message from the National Gay Task Force."

The next stage emphasizes the necessity to attack Christianity and its believers. And the way in which they would film this suggested attack is instructive:

> We have already indicated some of the images which might be damaging to the homophobic vendetta: ranting and hateful religious extremists, neo-Nazis, and Ku Klux Klansmen made to look evil and ridiculous (hardly a difficult task). These images should be combined with those of their gay victims by a method propagandists call the "bracket technique."

> For example, for a few seconds an unctuous beady-eyed Southern preacher is seen, pounding the pulpit in rage about "those sick, abominable creatures." While his tirade continues over the soundtrack, the picture switches to pathetic photos of badly beaten persons,

or to photos of gays who look decent, harmless, and likable; and then we cut back to the poisonous face of the preacher, and so forth. The contrast speaks for itself. The effect is devastating. (pp. 13–14)

Again, no need for the gay rights movement to expend its funds in such a manner. The major TV networks are continually flashing these same images on the screen in prime time dramas and sitcoms, and sympathetic corporations like AT&T are sponsoring such shows with their advertising campaigns. How often does the beady-eyed preacher appear? And how often does one see the idealized portraits of homosexuals prescribed above?

In addition to adopting the strategy proposed by Kirk and Pill, the homosexual activists preyed on the illusion among corporate executives that science can save the world. Produce enough studies, surveys, reports, and statistics and you can bowl over the most hard-boiled CEO that ever drove a competitor into bankruptcy. And often enough you don't need to produce the study. Just state boldly and unequivocally that such a study exists and refer to it in your literature and conversation. Such has been the case with Kinsey's famous 10 percent. That the ten percent figure was a fraud apparently never occurred to the leadership of multinational corporations, so it mattered little whether or not there were, in fact, 25 million homosexuals in America.

I am reminded of the young woman who was visiting in Maine and came back from a solitary walk bruised and bloody. "Good heavens," said her hostess, "What happened to you?" "I was chased off a cliff by a snake," the young woman replied." "But there are no poisonous snakes in Maine," said her hostess. The young woman shrugged her shoulders. "They don't have to be poisonous when they can chase you off a cliff." And so it is with the gay rights movement. Homosexuals don't have to constitute ten percent of the population if they can force giant corporations to use corporate assets to fund their agenda and to attack traditional sexual morality.

And this is precisely what they have done, as the following examples illustrate.

PHILLIP MORRIS

In April of 1990, homosexual activists launched a boycott against the Phillip Morris Corporation, producers of Marlboro cigarettes and Miller beer. Phillip Morris's crime: donating money to the 1990 campaign of Senator Jesse Helms, who has stoutly opposed the gay rights agenda in the U.S. Senate. Phillip Morris protested that their support of Helms was purely for business reasons. Helms, the senior senator from North Carolina, has perennially supported the tobacco industry. It was legal extortion—a ploy to punish Phillip Morris for its political incorrectness and to shake down the company in behalf of gay rights organization.

The boycott was particularly effective against Miller beer. According to *Overlooked Opinions,* a polling firm that specializes in homosexual market research, 51 percent of U.S. homosexuals, male and female, stopped drinking Miller as a consequence of the boycott. After a year, Phillip Morris finally settled with the gay rights organizations leading the boycott. They did not promise to withdraw support from Senator Helms, but they did issue a statement saying that their endorsement "should not be seen as an endorsement of any other of his positions." More importantly, the company promised to double its annual contributions to AIDS charities and to "lesbian/gay organizations." At that point the corporation had already donated $1.3 million to homosexual groups and AIDS activities. In a statement, Phillip Morris announced that the company "and representatives of ACT-UP and the gay and lesbian community have agreed on a plan to encourage community-based organizations to apply for grants from Phillip Morris. . . . All agencies providing [services] to the gay and lesbian community are encouraged to apply."

Using the language of gay activism, the company went on to say: "To fight AIDS is also to fight both discrimination against people living with AIDS and homophobia. Education efforts to combat these forms of discrimination may also be funded by Phillip Morris, which continues to stand against all forms of intolerance." One wonders what Phillip Morris means here by "homophobia" and "intolerance." Does the company mean, for example, the belief that homosexual conduct is immoral?

In which case, those who believe in the authority of the Bible on such sexual matters, including orthodox Christians and Jews, would be among those whom Phillip Morris would be donating funds to "combat." A bold gamble for the company—to risk alienating a significant portion of the population in order to please a considerably smaller segment, even if corporate executives believed them to constitute 10 percent. It was another victory for the gay rights movement, and another corporate scalp to brandish (*Philadelphia Gay News* June 7–13, 1991).

THE ADOLPH COORS COMPANY

The Adolph Coors Company was also the target of a lengthy boycott, one that lasted for over a decade, and continues in some segments of the homosexual community. Coors was singled out because of corporate and family gifts to such conservative organizations as the Free Congress Foundation.

Although the company is the third largest brewer in the country, with 1991 sales of $1.53 billion, and though its leadership is strongly conservative, Coors eventually made major concessions to the gay rights movement. You now see Coors beer advertised in homosexual publications, and the corporation has made substantial contributions to homosexual organizations and charities.

LOTUS

Perhaps the most "gay friendly" corporation in America is Lotus Development, which several years ago offered to its homosexual employees complete spousal benefits for their long-term, live-in sex partners. With 3,100 on its payroll, Lotus is by far the largest corporation to take such a step, though a few others (e.g. Ben and Jerry's Homemade, the *Village Voice*) have offered similar packages. It is important to note that Lotus does not offer benefits to the lovers of heterosexual employees, no matter how long they've been around the house. Russ Campanello, Lotus vice president of human resources, explained in a *Fortune* interview that since homosexuals do not have the option to marry, they alone are eligible. They must sign an affidavit saying that they live together, plan to continue the relationship, and assume responsibility for one another. Then they receive the full package, including health coverage—a crucial point to an AIDS-riddled community. (With typical disregard of medical literature, Campanello claims that long-term homosexual couples are no more at risk of AIDS than married heterosexual couples.) Of course, this policy requires that homosexuals come out of the closet, but Campanello says this is not discrimination, since "by requiring straight people to be married, we make them come out of the closet too." It is interesting to note that as of December, 1991, when *Fortune* reported on Lotus's program, only eight of the 3,100 employees had signed up (which, you'll notice is 0.26 percent—right in line with the Census Bureau study that counted 0.2 percent gay and lesbian couples nationwide [see chapter 1]).

OTHER CORPORATIONS

In addition to extorting money and support from corporations by boycotts and threats of boycotts, the gay rights activists were also making inroads in other ways. For one thing, some, after rising to the highest echelons of business, came out of the closet. A few years earlier, such a move might have meant their jobs. Now, with the gay rights movement masquerading as a 900-pound gorilla, they were able to flaunt their homosexuality with relative impunity. In December of 1991, *Fortune* took note of the phenomenon in a sympathetic cover story that quoted the 10 percent figure twice and cited exemplary success stories to reinforce the idea that corporate America was beginning to fall in line with the gay rights agenda:

- Levi-Strauss encouraged their gay employees to organize and to put up a banner in June that proclaimed: LESBIAN AND GAY EMPLOYEE ASSOCIATION CELEBRATES PRIDE WEEK.

- Employees at AT&T, Boeing, Coors, Du Pont, Hewlett-Packard, Lockheed, Sun Microsystems, U.S. West, and XEROX are also out of the closet. Al Lewis, a planning manager active in the XEROX gay employees organization, boasted: "Official or unofficial, there's a group in every large company in America."

- These groups use electronic bulletin boards to post personal messages, inform members of their legal rights, and even to pass along news of homosexuals in other corporations. According to *Fortune*, when Lotus announced spousal benefits to long-term partners of homosexuals, the word was passed around the country "within minutes" via homosexual bulletin boards.

- All over the country homosexual businessmen and businesswomen have formed informal clubs that transcend corporate boundaries and establish bonds between like-minded people. These groups often promote business contacts based on sexual orientation. In New York a coalition of such groups is known as "the Network." The Network's Christmas benefit has been known to attract 1,000 people, according to *Fortune*.

But corporations do not stop at employing homosexuals and allowing them to form groups within the organization. Many have determined that employees who disapprove of homosexuality are either ignorant or bigoted and must be "educated" to make certain they approve of homosexual relationships—regardless of what their churches may teach. These "education" programs are known as "diversity or sensitivity training" and are often taught by homosexuals, who appeal both to pity and to anti-Christian bigotry. They are almost always undergirded by erroneous scientific pronouncements and are conducted with the express purpose of "work[ing] together to 'demystify' homosexuality, help straight employees feel comfortable working alongside openly gay ones, and cleanse the work place of offensive jokes and insults."

AT&T has operated "homophobia workshops" since 1987. According to Thomas A. Stewart, who wrote this credulous and poorly researched story, "[Employees] receive accurate information to replace myths they may have swallowed, such as that homosexuality is 'curable,' or that gay men are sexual predators." The AT&T workshop is run by Brian McNaught, a homosexual himself, and his presentation is worth analyzing, since it illustrates just how ideological a corporation like AT&T can be.

As the Brian McNaught video opens, we see a living room, quietly but elegantly appointed. On a stuffed leather sofa sits a clean-cut young man who looks like a 1990's version of Wally Cleaver. He is dressed in slacks, an open shirt, and a sweater. He is clean-shaven and strikingly wholesome. If you had a golden-haired daughter who had just graduated from college, you would think seriously of arranging an introduction with this young banker or doctor or clergyman. When he begins to speak, he comes across as reasonable and prudent, the sort of fellow you'd ask to handle your stock portfolio, if you had one. It is only after he has been talking for a few minutes that you begin to see the bitchiness behind his genial exterior, the hostility that simmers just beneath the surface. But by then you may have been beguiled by his appeal to your natural capacity for pity, your Christian charity, your gullibility.

He immediately asks you to enter a fantasy world of his own creation—a society that is predominately homosexual. How would you like it, he asks, if your parents were gay, your teachers were gay, your siblings and playmates were gay, television shows were gay, the whole society were gay—and you were heterosexual? He doesn't merely raise the question and then make his point. He goes on to involve you in a romantic story of forbidden fantasies, shy discovery, tender affections, and idyllic love. The heterosexual lovers in his homosexual world, despite a mean-spirited society, find brief happiness together only to be wrenched apart by sudden death, a tragedy the bereaved lover cannot openly mourn.

Narrated with all the sweetness of a Mother Goose story, this little tale is guaranteed to entrance the thoughtless viewer, who would never think that the same approach could be used to sentimentalize pedophilia, bestiality, and necrophilia. ("How would you feel if you grew up in a place where everyone fell in love with the dead?") Certainly it would terrible to live in a world completely dominated by sexual perversion, just as it would be terrible to be homosexual in a normal society. No one denies the pain that such people suffer, and no one should be hard-hearted or pitiless in the face of such a plight. On the other hand, it is a non sequitur to conclude, as McNaught does before he is finished with his presentation, that homosexuals are just as normal and healthy as heterosexuals—and perhaps even more so, because they may be just a little higher on the evolutionary scale.

After offering his lengthy parable, he reinforces it by repeating all the quasi-scientific cliches that have become standard rhetoric among gay rights advocates. Indeed, McNaught is well on his way to becoming the Joseph Goebbels of the gay rights movement, with his plausible repetition of the movement's familiar lies and factoids.

- He cites both Kinsey studies—*Sexual Behavior in the Human Male* (1948); *Sexual Behavior in the Human Female*

(1953)—as evidence that "10 percent of the population is gay." (see chapter 1).

- In response to the idea that homosexuals are promiscuous, he says: "I would guess gay men probably have more sex than straight men."

For a man fond of citing scientific studies, he is curiously vague here. For the past 25–30 years, medical studies have consistently demonstrated a gap as wide as the Grand Canyon between the average number of male homosexual contacts and the number of male heterosexual contacts. One study of AIDS victims showed that "homosexual men . . . reported a median of 1,160 lifetime sexual partners, compared with . . . 40 for male heterosexual drug users." Another study reported that the median number of lifetime partners for homosexuals was 200, as opposed to 14 for heterosexuals. In yet another study, this one of 93 homosexuals, the "mean number of estimated lifetime partners was 1,422 (median, 377, range, 15–7000)." McNaught's casual dismissal of homosexual promiscuity is the equivalent of saying, "I would guess rabbits probably have more sex than three-toed sloths." He knows very well they do.

- In trying to prove homosexuals and heterosexuals are "alike" sexually, McNaught states that "according to all the women's magazines," the "number one favorite form of love making" for both homosexuals and heterosexuals is oral sex. None of the scientific studies so indicate, from Kinsey to the present, nor, indeed, do "all the women's magazines." It is significant that in so important a matter as exotic sexual behavior, he would become so slovenly, particularly since, earlier in his presentation, he has warned his audience against accounts of sexual conduct in the popular press. It is important to remember that homosexual conduct and heterosexual conduct are quite different in kind and quantity. Many homosexuals do things that are almost never done by heterosexuals, including urinating on one another and the ingestion of human feces.

- He says: "In every species of mammal, from the hyena to the baboon, there is homosexual behavior, whether in captivity or in the wilds."

This statement is either deliberately deceptive or naive. The study he cites here is over 40-years-old and, contrary to what he suggests, was not written by anyone who understands sexual behavior in animals. Anthropologists and sexologists often interpret the sexual behavior of animals as analogous to human behavior. Responsible students of animal sexuality seldom if ever make that mistake, because they know that animals are aroused in entirely different ways than are humans. Recent U.S. Department of Agriculture research on sexual behavior in sheep prompted the popular press to cite the study as one more bit of evidence that homosexuality is "natural" and to be found in sheep. However, the government researcher himself, when I questioned him, said there was absolutely no relationship between the conduct of the sheep and human sexual conduct. In fact, he would not use the term "homosexual," but rather referred to "dud" sheep, because they couldn't breed with females.

- McNaught's maintains that "transsexuals" are, for the most part, "heterosexuals."

This statement is nothing more than a trifling play on words. Anyone who wants to become a member of the opposite sex in order to have sexual relations with people of his or her own sex is anything but heterosexual, though perhaps it is too simplistic to call them "homosexual."

- He says, "the overwhelming majority" of men who dress in women's clothes are heterosexual. Homosexuals do cross-dress, he maintains, as "a joke, a tool." This explanation is wistful evasion of the truth. The whole mystique of "drag" is homosexual in origin and a significant and serious phenomenon in the gay community. To suggest otherwise is to strike an absurd pose in the face of overwhelming evidence to the contrary.

- He confidently asserts: "According to police statistics, the overwhelming number of people who engage in sex with children or who abuse children sexually are heterosexual."

This is a carefully crafted statement that may be technically true, while unconscionably misleading to the average viewer. Statistically, as noted above, a homosexual is 10–20 times more likely to abuse a child sexually than is a heterosexual, though, of course, a heterosexual is more likely to be physically abusive, since the overwhelming number of battered children are the victims of their parents. According to the most objective and comprehensive studies, between 20–40 percent of all molesters are homosexual, though they constitute at most 1–3 percent of the population. (It is perhaps significant to note that heterosexual pedophiles don't have a national organization like the North American Man-Boy Love Association, a group of homosexual child molesters who seek to alter age-of-consent laws and whose members march annually in the New York Gay Rights Parade.)

- Finally, his citation of the Evelyn Hooker study as evidence you can't identify a homosexual in a crowd displays his ignorance of the material. (see chapter 1)

McNaught, whose clients include some of the largest corporations in the world, makes appearances in mainline churches and on campuses; and some of the segments on his videotape were obviously filmed on tour. At the end, he answers a series of questions with the same cavalier attitude towards the research, and then receives a standing ovation from his audience. A close scrutiny of this cheering crowd reveals that the couples present are mostly of the same sex. The fact that McNaught is employed by AT&T and other Fortune 500 companies is ample evidence that major corporations are either managed by people who have little impulse to investigate the credibility of those they hire, or else are as ideologically motivated as McNaught and therefore willing to promote his appearances despite the fact they know his presentation is filled with errors and misrepresentations. Either explanation raises serious questions about the role of corporate America in endorsing the gay rights movement.

MUTUAL FUNDS

Among the most influential forces in the financial marketplace are the mutual funds, which buy and sell stocks on a grand scale, managing the funds of millions of small investors and using their buying power to make advantageous deals for their clients. In recent years, some have also become Politically Correct and have used the billions of dollars in their control to force corporations to follow certain ideological guidelines in establishing company policy. By the late 1980's these "socially responsible mutual funds" were beginning to pressure corporations to adopt "gay friendly" practices. Homosexual activists are particularly pleased with Working Assets Common Holdings and the Calvert Social Investment Fund, both of which have favored the stocks of companies that encourage homosexuals and homosexuality. Writing in *Genre* (October 20, 1992), Bob Nelson says of Calvert's:

> Siobhan Gallagher, senior research analyst at U.S. Trust Co. in Boston, researches the stocks that go into Calvert's $600 million fund, which includes balanced, money market, bond and equity portfolios. She uses a variety of reports, newsletters and press clippings, but sometimes she'll query companies directly on sexual-orientation discrimination and on domestic-partner benefits, and finds that top management takes a question about a firm's hiring practices seriously when it comes from a mutual fund that may own millions of dollars worth of the firm's stock. Firms can tell the public and research analysts what they want about their hiring practices, Gallagher said, but a good indication that they're taking gay issues to heart is whether the higher echelons are required to attend sensitivity training. "Senior management has to buy into this," Gallagher said. "If they don't, the employees are up the creek."

Of Working Assets Common Holdings, Nelson says:

The Working Assets money fund recently sold off its stock in the Nordstrom's department store chain when it learned that an employee with AIDS had been discriminated against, [Working Assets CEO Sophia] Collier wrote in the 1992 New York Pride Guide. . . . Mitch Rofsky, president of Working Assets in San Francisco, confirmed that the funds screen on gay issues and have more than $230 million under management.

The promotion of gay rights by the marshals of high finance indicates the degree to which the homosexuals have made an impact on the business community. This is no accidental phenomenon but a conscious choice by some of the most powerful people in corporate America to take sides in the sexual revolution, a commitment to a policy at odds with traditional family values and religious precepts. It is no less than a declaration of economic war, with few corporations willing to line up against the orthodoxy of the New World Order. Small wonder. Those that do are swiftly disciplined.

A case in point is Cracker Barrel, a Tennessee-based restaurant chain that attempted to take a stand in favor of family values. First the company was jumped by gay rights activists, and then by the establishment itself. The gay rights assault was led by a group called the Wall Street Project. This organization, founded by Nick Curto, is a homosexual initiative designed to promote "corporate responsibility"—that is, Politically Correct attitudes and behaviors toward homosexuality. One of its chief targets over the past two years has been The Cracker Barrel Old Country Store Inc., which operates 117 restaurants nationwide, with 1991 sales of over $200 million. In 1991, the company issued a directive that all identifiably homosexual employees should be fired. In a press release, the company said: "[I]t is inconsistent with our concept and values . . . to continue to employ individuals whose sexual preferences fail to demonstrate normal heterosexual values which have been the foundation of families in our society."

Of this action, Curto said: "We were developing this share-holder emphasis and knew it was needed. But we were hoping for a really egregious example of corporate malevolence, and guess what, along came Cracker Barrel." Homosexuals began boycotting and picketing Cracker Barrel locations. Queer Nation, the National Gay and Lesbian Task Force, and several unions became involved in the fight. Cracker Barrel, while rescinding the order, refused to rehire some 15 employees affected nationwide. At this point, Elizabeth Holtzman, comptroller of New York City, came up with a different approach to the "Cracker Barrel problem." As the official responsible for investing some $38 billion resting in the city's pension fund, Holtzman was in a position to use this powerful weapon to further her convictions on social and sexual matters. Since the pension fund contained $6 million of Cracker Barrel stock, she badgered the company with requests and demands; and when they didn't jump through her hoop, she drafted a stockholders' resolution calling on Cracker Barrel to prohibit discrimination on the basis of sexual orientation; and she persuaded the New York pension fund's board of directors to pass her resolution. Then she sent an emissary, Patrick Doherty, down to Tennessee, accompanied by a gaggle of gay activists to let the company know precisely how New York wanted things run. Cracker Barrel officials met them with cool courtesy.

As the emissary reported: "It was pretty shocking. One of the Cracker Barrel lawyers checking credentials was wearing rubber gloves. It was directed against the representatives of gay groups who were there."

The outcome of the meeting: no capitulation by Cracker Barrel. Even though Securities and Exchange regulations forbade the New York pension funds from contacting more than 10 other shareholders to discuss its resolution, the word went out to other groups, with the Wall Street Project coordinating the efforts. As a consequence, the Philadelphia Municipal Retirement System, with its $200,000 worth of Cracker Barrel Stock, agreed to support the resolution. Other pension funds and mutual funds were expected to come aboard. As 1992 came to a close, it appeared as if Cracker Barrel was holding firm.

However, in 1993, the company will be facing a major fire-fight with perhaps the most powerful coalition of ideologues to take the financial field since the South African boycott. As Doherty put it: "This is the first time an action like this has been taken at the stockholder level. It will set a precedent because most of the funds, public and private, will have to take a position."

So the lines will be drawn in the sand, and major financial institutions will be forced to step to one side or the other. They will be asked to make decisions based on sexual ideology rather than merely on what's good for their investors. And they will be at war with one another, unless all agree to be Politically Correct.

Of course this polarization is precisely what homosexual activists want. They know full well that no one is so-well organized in defense of traditional values and that the most likely outcome is the recruitment of more investment groups willing to commit themselves to Politically Correct manipulations of the stock market. However, before everyone jumps aboard the bandwagon, they would be advised to study the outcome of another such struggle in California—this one involving the Boy Scouts of America.

THE BOY SCOUT BOYCOTT

Perhaps the most widely publicized example of corporate commitment to the gay rights movement is the attempt on the part of a coalition of California gay rights activists, politicians, and giant corporations to force the Boy Scouts of America to rescind their perennial ban on homosexual scoutmasters. In the course of this battle, which is by no means over, both sides mobilized. Middle America showed a surprising strength, and one major bank was rumored to have lost over $200 million in deposits because of its ideological promotion of gay rights among Scouts.

The confrontation began in earnest as far back as 1980, when Timothy Curran, a 19-year-old from Mt. Diablo, California, was told he could not be an assistant scoutmaster because in a local newspaper article he had announced that he was a homosexual, was proud of the fact, and intended to take his boy friend to the local high school prom. The Mt. Diablo Council for Boy Scouts promptly said that Curran would not be allowed to help lead a local troop. The Southern California chapter of the ACLU joined Curran in an 11-year court battle to force the Scouts to abandon their prohibition against homosexuals. On May 21, 1991 a superior court judge ruled that the Boy Scouts could legally exclude Curran because of the organization's "expressive right" of association derived from the First Amendment, a right that negated the "Unruh law," California legislation that prohibited businesses in the state from discriminating against people on the basis of sexual orientation. At that point homosexual activists, unused to losing court battles in California, began to thrash around in anger, looking for some way to punish the Boy Scouts for their clear-cut victory on behalf of wholesomeness. The first thing the activists came up with was a move to pressure the United Way to defund the Scouts in general and the Mt. Diablo Boy Scouts in particular. Stamping their feet, nostrils flaring, they also took note of the fact that homosexuals were getting a smaller piece of the United Way pie than they deemed proper. As one commentator for the *Bay Area Reporter* wrote in linking the two issues:

> The recent court ruling that allows the Scouts to exclude gays would seem to put that group on a direct collision course with the written non-discriminatory policies of the United Way, their principal funding source. Many activists and leaders are calling upon the United Way to either "put up or shut up" about those policies. United Way funding of lesbian/gay services amounts to about $370,000 in the entire five-county Bay Area, with none for les-

bian/gay agencies in Contra Costa, San Mateo or Marin counties.
And only one agency in Alameda County, the Pacific center, gets
UWBA funds.

San Francisco Supervisor Roberta Achtenberg, a lesbian activist, joined the United Way board in July of 1991; and soon
earned a reputation for being, in conservative activist Bob
Knight's phrase, "the nation's No. 1 Boy Scout basher." In her
dual posts as Supervisor and United Way board member,
Achtenberg led the fight that resulted in the action by United
Way to defund the Scouts. (President Clinton later rewarded
her for these high-profile activities with an appointment as
HUD's chief fair-housing enforcer.)

But even though Achtenberg promised quick action from
United Way, homosexual activists were not yet satisfied. The
court defeat still rankled in their breasts. Indeed, the Boy
Scouts were receiving support from all over the country, as
thousands of traditionally minded families urged them to stick
to their guns. So a few months later the homosexual groups
persuaded three major California-based corporations to cease
their support for Scout activities. These three were Levi
Strauss, Wells-Fargo, and BankAmerica. Levi Strauss had been
known as a corporate supporter of gay rights for years, having
instituted "gay friendly" policies internally and contributed to
gay rights organizations. However, most observers were unfamiliar with the policies of the other two companies and were
surprised to see them come out of the closet.

At this point, an astonishing thing happened. With little initial organization from conservative groups, people all over the
country began to withdraw their funds from the two banks and
to boycott Levi-Strauss products, including the traditional Levi
jeans. Within a month, groups like Don Wildmon's American
Family Association had begun to give the boycott efforts direction. The companies were denounced daily on 1,500 Christian radio stations, and suddenly the two banks were caught on
the horns of a dilemma: either stick by their original decision
and face the wrath of Middle America, or else reverse them-

selves and stir up the homosexual activists to a new level of frenzy.

This dilemma was by no means an academic one. While BankAmerica would officially deny it, a source within management told the Wildmon organization that depositors had withdrawn more than $200 million from the bank in the space of a few weeks. Whatever the amount, the bank's leadership began to have serious reservations about its policy. They had contributed only a few thousand dollars to the Boy Scouts through the BankAmerica Foundation. All of a sudden that amount seemed like a modest enough investment—and an extremely wise one.

> Bank representatives met with the Boy Scouts in an effort to find some way of wiggling out. The Scouts, terrified by the growing controversy and none too stout in their own defense of their policy, were eager to be accommodating. So on August 8, BankAmerica issued the following press release: BankAmerica said today that, as a result of a clarification of the membership policy of the Boy Scouts of America, the organization would once again be eligible for charitable donations. BankAmerica said its understanding, based on communications which it initiated with the national leadership of the organization, is that the opportunity to join the Boy Scouts of America is open to all boys who subscribe to the Scout oath and law, Cub Scout promise or Explorer code (Exploring includes teenage girls). BankAmerica's contributions policies allow it to make donations only to those organizations that provide full access and equal opportunity to all members of the class that the organization is designed to serve. Boy Scouts of America, being open to all boys, which is the class it is designed to serve, meets the bank's contributions criteria.

The bank said it understands the Scouting organization's requirement and necessity to set guidelines for those qualified to serve as adult leaders. The Boy Scouts' eligibility for charitable contributions from BankAmerica is determined by its policy regarding youth membership. "For over a half century, Bank of America has been a friend and supporter of the Boy Scouts," said Executive Vice President Donald A. Mullane, chairman of the BankAmerica Foundation. "We're pleased to have reached this understanding that will allow that support to continue and be consistent with the corporation's long-held belief in equal opportunity."

No one was fooled by this bit of circumlocution. BankAmerica had backed down. They were eating a large, steaming plate of old-fashioned crow. It was a rare victory for traditional values in a season when the homosexuals were winning battle after battle. And perhaps it was more significant than most people realized.

Though Wells-Fargo and Levi-Strauss refused to cave in, BankAmerica, the third largest bank in the country, had been brought to its knees by a groundswell of protest. The lines had been drawn in the sand, more Americans had rallied to the side of normalcy than to the side of perversion, and up in the tower suite of the Warbucks Building, "Daddy" was staring out of the window at the winking lights below—frowning, clearly worried. It appeared as if the pathway to the New World Order might not be as smooth as he and his good friends had anticipated. Tonight the American people seemed restless and quarrelsome. They still worshipped old idols and paid allegiance to outworn creeds. Down there in the gathering gloom they were saying grace at table, attending prayer meetings, reading their Bible.

Far from preparing themselves to enter into the emerging global marketplace, they were worried about their children's sex lives, about militant homosexuals, and the advent of the New Morality, with its fairness and tolerance of all behaviors. Were they, after all, incorrigible?

The television networks were doing their very best to broaden the moral vision of the general public, and they were having enormous success, as were the mainline Protestant clergy and the educational system. Indeed, everything had been progressing nicely—according to schedule. Then, just when the sea change seemed complete, something like this had to happen.

Suppose instead of surrendering to reason, the American people began to organize themselves into an angry mass of people? Suppose, instead of allowing the sexual revolutionaries to effect change through boycotts and picketing, middle-class Americans resisted the inevitable and began to punish American business for supporting sexual license and the gay rights agenda? Suppose they forced every corporation to make the same choice that BankAmerica had to make?

Instead of a brightening future, in which all conflict was removed from the work place and all morality was removed from sexual conduct, multinational corporations might be facing a genuine crisis right in their own back yard—and a serious economic crisis at that.

"Daddy" felt a cold nose on his palm and stroked Sandy's head abstractedly. "We'll find a way to save them in spite of themselves," he said.

3

THE FEDERAL
GOVERNMENT JOINS
THE REVOLUTION

As John C. Calhoun pointed out more than 150 years ago, a democracy is not run by the majority but by the active minority with the concurrence of the majority. Or to put it in simpler terms, pressure groups control the government while the rest of us sit around and watch. Certainly that has been the case with the sexual revolution. A few activists have forced cowering public officials to further a radical sexual agenda while the majority has remained silent. The progress of the gay rights movement is a case in point. The homosexuals have convinced members of Congress and the White House that they number 10 percent of the population. As noted above, no study supports such a figure; yet the press reports almost daily that there are 25,000,000 gay men and lesbians nationwide—more than enough to sway almost any federal election. As a consequence, politicians follow the lead of groups like the National Gay and Lesbian Task Force and the Human Rights Campaign Fund—at least when they can do so without exposing themselves to the wrath of the sleepy majority. Yet even this suc-

117

cess is unjustified, given the clear evidence that there are comparatively few gay rights activists in the field. Consider the following facts:

- Phyllis Schlafly's Eagle Forum numbers around 80,000 members.
- The Rev. Donald Wildmon's American Family Association has a membership of around 925,000—most of them active.
- Concerned Women for America reports a membership of around 700,000.
- James Dobson's *Focus on the Family* has about 2 million members.

All of these organizations, and many more oppose the gay rights agenda. Now compare those figures with the following:

- The largest gay rights organizations in America, the Human Rights Campaign Fund and the National Gay and Lesbian Task Force, report a combined membership of fewer than 80,000.
- One of the largest chapters of ACT-UP is in Washington, D.C. Their weekly meeting is reported regularly in the *Washington Blade*. Attendance averages between 30–40 people.

This is the group that is constantly making the front pages of the newspapers and the Six O'clock News. This is the bunch that invades meetings of those with whom it disagrees, shouts down speakers and closes off debate. This is the ragtag mob that strikes terror in the hearts of Congressional committee chairmen and campaign managers. And they can only muster about 35 people at their planning sessions. Yet the victories of these screaming, cursing activists have been extraordinary, among the most impressive in the history of advocacy politics.

Take the case of AIDS.

The advent of this disease should have signalled the death knell of the gay rights movement. From the beginning AIDS was predominately a homosexual disease—one that first appeared among homosexuals, infected mostly homosexuals, and spread into the rest of the community largely as the result of homosexual contacts—needle sharing, women having sex with a bisexual male, a transfusion using infected homosexual blood. Suddenly the truth became obvious to everyone: it was enormously unhealthy to be a homosexual and to engage in the extravagant behaviors that were habitual to so many members of the gay community, particularly in New York, Los Angeles, and San Francisco. If homosexuality had seemed a repugnant but relatively harmless "lifestyle" to many Americans, it could no longer be so characterized. Objective viewers now understood that homosexual behavior was life-threatening.

As for AIDS, the medical strategy seemed obvious: routine testing, mandatory reporting, contact tracing, some means of isolating or controlling those infected. These measures had been traditionally employed in handling other infectious and sexually transmitted diseases. For generations health authorities either quarantined or colonized victims of Hansen's Disease (leprosy), we tested the adult population of an entire state for syphilis, and we forbade young people from assembling publicly during polio epidemics. Had these traditional public health measures been followed at the first onset of AIDS, the disease would have been checked, tens of thousands would have never been infected, and tens of billions of dollars would have been saved.

At a point early in the course of the epidemic, the gay rights leadership had a choice to make: Either keep the gay rights revolution barreling down the highway or save the lives of the vast majority of homosexuals still uninfected. You couldn't do both. As late as 1986, this was a real choice. The leadership chose to throw away tens of thousands of lives—primarily the lives of their own kind—in order to avoid the possibility that they might be singled out for special medical scrutiny. Terrified that they would be "stigmatized," they threw a collective tantrum and the whole course of medical history was altered.

Standard medical procedures were set aside. First they fought routine testing with a vehemence that startled and intimidated the medical profession, whose leadership was as cowardly as the politicians. In 1987, a poll conducted by *MD* magazine indicated that 78 percent of practicing physicians believed testing and contact tracing should be followed in confronting the growing epidemic. Yet the leadership of the medical profession surrendered to the leadership of the gay rights movement. This surrender occurred in large measure because the Centers for Disease Control and the Surgeon General of the United States were either cajoled or bullied into speaking out against standard medical practice. So the federal government was already beginning to buckle under pressure—already willing to risk lives in order to avoid trouble. Having ensured that the disease would spread without significant check, the homosexual activists next sought to corral as much money as possible for education and medical research—education to discourage discrimination against homosexuals and AIDS victims, medical research to save the lives of the many who should never have been infected in the first place.

By 1992, more money was being spent on AIDS than on heart disease or cancer, despite the fact that in one year each of these diseases kills many times the number of people who have died from AIDS since its first appearance. In fact, cancer and heart researchers are now complaining that HIV projects have cut deeply into their traditional sources of funding. Yet at both the 1992 political conventions, gay activists were screaming that the federal government wasn't doing enough, that more money was required, that a cure must be found immediately.

When preliminary research indicated that the medication AZT might delay the onset of the deadliest stage of the disease, gay activists demanded that the FDA drop its standard procedures and put the drug on the market immediately. For years, this policy had driven the terminally ill to despair. Victims of incurable disease had perennially been heartened to hear of a new medical breakthrough, only to learn in the next sentence that the new medicine or treatment was still undergoing FDA evaluation and would not be allowed on the market for years. It was a maddening policy, but no one successfully challenged it. Homosexuals, however, weren't about to go gentle into that good night. They began to shout their disapproval at public forums. Then ACT-UP appeared at a meeting where the FDA director was scheduled to speak. He rose, opened his mouth, and was drowned out by a chorus of shrieks and boos. He struggled for a while, then finally gave up. The incident received wide and sympathetic media coverage. The FDA immediately amended its policy—but only for AIDS. People who have cancer and other terminal illnesses must still wait for many years to take advantage of new medical discoveries—if they live that long.

But preferential legal and medical treatment for AIDS was not enough. Homosexual activists demanded much more: a national outpouring of sympathy for their disease—and their disease only. The American people had to show special feelings for AIDS victims, make an extraordinary act of contrition for somehow allowing this terrible plague to descend on the homosexual community. Because, as establishment propaganda began to make clear, homosexuals weren't responsible for their infection. It was Ronald Reagan's fault, and later George Bush's. It was lack of compassion. Lack of concern. An ignoring of the epidemic. To whip the nation into a communal display of sympathy, they orchestrated the Spectacle of the Quilt, the Order of the Red Ribbon, national support groups, gala benefits, profane diatribes by Elizabeth Taylor, television melodrama, public service announcements, tax-funded polemics, newspaper and magazine articles, street demonstrations, and speeches at political conventions.

It is significant that victims of other dread diseases have never required this kind of public display—in part, one suspects, because no sense of guilt and shame existed to demand it. Everyone who is stricken with a fatal disease deserves our deepest compassion. We share in their suffering if only because we too are doomed—all of us—to pain and sorrow and death. Given the peculiar horrors of AIDS, we are perhaps more inclined to feel pity and terror. But the manner in which the nation has been scourged and blackmailed into public displays of sympathy is unique in our history.

The participation of the federal government in the orchestration of public sentiment has been significant and disturbing. A good deal of the funding that might have gone to medical research and legitimate education has gone to propaganda—government studies and tracts demanding that no one blame homosexual AIDS victims for their plight, that AIDS is a disease that can strike "anyone" (including Billy Graham and Mother Theresa), that we must somehow recognize the propriety of homosexual behavior because of the AIDS epidemic, rather than in spite of it. Some of these government materials have been sent out to millions of Americans (e.g., *The Surgeon General's Report,* the national AIDS mailing), and some have been developed for "special markets." One thing is certain: The federal government during two "conservative" Republican administrations has promoted the gay rights movement in ways without precedent. Consider the following examples.

THE REPORT OF THE SECRETARY'S TASK FORCE ON YOUTH SUICIDE

The Secretary's Task Force on Youth Suicide was created by authority of Otis Bowen, Secretary of Health and Human Services under Ronald Reagan. Ostensibly established to confront a serious problem—the increase of suicide among the very young—it soon became a vehicle for several agendas, including that of the gay rights movement. The Task Force, like most such ad hoc committees, was composed of a swarm of drones and a few well-chosen workers. The drones attended a huge meeting in Washington, paid for by the federal government, heard speeches by experts in the field, then returned to their usual occupations. Then the workers crafted a report, sent it out to the drones for pro forma approval, made necessary corrections, and then published the final report as a work of the entire Task Force, drawing on the prestige of many of the drones to reassure the public that these materials were assembled by responsible people.

It is important to note that among the hundreds of drones invited to the Washington conference, not a single legitimate clergyman was listed. (One participant taught in a liberal theological seminary.) The significance of this fact will be apparent as the discussion develops, though suffice it to say that a major segment of the conference was devoted to the role of religious institutions in the prevention of youth suicide, a segment in which the inadequacy of the clergy to deal with this problem was one topic scheduled for discussion.

When the Report was published in January of 1989, just as Reagan and Bowen were leaving office, it contained enough words to fill four large volumes and was all but lost in the coverage of the new administration. However, there was one segment of the Report that had a life of its own—a lengthy, ill-documented polemical essay by one Paul Gibson, described as a "therapist and program consultant" in San Francisco, California. This essay, entitled "Gay Male and Lesbian Suicide" and carrying the imprimatur of the federal government, has been cited time and again by gay rights advocates as "proof" that homosexual youths are killing themselves in large numbers and that the chief cause of this unfortunate phenomenon is society in general—and the Christian church in particular. Gibson makes a number of recommendations designed to correct this societal error and to put religion in its place. Again, these recommendations are given additional credence because they are published in an official federal document. (After religious and pro-family groups complained, the Department of Health and Human Services announced that the Gibson essay was a "position paper" rather than a part of the official report, and Secretary Louis Sullivan repudiated it. He even stated that the Report had been withdrawn from the market. However, the Report was still for sale until all the copies were sold in mid-July, 1992.)

The problems with Gibson's polemic are scientific as well as religious. Consider, for example, the following statement:

> [Kinsey] found that approximately 13 percent of adult males and 7 percent of adult females had engaged in predominantly homosexual behavior for at least three years prior to his survey. This is where the figure that 10 percent of the population is homosexual comes from. (*Report of the Secretary's Task Force on Youth Suicide,* vol. 3, p. 115)

As already noted, Kinsey found no such thing: yet Gibson has forever established authority for the 10 percent figure in the literature of the federal government. As for young people, he uses his own misreading to make the following statement:

> It is apparent, however, that a substantial minority of youth—perhaps "One in Ten" as one book suggests—have a primary gay male, lesbian, or bisexual orientation. Given the higher rates of suicidal feelings and behavior among gay youth in comparison with other young people, this means that 20–30 percent of all youth suicides may involve gay youth. Parris believes that as many as 3000 gay and lesbian young people may be taking their lives each year. (p. 115)

This statement is simply not born out by hard evidence. In 1990, the Gallup organization ran a poll on youth suicide to determine how many young people had contemplated or attempted suicide. Using both a written questionnaire and a follow-up phone interview, the Gallup organization listed a number of causes for youth suicide—from trouble with parents to Satanism. Homosexual orientation did not make a blip on their radar screen. It was apparently included among the 3 percent who gave "other reasons." (Satanism was listed as a factor in contemplating or attempting suicide by 7 percent of young people polled. One has to wonder when the Secretary of Health and Human Services will convene a Task Force to consider that question.)

The Gallup findings would seem to support a recent and comprehensive study conducted in Minnesota[1] that reported only "1.1 percent [of adolescents] described themselves as bisexual or predominantly homosexual." The anecdotal evidence likewise indicates that few adolescents are homosexual. The highly publicized Project 10, a homosexual "support program" sponsored by the Los Angeles Unified School District, has, according to the San Francisco school superintendent, only served about 18 students from among hundreds of thousands attending L.A. public schools. Quoting his own anecdotal evidence and citing selectively from studies written by sexologists and activists, Gibson builds a case that there are huge numbers of homosexual youths in the country, that they are all experiencing vehement persecution, and that they are at risk of suicide. Then he lays the blame for this deplorable state of affairs at the doorstep of the family and the church. Of the family he writes:

> Gay and lesbian youth face more verbal and physical abuse from family members than do other youth. The National Gay Task Force found that more than 33 percent of gay males and lesbians reported verbal abuse from relatives because of their orientation and 7 percent reported physical abuse as well. These figures are substantially higher for youth open about their sexual orientation while still living at home. (p. 127)

He has this to say about religion:

> Religion presents another risk factor in gay youth suicide because of the depiction of homosexuality as a sin and the reliance of families on the church for understanding homosexuality. Many traditional (e.g., Catholicism) and fundamentalist (e.g., Baptist) faiths still portray homosexuality as morally wrong or evil. Family religious beliefs can be a primary reason for parents forcing youth to leave home if a homosexual orientation is seen as incompatible with church teachings. These beliefs can also create unresolvable internal conflicts for gay youth who adhere to their faith but believe they will not change their sexual orientation. They

may feel wicked and condemned to hell and attempt suicide in despair of ever obtaining redemption. (p. 127–128)

This passage raises several points. First, one must ask: "Where is the famous 'wall of separation' we hear so much about when discussing such issues as prayer in schools? If the state is forbidden to promote religion, then, according to the Lemon test, it is also forbidden to attack religion—and especially specific denominations. To identify religion as a "risk factor" is itself an outrageous tactic for a government-sponsored publication, but to single out two specific communions for special blame seems deliberately provocative, particularly when they are the largest Christian denominations in the country. In fact, Professor Edward Wynne of the University Illinois at Chicago, a keynote speaker at this same 1987 Youth Suicide Conference, has published a study demonstrating that religion is one of the chief deterrents to suicide among young people.

Like many social scientists, Gibson neither understands the Christian concept of sin (everybody commits it) nor what is required for redemption (not "right conduct" but the undeserved grace of God). If some families fail to understand the Christian imperative of forgiveness or fail to love their children properly, then these failures can hardly be blamed on Christianity, much less on two of its most substantial branches. More to the point, the federal government has no business funding such ignorant expressions of bigotry. The Department of Health and Human Services has used the tax dollars of tens of millions of Catholics and Baptists to fund attacks on their respective churches. Had HHS used the same funds to say something positive and complimentary, the agency would have been long since hauled into federal court by the ACLU, People for the American Way, and other ideologues of the Left. But in his Report essay, Gibson is not content merely to criticize and defame. He also prescribes radical reform of society, the family, and the church—with all the borrowed and magisterial authority of the Department of

Health and Human Services, the largest bureaucratic agency in the world.

For society he offers the following prescription—a mandate that goes far beyond the limits of an essay on youth suicide:

> Gay males and lesbians need to be accepted as equal partners in our society. Laws should safeguard their individual rights and not permit discrimination against them in housing, employment, and other areas. Laws prohibiting homosexual relationships between consenting adults should be repealed and marriages between homosexuals should be recognized. Special attention should be paid to the enforcement of laws that punish those who commit violence against homosexuals. Laws can help to establish the principle of equality for lesbians and gay men and define the conduct of others in their interactions with them. (p. 133)

But Gibson believes that laws conferring special privileges and special protections are finally insufficient to solve the vast problem he has described. We must positively endorse homosexuality as a way of life:

> We must promote a positive image of gay males and lesbians to reduce oppression against them and provide gay youth with role models to pattern themselves after. Massive education efforts need to take place that would provide people with accurate information about homosexuality. These efforts especially need to be directed to those who have responsibility for the care of the young including families, clergy, teachers, and helping professionals. (pp. 133–134)

What he proposes here is nothing less than a massive brainwashing of the American people, particularly families and clergy, where he has found the greatest resistance to the acceptance of homosexuality. Parents and the church, after all, are the ones most likely to find objections to the idea that children should adopt such a dangerous and disturbing way of living. Adults in authority must be taught that their most deeply-held convictions are wrong-headed and destructive— and undoubtedly with the same flow of tax dollars that has funded Gibson's essay.

He reveals his own bias even more clearly when he writes:

We need to recognize that youth are sexually active from an early age and that sexual orientation is frequently formed by adolescence. All youth need to be provided with positive information about homosexuality that presents it as a viable adaptation. We must accept a homosexual orientation in young people in the same manner we accept a heterosexual orientation. (p. 134)

This passage is all the more significant because Gibson suggests that what happens by adolescence actually "forms" sexual orientation. He gives some concrete examples of what communities can do to affirm this equality.

Gay and lesbian youth need access to the same social supports and recreational activities that other youth have. This would reduce their isolation and enhance their positive social development. Communities need to develop social groups and activities (i.e., dances) specifically for gay and lesbian youth as a way of meeting others like themselves and developing relationship skills. Existing youth programs such as the Boy and Girl Scouts should incorporate gay youth into their activities. Youth programs such as Big Brothers and Sisters should enlist gay and lesbian adults to work with gay youth. It is very important for gay youth to see the potential of a happy and stable lifestyle as adults. Lesbians and gay men need to become more involved in supporting gay youth and being positive role models for them. This requires assurance for gay adults that they will not be harassed and accused of "recruiting" youth in doing so. (p. 135)

His federally funded lecture to the American family is equally prescriptive. It presumes to mandate that parents revise their own values and adopt an entirely new way of looking at right and wrong, good and evil:

Parents should know that homosexuality is a natural and healthy form of sexual expression. They do not need to feel bad about something that is good. . . . Families need to take responsibility for presenting homosexuality in a positive context to their children. (p. 134)

As for religion, the churches and synagogues also get their marching orders:

Religions need to reassess homosexuality in a positive context within their belief systems. They need to accept gay youth and make a place for them in the church and include them in the same activities as other youth. Religions should also take responsibility for providing their families and membership with positive information about homosexuality that discourages the oppression of lesbians and gay men. Faiths that condemn homosexuality should recognize how they contribute to the rejection of gay youth by their families and suicide among lesbians and gay male youth. (p. 135)

It is important to note that Gibson, like too many people ignorant of religion, want to regard faith and doctrine as no more than a "system," something ultimately mechanical or electronic that can be rewired or reprogrammed with the same ease one would repair a TV or a computer. Traditional religious convictions don't lend themselves so easily to pragmatic tinkering. For example, the Southern Baptists (with about 15 million members) derive their religious views from the Bible, which, they believe, is the best authority for tenets of faith and ethical principles. Of course, through linguistic distortion and elaborate rationalization, some clergy (principally homosexual Episcopalians) have been able to argue that the Bible does not denounce sodomy. However, the fact is that scripture repeatedly condemns homosexual behavior—and in unequivocal language. It is well nigh impossible for those who live by the inerrancy of Holy Scripture to reprogram their "belief system" to accommodate the gay rights movement or even the federal government.

As for orthodox Roman Catholics, they tend to accept the authority of the Mother Church in matters of morals and dogma. The Catholic Church, which predates both the gay rights movement and the U.S. government, has always taught that sex should be primarily (though not exclusively) for procreation and that any sex outside of marriage is a sin. So how are Catholics to "reassess homosexuality in a positive context" when their "belief system" rests on assumptions about sex that are irreconcilable with anal and oral intercourse?

The obtuseness of Gibson's essay, its misuse of scientific data, and its ideological cast render it useless as a commentary on the problems of homosexual youth, which are formidable and deserve serious consideration by families, churches, and qualified physicians and counsellors. What marks it as significant is its inclusion in a major report issued by the Department of Health and Human Services, the lead federal agency for all matters relevant to AIDS and adolescent sexuality. The choice of Paul Gibson to discuss this particular issue was surely no accident. His views must have been known, his biases duly noted by those who picked him to discuss this particular topic. His credentials are by no means awesome: "L.C.S.W., Therapist and Program Consultant, San Francisco, California." No long list of degrees. No major publications. No university affiliation. His name is not a household word— even in Greenwich Village. So why was he chosen, except for his personal experience as a counsellor in San Francisco and the political correctness of his sympathies?

The fact that Gibson's essay was commissioned and published in an official government document is ample evidence that the Department of Health and Human Services has been heavily involved in the promotion of the gay rights agenda, whatever the social and political beliefs of the Republican appointees who ostensibly ran the Department. Either Otis Bowen and his staff were doing a poor supervisory job or else they were well aware of what was going on and condoned it. But regardless of the intent of those in authority, the document is immortal now. It has already been cited in articles and in debates nationwide. It is no longer an expression of one man's opinion but a fact, certified by the U.S. government, finally and irrevocably True in a way beyond the dispute of those who would disagree. For scientists, polemicists, and activists all over the country, religion is to blame for the misery of homosexual youths, we must somehow make Catholics and Baptists stop behaving that way, and homosexual men and women should be Big Brothers and Big Sisters. It's all true because Uncle Sam said so.

AIDS, SEXUAL BEHAVIOR, AND INTRAVENOUS DRUG USE

If the Department of Health and Human Services were the only government agency involved in promoting gay rights and denigrating age-old religious beliefs, then we could dismiss the Secretary's Report as an aberration, a problem existing in only one locality of the vast empire of government. But such, alas, is not the case. A number of government agencies have exhibited the same bias, particularly those that have some scientific pretentions—for example, the National Research Council.

The National Research Council (NRC) is one of those freestanding agencies that is funded by tax dollars but really doesn't report to those who pay the bills. In that respect it is like both the National Endowment for the Arts and the Corporation for Public Broadcasting.

In 1989—in its capacity as advisor to the government, the public, and the scientific community—the NRC decided to issue its own report on the AIDS epidemic.

To carry out this grand scheme, they also required money, which they received from three sources: the U.S. Public Health Services, the Russell Sage Foundation, and one more body perennially interested in transforming American sexual behavior—the Rockefeller Foundation. With this funding, the NCR assembled a group of scientists to constitute a Committee on AIDS Research and the Behavioral, Social, and Statistical Sciences. It is this Committee that produced the study.

The results of such a study should have been impressive by anybody's standards. Those chosen were academic figures of some reputation.

They were supported by a Panel on Statistical Issues in AIDS Research, and they had the cooperation of the U.S. Public Health Services, as well as a string of additional consultants. However, the result—a stout volume called *AIDS, Sexual Behavior, and Intravenous Drug Use*—was a more sophisticated and intellectually challenging piece of propaganda than the Gibson essay, but propaganda nonetheless. Indeed, after reading the report, one is struck by the degree to which the scientific community is walking in lockstep towards the same long-term common goal—a nation, perhaps a world, in which neither custom nor traditional social morality nor religion has any place. The short-term goal was predetermined as well— the transference of all blame for the AIDS epidemic from the homosexuals to normal Americans and to their religious institutions.

Education

From the beginning, gay rights activists have insisted that the only proper role for government in preventing the spread of AIDS is to provide education—education of the right sort. Now the "right sort" of education is a curious mixture of ingredients, one that makes little sense to anyone who isn't familiar with the gay rights agenda. Here are some of its key elements:

- the assumption that virtually everybody engages in casual sex and that people couldn't stop if they tried.
- an invincible belief in the efficacy of condoms.
- the assertion that homosexuality is normal, immutable, and that homosexuals make up a significant proportion of the population.
- a commitment to instructing people in great detail how the disease is NOT transmitted.
- homilies on the wickedness of blaming anyone for the epidemic, other than the federal government.

This NRC study was designed to support such an educational program. For example, in a segment of the report entitled "Social Barriers to Prevention," the authors discuss what seems to them a clear-cut case of science versus religiosity:

For several years, federal AIDS education efforts have stumbled over disputes about the need to offer "realistic" advice about the protective value of condoms (and bleach) versus counterclaims that the AIDS epidemic requires moral education to promote abstinence from sex prior to marriage, fidelity within marriage, and avoidance of drugs. Evidence of this conflict can be found by comparing the statements issued in 1986 by the surgeon general (U.S. Department of Health and Human Services, 1986) with those distributed to every school district by the U.S. Department of Education in 1987. The surgeon general's brochure recognized the protective value of sexual abstinence and monogamous relationships with uninfected partners, but it also advised the following:

> If your partner has a positive blood test showing that he or she has been infected with the AIDS virus or you suspect that he or she has been exposed by previous heterosexual or homosexual behavior or use of intravenous drugs with shared needles or syringes, a rubber (condom) should always be used during (start to finish) sexual intercourse (vagina or rectum). (1986:17)

Dr. Koop had absolutely no scientific evidence to support such an extravagant claim for condom use—that they were "adequate to safely protect yourself and others from infection by the AIDS virus." He was merely drawing on his own "faith" in the efficacy of this paltry product of not-so-modern technology. While the Koop report was being sent to millions of Americans, assuring them they could safely have vaginal and anal intercourse if they used a condom, researchers were beginning to build a case against the efficacy of condoms in preventing AIDS.

- Dr. Margaret Fischl, speaking at the 1987 International AIDS Conference, reported on 18 married couples who used condoms in intercourse because the male was HIV positive. In an 18-month period, three of the wives became infected with the virus, despite condom use. (It is interesting to note that the infection rate she reported was almost exactly the pregnancy rate reported by teenage condom users.)[2]

- Dr. James Goedert of the National Cancer Institute, writing in *The New England Journal of Medicine* (May 1, 1987, p. 1340) said of condom use with an HIV-infected partner:

"there is no acceptable level for this risk. 'Lower' risk is an inadequate goal and perhaps even a vacuous notion."

- Dr. Bruce Voeller—gay rights advocate and president of the Mariposa Research Foundation, who was then researching the efficacy of condoms—said to the *New York Times* (August 18, 1987): "The safe sex message just isn't true. You're still playing a kind of Russian roulette."

- Dr. Harold Jaffe, the Centers for Disease Control's chief of epidemiology, was quoted in the same *New York Times* article as saying: "You just can't tell people it's all right to do whatever you want so long as you wear a condom. It's just too dangerous a disease to say that."

- Studies appeared in British and Dutch medical journals that showed a high breakage rate for condoms used in anal intercourse. (See Wigersma and Oud in *British Medical Journal*, July 11, 1987; and *The Lancet*, December 21/28, 1985).

- Finally, in the wake of growing controversy, the NIH commissioned a definitive study to determine the effectiveness of condoms when used by homosexual couples. The results were catastrophic.
  - First, on store shelves researchers discovered "rogue condoms" that came apart in the hands of those about to use them. (Allan Parachini, *Los Angeles Times* January 27, 1988)
  - Then they found that the infection rate in L.A. among condom users appeared to be so high that, according to Dr. Jeffrey Perlman of NIH, "one would really be talking about delaying infection rather than preventing it." (*Los Angeles Times,* August 10, 1988)
  - As a consequence of the obvious risks incurred by those involved in the study, the NIH quietly canceled it—an admission that Dr. Koop was wrong. When *Los Angeles Times* reporter Allan Parachini attempted to get a quote from the Surgeon General, he was told Dr. Koop was on vacation.

Religion and the NCR

Yet a year after the collapse of the NIH study, the National Research Countil was still advocating condom-centered education for young people. This message was accompanied by a direct assault on the influence of religious institutions in "stigmatizing" homosexuality and drug use. This attack begins with a long quasi-anthropological discussion of "stigmatization" in the abstract, which says, among other things:

> Rather, in its sociological meaning, the stigma is the set of ideas, beliefs, and judgments that the majority or dominant group holds about some other group. These beliefs are not merely negative; they often characterize members of the stigmatized group as dangerous or deserving of punishment for some vague offense or moral improbity. Group members may be considered dangerous because their very existence threatens the dominant group's sense of primacy, power, or safety. By simply being different, they may cast doubt on the rightness or perfection of the dominant group's way of life. The characteristics imputed to the stigmatized group—for example, inclination to crime, laziness, inferior intelligence, and the like—result from biased, limited observation and are supported by illogical, tortuous arguments. The stigma becomes a predominant description of members of the group, effectively hiding most of their real features. Stigma thus becomes not merely a cliche but a menacing, mean cliche. (pp. 390–391)

Harumph! This pretentious, quasi-scientific passage was clearly framed to appeal to politically correct opinion. The example of stigmatizing characteristics is clearly meant to suggest a specific minority and to stir up the reader's sense of racial injustice. "So that's what stigmatization is," the reader says. "Well, I'm certainly against that kind of thing!" However, the passage is subject to a different interpretation in the light of another frame of reference. Isn't this "stigmatization" precisely what scientists do to those they find different and odd and threatening? Isn't this the way they treat . . . religious people? Christians? No question about it: Scientists are the "dominant" group in our society. It is to scientists that government turns when it wants answers to the most pressing problems, whether military or medical or social. It is scientists who receive the lion's share of our tax dollars to invent and launch new things, to fix old things, to study every phenomenon from the anemone at the bottom of the ocean to the behavior of the farthest stars. They predict the future of the economy; they explain its past failures; they make us understand why we are really nothing more than economic automatons. Politicians hesitate to make speeches without quoting the latest report or the most comprehensive study. Scientists are the high priests of our culture, the messiahs of our destiny, the counters, classifiers, and explainers of everything that was, is, or ever shall be. And whom do scientists regard as "dangerous?" The answer is obvious: religious people—those whose very existence is a reproof to science, who suggest that scientists can never discover the answers to the most important questions, which are theological and spiritual and therefore beyond measurement and quantitative analysis. As long as traditional religion exists in our society, the primacy and power of the scientist is threatened. By simply being different, religious people cast doubt on the rightness or perfection of the scientific vision. For these reasons, many scientists stigmatize those who believe in God and Mystery and Transcendent Truth. As a consequence, they impute characteristics to Christians—for example, cold-heartedness, lack of compassion, ignorance, emotionalism, self-righteousness, superstition, irrationality—characteristics that result from bias, limited observation and are supported by illogical, tortuous arguments. If you don't believe scientists stigmatize religious people in general and Christians in particular, consider the next paragraph on stigmatization of AIDS victims:

> In this epidemic, the rationale rests on the fact that AIDS is transmitted by seemingly voluntary behaviors that are widely disapproved of in the broader society. In the vocabulary of some religions, these behaviors are called "sinful." Accusers can say to victims, "If you hadn't behaved in this or that shameful or sinful way, this wouldn't have happened to you." This direct attribution of responsibility feeds one of the essential features of stigmatization: blameworthiness. It allows the society to feel justified in excluding victims from concern or banishing them from the community. One group that is especially prone to stigmatization is gay men. (p. 393)

A clever passage indeed—to stigmatize those one hates and fears while denouncing them for using the same tactic. And after a thinly veiled attack on the Supreme Court for ruling that the states could outlaw sodomy, the committee—apparently comfortable in making absolute pronouncements on any subject (they are scientists, after all)—returns to the subject of stigmatization and now terms it "pathological."

> The deeply rooted social *pathology* [emphasis added] of stigmatization is not easy to dispel. Even when revealed for what it is, the psychological and social mechanisms that support stigmatization may resist eradication. Rational appeals to understanding are necessary and sometimes useful, but they are often frustrated by forces deeper than reason. (p. 397)

What the committee is really saying here is that a Christian morality that denounces drug addiction and homosexual behavior as immoral is "social pathology"—that is, a disease of society—and that it must be stamped out, or else brought under control. Of course, it can't be cured by appeals to rationality, because such appeals are too often frustrated by "forces deeper than reason." It may be, the committee suggests, that Christians "must begin to recognize that the maintenance of stigma has a deleterious effect on [them] as well as on [the homosexuals and drug addicts] who are stigmatized." In other words, perhaps Christians can be persuaded that it is in their own best interest to discard traditional Biblical principles, that they are only hurting themselves in maintaining such an "outmoded" point of view. And if Christians don't get the big picture, then perhaps the scientists and their friends in government can help them see more clearly their own enlightened self-interest. In that generous spirit, the committee offers some unsolicited advice to Christian Churches and their benighted preachers:

> Churches, whose involvement in stigma has historically been great—both as objects and agents—can preach an enlightened view and demand of their adherents sympathy and justice. (p. 398)

Surely this is unprecedented from an agency of the federal government—an order to Christian preachers to demand a particular social attitude from their congregations. The word "demand" is singularly harsh and suggests how ignorant the committee is of the relationship between most clergy and their "adherents." Christian preachers do not carry the same authority as the federal government. They have no police powers— no FBI, no Armed Forces, no regulatory agencies at their beck and call. They cannot even empower a committee to mandate obedience to these fine old abstractions. Indeed, unless they can appeal to the Sermon on the Mount or to the other red-letter passages in the Bible, many of them command little respect from their congregations, who do not idolize men or learning, but respect only God and His Word. But an appeal to the Bible would be unacceptable, since it is there that Christians would also find those "stigmatizing" prohibitions against promiscuity and perversion. In such passages as these, the committee reveals its true motives for compiling this report: It is to give scientific respectability to public policies that favor gay rights advocates and to attack the basic religious tenets that inform American society—assuming that these tenets have not already been destroyed by such forces.

NONCONFORMING SEXUAL ORIENTATIONS AND MILITARY SUITABILITY

The report of the National Research Council is by no means the most overt federally funded attack on Christians or their beliefs. Far worse is a 1988 report commissioned by the Department of Defense and prepared by a group called the Defense Personnel Security and Education Center. This group defines itself as follows:

> The Defense Personnel Security Research and Education Center (PERSEREC) performs research and analyses in support of DOD's personnel security programs. One of its top priority projects approved by OSD is to validate existing criteria for person-

nel security clearance determinations and to develop more objective, uniform, and valid adjudication standards, e.g., clarify relationships between risk and various personal characteristics. (p. i)

If you don't understand what you've just read, PERS-EREC's Director, Caeson K. Eoyang, clarifies the group's assignment in the following terms:

In exploring the range of antecedent conditions related to trust violation, PERSEREC is examining such factors as drug and alcohol abuse, credit history, psychiatric disorders, and nonconforming sexual behaviors. In this context, a comprehensive review of the scientific literature on homosexuality was undertaken to illuminate the relationship between homosexuality and security. It quickly became apparent that security risk per se is also related to a larger problem; namely, the suitability of homosexuals for military service. This report provides a historical review of the various social constructions that have been placed on homosexuality, the effects of legal decisions and changing folkways, and a summary of the scientific literature. Current employment practices within DOD are reviewed in the light of conclusions drawn from this study. (p. i)

An ambitious statement that promises a study of considerable depth and scope. What the reader finds instead is a short, slovenly report that looks as if it were thrown together over a long weekend on Fire Island. It draws on few sources, all of which support a single position, and it covers all areas of the subject superficially. It is predictably and militantly pro-homosexual. The section on "Judicial Trends and Shifting Folkways" covers a few recent legal cases relevant to the question of homosexuals in the military. Picking among the bones of old rulings, PERSEREC finds evidence to support the idea that times are changing, that the courts are beginning to recognize the rights of homosexuals, that a trend toward acceptance is discernible. The report identifies that trend in slightly more than three pages.

To be sure, traditional attitudes are resistant to change. Not all legal rulings and social practices are favorable to policies supporting nondiscrimination on the basis of sexual orientation. Nonetheless, the instances quoted above are more than straws in the wind. One interpretation to place on these judicial decisions is that folkways are shifting from intolerance to indifference, if not to openminded tolerance. This shift in folkways is reflected, in part, in the repeal of vaguely written and differentially enforced sodomy statutes in nearly half the States, thus decriminalizing homosexual conduct (not to mention decriminalizing unconventional but widely practiced forms of heterosexual conduct). (p. 6)

It is interesting to note that in 1993 Major Melissa Wells-Petry discusses the same question in *Exclusion,* a book on the subject and comes to a different conclusion, reaffirming the idea that the military has a legal and constitutional right to discriminate against homosexuals. Major Wells-Petry's well-researched and well-written book is over 200 pages, with hundreds and hundreds of citations. The text of PERSEREC's report is just over 36 pages, and the bibliography is just over 4 pages.

After reviewing the legal status of homosexuals in the military, PERSEREC reports on "Scientific Status of the Homosexuality Concept." Again, the survey of scholarship runs slightly more than three pages and presents only evidence supportive of the idea that homosexuality and heterosexuality are not discrete categories but are "best described in terms of gradations or dimensions" (p. 10)—in other words, that a large proportion of people are to some degree sexually attracted to people of the same gender and have experiences with members of both sexes. The primary source: Kinsey.

Perhaps the most thorough research undertaken to advance the frontiers of knowledge about sexuality was that of Alfred Kinsey (Kinsey, Pomeroy, and Martin, 1948; Kinsey, Pomeroy, Martin, and Gebhard, 1953). A zoologist, Kinsey organized his research program along ethological and epidemiological lines. The variable of interest for Kinsey was sexual acts. The raw data for his studies were obtained through structured intensive interviews. In contemporary scientific fashion, quantitative analysis guided his work and influenced his conclusions. He employed a rating scale that allowed him to rate subjects from 0 to 6. (A category "x" was used to identify persons with no "socio-sexual" response, mostly young children.) From the interview data, he compiled ratings on the hetero-homosexual dimension for a large sample of respondents. . . . Kinsey reported many significant findings, among them that 50 percent of the white male population were exclusively heterosexual and 4 percent were exclusively homosexual throughout adult life. Forty-six percent had some homosexual experience throughout adult life. Between the ages of 16 and 65, 10 percent of the men met Kinsey's criterion of "more or less exclusively homosexual." (pp. 7–8)

It is important to note the degree to which the PERSEREC report misrepresents the findings of Kinsey. For example, in discussing the 10 percent figure, the report leaves off the qualifying phrase "for a period of three years."

Perhaps the most ill-conceived and ill-wrought section of the report is the third part, entitled "The Social Construction of Sexual Deviance." Relying heavily on historical commentary by such sexual revolutionaries as Kinsey, Bullough, and Ruse, the authors attempt to suggest that Christian civilization is just an ill-conceived web of tribal superstitions that are irrational and arbitrary.

In the Judeo-Christian traditions, Good and Evil are the categories that provide the background for declaring value judgments on sexual nonconformity. Arising from primitive taboos, the powerful image of "sin" was employed to define the unwanted conduct. Fundamentalist preachers who take the Scriptures as the literal revealed Word of God are contemporary advocates of the belief that nonconforming sexual behavior is sinful. The attribution of sinfulness carries multiple meanings: among some groups, sin is explained as voluntary acceptance of Satanic influence; among others sin is believed to produce a flawed or spoiled identity. Societal reactions to sin include ostracism, corporal punishment, imprisonment and in more draconian times, torture, stoning, hanging, burning at the stake, and even genocide. (p. 13)

It is difficult to see how a summary of the meaning of sin could be more simplistic or narrow-minded. The authors ignore all the great Judaic and Christian authorities on the subject and choose instead to construct a description based entirely on social scientists ignorant of theology and church history. For example, fundamentalists are not the only Christians who believe that oral or anal intercourse between men is sinful. It is a position that has been held by the greatest intellectuals in Western civilization, from Dante to Thomas Jefferson to C.S. Lewis. As for the list of punishments prescribed for sin over the history of Judeo-Christian civilization, punishments at least as severe have been meted out even more cruelly by modern totalitarian states whose rulers rejected Christianity—including Nazi Germany, the Soviet Union, and Red China. In addition, Christians believe that all human beings are sinners, not just sexual deviants. They also believe that they must forgive the sins of others, otherwise their own sins will not be forgiven. It was Christ rather than Kinsey or Bullough who said, "Let him who is without sin cast the first stone." Christians believe in condemning sins, in leading sinners to repentance, and in the maintenance of social order. Dante, who certainly knew a lot more about sin than anyone in the Department of Defense, places unrepentant sodomites in the same level of hell with unrepentant usurers, thereby telling us why the medieval church thought homosexuals were sinning—because they took a natural impulse and used it in a way that could not produce anything new or valuable. Usury, to Dante, was the economic equivalent of spilling your seed on the ground. The authors of this report take a different position:

> Sin is an attribution, a construction made by others or by oneself. Its force lies in its attachment to entrenched religious doctrine. Like taboos, the concept of sin is acquired by people before they reach the age of reflection. The argument that sin is a social construction is nowhere better illustrated than in the debates of theologians who have puzzled over the criteria for sinful conduct: under what conditions should an action be regarded as a venial sin or as a mortal sin? (p. 13)

Again, it is significant that a government report would presume to state in such a categorical manner that "sin" is an artificial concept, a creation of the individual consciousness that varies from person to person. Such a view rejects the idea of absolute values and, by implication, the existence of God. Some of the greatest philosophers in history have agonized over this question, including such "ancients" as Plato and Aristotle; such medieval figures as Augustine, Aquinas, and Occam; and such modern giants as Locke, Berkeley, Hume, and Kant. How convenient to have the whole matter resolved in a few sentences by the U.S. Department of Defense. It is untrue, incidentally, that theologians have argued extensively over what is and isn't mortal or venial sin. The Catholics are the chief religious body concerned with this distinction, which, for them, was essentially settled long before Dante wrote the Divine Comedy, that is, before the 12th century. Protestant theologians have generally ignored such a distinction, literally for centuries. As for specific real-life cases of sin, "theologians" don't often argue about such matters, since most orthodox Christians believe degrees of guilt and innocence are a matter for God to determine ("Judge not, lest ye be judged.")

What follows this muddled and illiterate discussion of sin is an abbreviated and highly selective history of English jurisprudence which suggests that laws against "nonprocreative sexual behavior" stem solely from the Judeo-Christian belief "that sex served only one purpose: procreation." One is compelled to ask: "What purposes would sex serve for those who are not orthodox Christians or Jews? Pleasure? Intimacy?" These purposes are commended in the Bible as well, and in Christian literature from the earliest times. They are a part of the complicated nature of human sexuality recognized by all sophisticated cultures. Medieval lyrics and narratives, inherently Christian in their structure and texture, explore all the ramifications of sexuality, its subtlest sensual and emotional facets, as does the *Psalm of Psalms*. Indeed, the only civilized people who might regard procreation as the sole purpose for sex would be the evolutionists, who see the survival instinct as the controlling force in life. They alone would tend to view the pleasurable aspect of sex as no more than an evolved stimulus to ensure the survival of the species. So the idea of sex as solely for procreation is a scientific one. When they come to the famous change in the official stance of the American Psychiatric Association, the authors of this report simply ignore the physical and emotional intimidation of gay rights activists in favor of their own more serviceable fantasy:

> In 1974, the diagnosis of homosexuality was deleted from the Diagnostic Manual of the American Psychiatric Association under pressure from many psychiatrists who argued that homosexuality was more correctly construed as a nonconforming life style rather than as a mental disease. (p. 16)

They go on to describe the surrender of other major organizations, who fell in line as abjectly as did the psychiatrists under pressure from an active minority of homosexuals who took advantage of the rising tide of political correctness sweeping over the intellectual and professional communities in America.

Finally, in their history of the New Enlightenment, they discuss the homosexual community as the latest in a series of "minorities" claiming the need of special rights as the result of special suffering, ignoring the per capita income of homosexuals (which, according to a recent survey, is more than $23,000 higher than that of the population as a whole) and their disproportionate representation in the higher echelons of corporate America and in the professions.

> Similarities to more widely recognized minority groups are not hard to find. Prejudice against persons with nonconforming sexual orientations is like racial prejudice in that stereotypes are created. Such stereotypes are often exaggerations of social types that feature some unwanted conduct, style of speech, manner, or style that purportedly differs from the prototype of the majority. The personality of an individual identified as a member of a minority group is construed not from his acts, but from his suspected or actual membership in the minority group. Racial and ethnic slurs help to maintain the partition between the minority group and the majority. Wops, Guineas, Japs, Spics, Kikes, Beaners, Polacks,

Sambos, and other pejoratives have only recently been discouraged as terms to denote the social and moral inferiority of selected minority groups. Fag, fairy, queer, homo, and pervert serve similar functions for persons who want to communicate that the homosexual is "inferior." At the same time, the slur is intended to characterize a social type that exemplifies a negatively valued prototype—the feminized man. (p. 18)

After beginning this paragraph by saying that similarities with other minority groups are not hard to find, the authors are only able to find *one*—the use of stereotypes—and this characteristic is also shared by the majority as well. Anglos, Gringos, Honkies, and Whiteys are also called by names and reduced to stereotypical descriptions. Watch television any night to find examples. What the authors cannot with authority say is the following:

- that homosexuals are undeniably born with their distinguishing characteristics.
- that homosexuals can be readily identified at sight, as can other minorities.
- that homosexuals have suffered widespread job discrimination because of their bedroom habits.
- that homosexuals are discriminated against for what they are rather than for what they do.

The extreme bigotry underlying this study is further reinforced by the authors' commentary on the "Resistance to Change."

In the foregoing analysis, we have tried to make the case that the military services should prepare for a shift in legal and public opinion on discrimination against homosexuals. Such a change in a time-honored practice is not likely to be accepted without active resistance. In the absence of compelling reasons, bureaucracies resist change. The first line of such resistance is the invocation of the concept of tradition. In general, the arguments against change contain declarations of the necessity for preserving such qualities as integrity, morals, morale, pride, fidelity, and so on.

In fact, few of these reasons have been given by those who argue in favor of a continued ban against homosexuals in the military. In this day of political correctness, appeals to abstractions such as "integrity" and "morals" invite ridicule and even persecution. Those who favor the ban often refer to morale, but they don't do so in a vague, misty-eyed fashion. They cite documented cases of sexual harassment by homosexuals in command, danger to the blood supply during combat (when all troops are potential donors), and the close proximity of personnel while in foxholes or on shipboard. This report considers none of these questions, while ranging widely over political and social questions that are only marginally relevant to the question of security. The public version of this report (minus the name of one of its original authors) appeared in an abridged form; but, like the Gibson essay, the full study has a continuing life of its own and has been cited often by advocates of homosexual entry into the military (e,g., a June 1992 report on the subject issued by the General Accounting Office of Congress, which most American fail to recognize as no more than an arm of the liberal wing of the Democratic Party).

CONCLUSION

These three studies—funded by three separate federal agencies—are by no means the only examples of active involvement by the government in the promotion of the sexual revolution. The National Institutes for Health, the Centers for Disease Control, the Office of the Surgeon General, the Justice Department, the U.S. Congress, and the White House itself have all funded projects or supported initiatives that in one way or another contribute to the new climate of sexual license. They have not done so carelessly or without knowledge of the implication of their actions. Indeed, both parties are to blame for the growing tendency of government to lend active support to the sexual revolution. The Democrats, of course, are more open and aggressive in their advocacy. Led by such teeth-clenching critics of traditional morality as Edward Kennedy, Pat Schroeder, Gerry Studds, and Barney Frank, the Congress of the United States stands poised to consider a National Gay Rights Bill. Indeed, 108 members of the last Democratic congress agreed to co-sponsor the bill. The Republicans, though less open in their advocacy, are increasingly willing to consider such legislation in order to end the controversy and split the homosexual vote. Undoubtedly they are under the delusion that ten percent of the population are homosexual and increasingly likely to vote as a bloc, despite no legitimate and convincing evidence of such a trend. From 1989–1993, President Bush opened the doors of the White House to homosexual activists, invited openly homosexual couples to White House dinners, and allowed a former cabinet member and 1992 campaign official, Robert Mosbacher, to "negotiate" with gay rights activists as part of his duties as campaign manager. It was only after polls showed him losing support among conservatives that President Bush stiffened his stance against gay rights and started emphasizing family values. It is clear, however, that the political establishment is beginning to coalesce behind laissez-faire sex in America, the doctrine that anyone can have sex with anyone else, provided both parties are willing. Of course, the corollary to that proposition, as we have seen over the past five or six years, is that, while the public has no right to forbid consensual sexual activity between adults, it does have the absolute obligation to pay for the consequences of indiscriminate sex, whether in the form of billions and billions for AIDS, or in the ever-increasing benefits for single mothers who give birth to out-of-wedlock children. When England passed its gay rights bill a few years ago, Lord Boothby was quoted as saying: "Now that it is legal, how long before it becomes mandatory?" Given the nature and scope of the reports above, Americans might well ask the same question.

4

MILITARY RETREAT

Many Americans, even as late as the early 1990's, preferred not to think about the gay rights movement. In the first place, because of the the stagey demonstrations of the peaceniks and feminists—with their non-negotiable demands, political posturing, and federal litigation—a lot of people were burned out with the "civil rights movement." To them, homosexual demands sounded more tiresome than threatening. Organizations like the *National Gay and Lesbian Task Force* were merely one more group attempting to renounce all responsibility and board the Freedom Train, whose destination these days is special privilege. Others just didn't want to think about homosexuality because it was disgusting. When they read in magazines that homosexuals engage in anal intercourse and the ingestion of human waste they became angry—not at the homosexuals but at the reporter or columnist who discussed such matters in public. How dare anyone bring up such aberrations in a publication habitually read in the den or the dentist's office!

While many gay rights activists resented such attitudes, they also profited politically by them. The success of their agenda depended on two things: first, the lack of any coherent and highly focused opposition to their movement, and second, widespread ignorance of the unhealthy acts that homosexuals habitually perform and the medical consequences of those acts. Their little drama had to be staged with lights dimmed and all sexual activity taking place in the wings. If the American people ever were to recognize the truth of what homosexuals are demanding and what they are doing, the gay rights movement would begin to face serious and organized opposition.

Yet from its beginning in the late 1960's, the movement had, from time to time, displayed a decidedly dark side, one that mirrored the deep pathology of homosexuality, its obsessive capacity for self-destruction. More reasonable leaders chose their battles carefully, making certain that they couched their demands in seemingly benign terms and kept the debate focused on civil rights rather than sexual behaviors. "Leave us alone," they said. "Whatever you may think of our behavior in bed, grant us the same rights of privacy that you enjoy. Stop being cruel and judgmental."

Others, however, did not stick to such prudent tactics. For example, by the late 1980's gay rights parades were growing more obscene and orgiastic with each passing year—particularly in California. And while the major networks could be counted on to air only segments that focused on the most respectable floats and participants, conservative Christian groups were filming everything—the sex acts, simulated and real; the nudity; the four-letter words; the obscene placards and banners; the deliberately offensive blasphemy; and the wild, frenzied fits of many of the marchers.

These films were being shown around the country, along with clips and stills of other excesses—and always to shocked audiences, whose anger was followed by hefty donations to anti-gay-rights activists. Indeed, by 1993 more and more people seemed willing to face the issue directly and honestly and to consider the implications of what the homosexual movement was demanding.

It was at this moment that the gay rights leaders may have made their first major blunder in an otherwise perfect long-range strategy. They decided to challenge the military's exclusion policy and demand from the Democratic Party a promise that if elected, its nominee would end the ban and allow open homosexuals, both male and female, to enlist in the services. There are two reasons why this move may have been a mistake. First, in focusing on the military ban, the homosexual activists declared war on a highly organized group of people who had hitherto remained neutral: the American military, both active and retired. And second, in raising this issue, homosexual activists for the first time made it possible for their opponents to introduce into the debate the legitimate question of what homosexuals do and how it affects their health.

Indeed, the military policy rested in large measure on the argument that homosexuals were so unhealthy they would impose an intolerable burden on service health care resources. Yet, according to many, unless they could continue to limit the debate to their own narrowly framed "civil rights" arguments, homosexual activists would risk exposure of their sexual practices to the general public and, as a consequence, the collapse of their entire agenda.

One thing was certain: If the majority of Americans knew the whole story about homosexuality, they would put an end to all the pretty talk about equal rights and mindless bigotry. Yet, either encouraged by their many successes or inflamed by the outrage of being denied access to such a happy hunting ground as the Armed Forces, they stepped up their campaign against the exclusion policy and won a commitment from Democratic nominee Bill Clinton to eliminate the ban.

On November 3, Clinton won the election, largely because George Bush had been a weak and vacillating president and because the country was in the grips of a sluggish economy. Clinton made one appearance before a gay-rights organization during the campaign; and the national media, ravenous for Bush's blood, carefully ignored the Democratic nominee's vague but potentially damaging speech. Certainly, Clinton's 43 percent vote did not indicate an overwhelming mandate for a national gay rights agenda. All the same, homosexual leaders claimed that their constituency played a decisive role in the victory and demanded that Clinton make good on his promises.

In January, prior to the inauguration, Bob Hattoy, described as "an openly gay member of President-elect Bill Clinton's transition team," was quoted in the *Washington Blade* (January 15, 1993) as saying that the President-elect had every intention of eliminating the ban. However, as in other areas where promises had been made, there was some rhetorical fudging. As the *Blade* put it:

> Hattoy said that Clinton is still studying the option papers dealing with the practical implementation of how to lift the ban. However, Hattoy said he is "confident that an executive order will be issued," and will come "very soon." Once the Commander-in-Chief has issued his order, it will strip the military of its "mandate to discriminate," as Hattoy put it.

In response to those service members who threaten a mass-resignation if the ban is lifted, Hattoy spared no words: "If they choose bigotry as more important [than taking an order], then get out."

Asked about the readmission of those already ousted by the military for being gay, Hattoy said that Clinton has never discussed the issue either publicly or privately. According to Hattoy, the executive order will stop ousters "from now on" and not reinstate anyone (p. 8). However, in the same issue of the *Blade,* other reports suggested that the new president might not issue an executive order after all. Some among his close advisers were beginning to realize the tremendous latent opposition to ending the ban and were trying to find a "middle ground" that would allow the President to share the burden of the decision. These advisers were recommending an "indirect" approach, a "directive" from Clinton's Secretary of Defense Les Aspin that would order the various services to drop the exclusion policy. According to the *Blade*:

Those pushing the directive say it would have the same legal effect as an executive order. They say it would be viewed as a "compromise" that would be more acceptable to angry military leaders who have opposed lifting the ban. (p. 10)

Gay rights activists objected to this modified approach:

"We believe this policy needs to be changed directly by the president of the United States through an executive order," said Kevin Cathcart, Lambda's executive director. Cathcart, who cited President Harry S. Truman's executive order integrating blacks into the armed services, said a similar order is needed now to set the tone for ending years of discrimination against gays (p. 21).

This stiff resistance led to more fudging. At a press conference, the chief fudger was Clinton's press spokesman, George Stephanopoulos, who said, "I expect it will be eventually by executive order, but the final decisions have not yet been reached—the exact structure of the decision" (p. 21).

Meanwhile, faced at last with a major initiative on the national level, the country began to sit up in bed, rub its eyes, and ask in a sleepy voice, "How did it come to this? What in heaven's name are we about to do to our military?" A good question indeed, and asked only at the 11th hour, when the executioner was already testing his equipment. How did we come to the point where politicians were willing to take such a drastic step without an act of Congress or a full national debate? In partial answer to this questioning, here is a brief history of how opponents to the ban on homosexuals organized their forces and how they paved the way for Bill Clinton's administration to take such a momentous step.

In the first place, in one way or another it has always been illegal to perform homosexual acts while serving in the military. As early as 1778, a decade before the U. S. Constitution, General George Washington ordered soldiers court-martialed for sodomy. Those convicted were publicly stripped of rank and subjected to a gauntlet of drummers and fifers who literally "drummed [them] from the corps."[1] As the U. S. military be-

came larger and older more rules were added. But the ban on
sodomy never changed. In the Uniform Code of Military Justice used in the 1940's, sodomy was punishable as a crime and
defined in article 125 in the Uniform Code of Military Justice:

> Sodomy is engaging in unnatural carnal copulation, either with
> another person of the same sex, or opposite sex, or with an ani-
> mal. Any penetration, however slight, is sufficient to complete the
> offense, and emission is not necessary.

> It is unnatural carnal copulation for a person to take into his or
> her mouth or anus the sexual organ of another person or of an
> animal; or to place his or her sexual organ in the mouth or anus of
> another person or of an animal; or to have carnal copulation in
> any opening to the body, except the sexual parts, with another
> person; or to have carnal copulation in any opening of the body of
> an animal.

> Proof. (a) That the accused engaged in unnatural copulation with a
> certain other person or with an animal, as alleged; and if alleged,
> (b) that the act was done by force and without consent of the other
> person or was done with a child under the age of sixteen.

The 1951 version of the *Uniform Code of Military Justice*
updated and further codified what had long been the practice
in our armed forces. Indeed, homosexual conduct was punished more severely in earlier times than it was in the 1940s
and 1950s, when widespread acceptance of psychological
theories identifying homosexuality as an illness had begun to
soften public opinion.

In 1982 a policy of exclusion was officially instituted under
the Reagan administration to rid the military of homosexuals,
who, in the wake of the sexual revolution, were more and
more open and promiscuous in their behavior. The ban also
prevented others with the same inclinations from enlisting.

Since that time, the few homosexual challenges to this ban
have ultimately been rejected by the courts on the grounds that
there was no legally significant distinction between being homosexual and engaging in homosexual behavior. And the case
histories of homosexuals in service indicate that almost with-

out exception, those who enter the armed forces soon enough violate the *Uniform Code of Military Justice.* The courts have therefore concluded over the years that the policy is both reasonable and constitutional.

The history of this legal struggle has been brilliantly outlined by Major Melissa Wells-Petry in her book, *Exclusion: Homosexuals and the Right to Serve,* (Regnery Gateway, 1993). Indeed, this battle, fought over the past decade in the federal courts, is all but over. The military has won; the homosexuals have lost.

The ban has been upheld in every single one of the 12 challenges to its constitutionality that have been finally resolved. There are cases still in litigation; but given the precedents involved, there is little doubt that the legality of such a ban will again be affirmed by the highest courts. Ironically, just when the courts had decided the issue from almost every conceivable angle and by so doing discouraged further litigation, the gay rights leadership moved to convince the general public that somehow the military establishment had been arbitrary and extra-legal in its defense of the ban, that homosexuals made perfectly good service members, that the exclusion policy was based on nothing more than ignorance and bigotry, that it therefore should be repealed at the executive level before the courts declared it unconstitutional.

Actually the reverse was true: Homosexual activists decided to put pressure on the executive branch because in successive court battles they saw the dark at the end of the tunnel. The federal courts would give them no relief. Members of Congress were also reluctant to vote openly for "gay rights" measures, since the folks back home overwhelmingly opposed special protection for homosexuals, unless a member happened to represent an urban district in Boston, New York City, or San Francisco. The only avenue left was the executive branch, and the only method for lifting the ban one that would not involve lengthy and probing public debate.

This push for the elimination of the military ban followed the predictable pattern of homosexual activists: They used discredited data to inflate the estimated number of homosexuals in the military; they began running articles on the subject in their journals; they persuaded allied interest groups like the ACLU to take up the cause; they asked their friends in the media to begin beating the drums for the elimination of the exclusion policy; and they began pouting and posturing in front of television cameras. They also pressed the Department of Defense to commission a study—one that would lay the groundwork for an all-out assault on the policy. They had always been able to manufacture studies to justify their cause. This time they wanted the Defense Department to pay the bill. And in a government agency that President Bush's Secretary of Defense, Dick Cheney, had top-loaded with homosexuals, they got their "study." (According to reports published in such mainline outlets as *Fortune* and the *Wall Street Journal,* homosexuals in high positions on Cheney's staff included his "chief headhunter" for the agency.)

THE PERSEREC REPORT

I have included a detailed analysis of this 1988 study, *Nonconforming Sexual Orientations and Military Suitability*—prepared by a group called the Defense Personnel Security and Education Center—in chapter 3. Suffice it to say, the report was a piece of brazen propaganda that drew heavily (and exclusively) on the research of a handful of gay rights cheerleaders. It contained passages that were little more than anti-religious bigotry—and it ignored the enormous body of legitimate legal and scientific opinion that supported the ban. What's more, its authors failed to confine themselves to their assignment, which was to address the narrow question of whether or not homosexuals were security risks.

When Pentagon officials saw the direction the report had taken, they were embarrassed by its partisanship and its lack of scientific evidence. As a consequence, they demanded that it be scaled back to fit the assignment; but the draft report had a life of its own. Gay rights advocates saw that it fell into sympathetic hands, and soon enough the press and members of Congress were citing it as authoritative and definitive. Brief, biased, and shallow, it became the banner around which gay rights activists rallied in their assault on the military ban.

THE GAO REPORT: THE STUDY THAT NEVER WAS

We don't always agree with U.S. government reports. But since we pay the salaries of the people who produce them, we should insist that they be fair and comprehensive, particularly when they are supposed to shed light on important public policy options. Yet for years the General Accounting Office (GAO) has had a reputation for developing highly partisan studies that hide or distort contrary evidence in the interest of political expediency. As one government researcher put it: "The GAO is simply a creature of the liberal Democrats in Congress. The agency might as well be called *Research a la Carte*. Its conclusions are all too often ordered up by a congressional staff. The GAO merely finds the supporting evidence—or else manufactures it. Everyone in Washington knows this. Only the American people are fooled."

To illustrate the truth of this observation, we need only look at the GAO report on gays in the military.

Here are the facts. On June 12 of 1992, a report on the subject of gays in the military was issued by the General Accounting Office (GAO) of Congress. (This is the same GAO report that Bill Clinton relied upon and quoted during his campaign). Among other things, the report:

- proclaimed not only that 5–10 percent of the population was homosexual, but also concluded that these proportions also held true for the military, despite the official exclusion policy,

- asserted that homosexuals are so easily integrated into the miliary that their large numbers cannot be detected,
- concluded that homosexuals have adjusted so well to military life that the current policy made absolutely no sense.

To arrive at these conclusions, the GAO claimed to have weighed all the available evidence on this controversial issue. And indeed GAO staff members went through the motions of requesting testimony from the Department of Defense:

> To determine what evidence exists to support DOD's rationale for its homosexual exclusion policy, we asked DOD to identify any research studies that had been conducted or commissioned and any reports or drafts that had been written to examine the rationale and premises underlying the existing policy. (p. 14)

Furthermore, the GAO announced that the Department of Defense "has not conducted specific research to develop empirical evidence supporting the overall validity of the premises and rationale underlying its current policy on homosexuality. . . ."

Indeed, the report maintained that "[D]efense officials stated that DOD's policy is not based on scientific or empirical data, but rather on the considered judgment of military professionals and civilian policymakers serving in various leadership positions throughout DOD and the services" (p. 27).

But, as a matter of fact, the Army *had gathered a significant body of* empirical work, and had *delivered the results* of that empirical work to the GAO! Further, DOD representatives *had frequently cited this empirical research* as buttressing their case against homosexuals in the military.

In effect, GAO staff members had ignored the two Army studies compiled by the Department of Defense and sent to the GAO, then in their report claimed that the Department of Defense had failed to offer any research on its policy of excluding homosexuals! The GAO further charged that, because of the absence of empirical studies, the DOD had no rationale for its ban.

To understand fully what really transpired, consider the following sequence of events:

First

On February 11, 1991 Irene Robertson, Evaluator-in-Charge of the gays-in-the-military project; Foy Wicker, a GAO Assistant Director; and Casey Barrs, another Evaluator, met with their research team—called in the grand jargon of the General Accounting Office a "Design, Methodology and Technical Assistance Group (DMTAG)." The purpose of this meeting: To fill the order of three Congressmen (Conyers, Studds, and Weiss) for a report that would discredit the current Department of Defense policy banning homosexuals from the military. Some kept fairly detailed notes outlining what happened; the notes wandered out of a GAO file and eventually fell into my hands. They reveal a shameless willingness to manipulate data and to ignore or obfuscate fact. The participants talked frankly and freely as they devised a recipe to cook the report.

> We briefed DMTAG staff on our original approach which involved getting the view of DOD policy-makers and implementors, DOD investigative organizations, DOD chaplains, and the view of the American Psychiatric Association. The results of our efforts led to the finding that the DOD has not done any research or conducted any studies in support of its policy, nor does DOD feel the need to since the courts have supported its policy. (p. 3)

This statement was simply untrue, though at this stage of the discussion, it is likely that at least some of those present were unaware of its falsity. The military had indeed commissioned studies, more detailed and relevant than anything the GAO would be able to produce.

It must have been obvious from the tone of the discussion what results had been mandated, as the following statement reveals:

> DMTAG staff asked if we were leaning toward making our bottom line in the report DOD needs to change its policy.

But those in charge knew better than to appear so overtly partisan:

Foy stated that, ultimately, GAO would not be taking a position one way or the other on the issue of "homosexuals in the military." However, we want to be as responsive as possible to the request in terms of providing evidence relevant to the policy claims." (p. 3)

The DMTAG crew fell right in with the strategy:

DMTAG stated that one hypothesis we may want to consider would be: *"There exists a large body of diverse, scientific evidence, that may or may not support the military's exclusionary policy toward homosexuals, which the DOD has not yet examined."*

There is a wide array of organizations which could contribute toward this project. Marilyn therefore suggested that we may want to classify the various organizations, rank them on various factors, and select a "representative" few.

This strategy, intended to play on the already-known position of several organizations, is ironic in view of the fact that it was the GAO rather than the military that ultimately ignored scientific evidence. Organizations the DMTAG staff suggested as "representative" were:

- ACLU, American Civil Liberties Union (has a Gay and Lesbian Task Force)
- APA, American Psychiatric Association
- APA, American Psychological Association
- AMA, American Medical Association

All had already gone on record in favor of the gay rights agenda, so there were no risks in meeting with this crowd. On the other hand, there was still a problem—the testimony of military personnel. Obviously somebody brought up the fact that such evidence would be forthcoming, because DMTAG offered a means of weakening or discrediting such evidence:

DMTAG staff noted that the anecdotal and historical views of career soldiers are valid evidence to be solicited, even if they are not "correct." The staff further added that we could protect ourselves somewhat by asking DOD "to name a few organizations, either in or out of the military, which they thought could provide relevant information for our investigation." We could then add selections of our own so as to cover all the "key constituencies."

DMTAG staff also noted that it would be appropriate to touch bases with gay rights activist organizations, indeed that not doing so could invite criticism. (p. 4)

Here the partisan nature of the meeting becomes painfully apparent. Note the word "correct," a first cousin to the phrase "politically correct." Already a "correct" position is assumed. Everything that follows is a way of overwhelming any such "incorrect" thinking.

Of course, everything depended on the inability of the military to come up with legitimate studies of its own. And while some at the meeting were obviously in the dark, a DOD spokesman says he had already talked to the GAO and told them that such studies did indeed exist.

Second

Lt. Colonel William A. Woodruff, Chief of the Litigation Division of the Army, in a February 27, 1991 letter to Ms. Irene A. Robertson, Evaluator-in-Charge of the GAO, noted that he included "a survey at the Sergeants Major Academy and the U.S. Army War College on the homosexual policy. I have included the results of that survey as well as Lieutenant Colonel Blades' deposition and trial testimony."

He further asserted that "the experience of commanders with those who served in contravention of the homosexual policy has been uniformly negative. Thus, there is a legitimate and rational basis to establish a broad exclusion policy." Col. Woodruff called this material "a compilation of documents and materials that explain the policy and its rationale. . . . There are several documents which I would like to draw your particular attention to. You will notice from the index of attached documents that we have included testimony from then Major General Schwarzkopf and a Lieutenant Colonel Blades. . . . General Schwarzkopf was the Acting Deputy Chief of

Staff for Personnel at the time of his deposition and testified as the Army spokesman on the basis and need for the policy. Lieutenant Colonel Blades was an action officer in the Deputy Chief of Staff for Personnel's office."

Third

Analysis of these studies had been at the heart of the 1983 deposition of General Norman Schwarzkopf which also was provided by Lt. Col. Woodruff. During this deposition, General Schwarzkopf referred to and agreed with a survey of commanders regarding their experiences with homosexuals.

Fourth

Irene Robertson phoned and asked to see the survey which General Schwarzkopf used, and on April 8, 1991, Woodruff sent her the 179 pages of testimony from 84 commanders and an analysis of that testimony by Dr. Ron Blades.

Fifth

On April 22, 1991 Harvey Finberg addressed an internal memorandum to Irene Robertson.

> The evaluation question, as we understand the congressional letter is "What evidence can the military provide to justify the exclusion of homosexuals?" We have suggested probing somewhat deeper and addressing the underlying question: "Does DOD have any support for its policy position concerning the sexual orientation of individuals?" Please note that this memo will be confined to a discussion of how to show that DOD needs to produce supporting material. We will be trying very hard to avoid judging the merit of the policy. The most difficult issue to address is how to respond to the potential charge by a commanding officer, "In my professional opinion as a commanding officer, the presence of these persons is detrimental to the good order and discipline of my unit." Our suggestion, as we have already indicated, is to identify impartial, i.e., neutral, "expert witness" groups who can testify based on their professional and practical experience. It is possible that this testimony may provide support that is both pro and con with respect to DOD's policy. However, we suspect that the testimony of these

neutral groups will demonstrate that support cannot be found for DOD's policy, i.e., the absence of this policy does *not* cause bad things to happen.

(Note that this memorandum—still questioning the existence of the DOD empirical studies—was written almost two months after the receipt of the Woodruff letter, the empirical studies, and the Schwarzkopf and Blades depositions, to say nothing of the Wells-Petry thesis. It was also written *two weeks after Irene Robertson had requested and received the empirical study of reports of commanders that Lt. Col. Woodruff had sent her on April 8, 1991.*)

Sixth

The Army had not merely relied upon empirical surveys of field commanders. Col. Woodruff had also sent on June 10, 1991, the GAO the most exhaustive research document ever written on the subject of gays in the military: the University of Virginia thesis of then-Captain Melissa Wells-Petry. The Melissa Wells-Petry document included:

* a comprehensive survey of pertinent legal opinion on the subject and an expert analysis of its implications;

* a survey of numerous medical studies of homosexual conduct, virtually all of which were written-up by leading clinicians and reported in such respected medical publications as the *Journal of the American Medical Association* and the *New England Journal of Medicine.*

Seventh

In a June 15, 1991 memo to file, Irene Robertson gave the following account of her one-on-one meeting with Col. Jim Schwenk at the Pentagon.

Purpose: To clear up points on the Department of Defense policy excluding homosexuals from the armed forces. Specifically, to find out why DOD has not conducted any studies to support its policy and why DOD is so against having homosexuals in the service.

As told to GAO in earlier meetings, DOD feels that it does not have to produce any evidence to support its policy. The fact that the courts have upheld DOD's position on the issue is evidence enough. Additionally, there are isolated cases that show that homosexuals do not fit in the units with heterosexuals. There are incidents of brawls among heterosexuals and homosexuals that have been documented.

(This memo was written by Irene Robertson—the very same Irene Robertson who asked for and received Dr. Blades' empirical studies on February 27, 1991, the Irene Robertson who phoned Col. Woodruff and then received the empirical study she requested on April 8, 1991. Yet four months after receiving the first set of empirical studies and two months after requesting the second empirical study she wrote that she hoped to "find out why DOD has not conducted any studies to support its policy and why DOD is so against having homosexuals in the service.")

Eight

On June 12, 1993, the GAO published its study. Tucked away in Appendix IV on the next to last page of its report, was this statement: "Tabulations of self-initiated letters are not valuable when, as in this case, stronger evidence is available in the form of more technically sound, public opinion poll evidence." The GAO did not explicitly refer to Dr. Blades' analysis anywhere in its report, yet this statement makes clear that the GAO not only received Dr. Blades' analysis of solicited opinions and experiences of Army commanders, but ultimately rejected it as "not valuable." The report also ignored the extensive study of Wells-Petry, which provided precisely the kind of empirical evidence necessary to validate the DOD ban.

Ninth

In March of 1993, congressional staffer Cheryl Crate went to the GAO to examine the evidentiary basis of the GAO report. She found almost everything neatly piled in stacks on the table: There was the Kinsey report, the testimony of the American Psychological Association representatives, even the February 27, 1991 letter from Col. Woodward was there—but *none of the attachments he provided*. The empirical studies had disappeared into the black hole of the GAO's memory. When Cheryl Crate asked to see them she was informed that they could not be found! She persisted, and eventually Irene Robertson asked for, and again received from the Army, on March 22, 1993, the entire packet that Lt. Col. Woodruff had sent in two segments over two years before!

Appalled by the patent dishonesty of this study, several researchers have called the GAO and asked to speak to Irene Robertson, only to be told that she's unavailable. Apparently she's perpetually "out of pocket," at least until this particular policy is resolved. In this respect she resembles the Congress itself, which never has to follow the rules or answer for its own mistakes or deceptions. When you try to bring accountability to the front door, nobody answers the bell, though you can see a shadowy figure peeping through the curtains of an upstairs window.

As of this writing, the GAO report is still waved about as the final word on the wisdom of the military ban. Yet anyone who bothered to compare this crude and sneaky little document with the materials Col. Woodruff presented would understand fully why the DOD's report simply *had* to be repressed. The testimonials of field commanders and Col. Blades' analysis constituted an eloquent and systematic military argument in favor of maintaining the current policy. Melissa Wells-Petry's scholarly review of the medical studies on homosexuality provided an irrefutable scientific argument in opposition to lifting the ban.

And so a committee of bureaucrats ignored the evidence and reported that the DOD had "not conducted specific research to develop empirical evidence." Would that we could resolve all the complex issues of the day with such mindless disregard of fact. It is this consciousless manipulation of public debate that more and more characterizes the society in which we live, the government for whom we all now seem to work. Small wonder that the Congress and its obedient servants are held in such fine contempt by the American people.

THE SCHMITT ARGUMENT

In a revealing report on homosexuals in the military, Eric Schmitt, writing for the *New York Times* (December 1, 1992), offered yet another argument for dropping the ban: The homosexuals were already there and in control; no use to try to root them out.

As he put it in his front-page article: ". . . there is a flourishing gay subculture in the military, despite the official ban on homosexuals in uniform. It underscores the way the military has already adapted to something its leaders say is impossible even to contemplate."

Schmitt, as much the polemicist as the reporter, wrote: "[A]t Camp Lejeune and many other military bases, [homosexuals] already coexist [with heterosexuals]. Individual base commanders vary widely in how strictly they enforce the ban on the thousands of gay men and lesbians in the services, particularly when it involves gay bars and organizations that are situated off base. The commanders of Camp Lejeune are clearly aware of the bar's existence but have not done anything to shut it down or round up its patrons for years. 'We don't sit and stake out these places and harass people,' said Maj. Jay Farrar, a camp spokesman." (p. A-1)

Schmitt did not explain how he knew there were thousands of homosexuals in the military or why he believed commanders of military bases had the authority to close down civilian businesses during peacetime.

However, he did go on to quote homosexual marines who said that there was an active homosexual network already in operation in the military, one that had connections with the homosexual movement at large. Indeed, he cited civilian groups that had been formed to offer "support" for homosexuals in the military:

- A few years ago, 20 junior Navy officers formed the San Diego Gay Naval Officers Association, an informal social club. (p. B-8)

- In Falls Church, Virginia, a West Point man organized an alumni association for the homosexual graduates of the service academy.

- In San Francisco, according to Schmitt, a majority of the 125 members of American Legion Post 448 are homosexual. Schmitt also wrote: "In addition, an array of large national organizations, from the American Civil Liberties Union to the Lambda Legal Defense and Education Fund, offer advice and legal counseling to gay members of the military who are threatened with being discharged for homosexuality. 'Don't tattle,' advises one pamphlet distributed by the Gay and Lesbian Military Freedom Project, an umbrella group of gay rights organizations. 'Giving names may actually make things worse for you. Investigators may try to bluff you into thinking that giving names will help you, when in truth they may have nothing against you unless you give names.' "

According to Schmitt, other groups, like the Gay/Lesbian/Bisexual Veterans of America, had 30 chapters around the country that continued to lobby for change in national and state laws to gain more rights for homosexuals. Needless to say, this organized subversion of authority could be devastating to military morale, particularly if it were to be increased exponentially by the lifting of the current ban.

There is no previous example in the American military of such a conspiracy, one that helps men and women flout rules, cover up lies, and legally harass the Armed Forces whose code they have sworn to obey. But these organizations were also helping homosexuals to make connections with new sexual partners wherever they went. Consider Schmitt's account on the subject:

Other gay soldiers and sailors say that tight-knit circles of friends reach out when a member transfers to a new base. 'When I went to San Diego from Norfolk, my friends here called their friends there, and I had a ready-made network when I arrived,' said a 34-year-old Navy lieutenant commander who is now in the Washington area.

And not only in Washington. The same kind of organized perversion was also present at Camp Lejeune:

One social group of about 30 gay marines and civilians, called Oasis, served as a social anchor and a fund-raising organization for some of the area's gay men. New members are closely screened to prevent military investigators posing as gay service members from infiltrating the group.

"There's a camaraderie here," said one 30-year-old sergeant who belongs to Oasis. "It's like we're all a family. And we can understand what each other is going through."

According to Schmitt, on some bases, homosexuals had even developed an "early warning system" to make certain they were cleared out of nearby gay bars when military police made a visit.

At the Oar House, a gay bar two miles from the Norfolk Navy base in Virginia, the bar's president, Frank Belcher, said surprise visits by the Naval Investigative Service ended several years ago. "Usually we had a call from the base telling us they were coming," said Mr. Belcher. "Homosexuals are everywhere in the military."

To summarize, Schmitt said, in effect: "The military is already full of these people, and they are getting along swimmingly, except for the unfair policies that discriminate against them. Eliminate the ban and you will have happy campers. Try to maintain it, and the clever, ubiquitous homosexual network will thwart you every time."

Randy Shilts, in his huge and hastily assembled *Conduct Unbecoming: Gays and Lesbians in the U.S. Military,* offers evidence to support Schmitt's contention. He writes: "Over the past twenty years, as the gay community has taken form in cities across the nation, a vast gay subculture has emerged within the military, in every branch of the service, among both officers and enlisted. Today, gay soldiers jump with the 101st Airborne, wear the Green Beret of the Special Forces, and perform top-level jobs in the 'black world' of covert operations. Gay Air Force personnel have staffed missile silos in North Dakota, flown the nuclear-armed bombers of the Strategic Air Command, and navigated Air Force One. . . . A gay admiral commanded the fleet assigned to one of the highest-profile military operations of the past generation. The homosexual presence on aircraft carriers is so pervasive that social life on the huge ships for the past fifteen years has included gay newsletters and clandestine gay discos. Gay Marines guard the President in the White House honor guard and protect U.S. embassies around the world. . . . At least one gay man has served in the astronaut program" (p. 3).

As for lesbians, Shilts claims that their presence was pervasive in the women's branches of the service. As he put it: "The upper echelons of the WAC's made it resemble an exclusive gay sorority." (p. 45) Indeed, Shilts's description of our Armed Forces in Vietnam, were it accurate, would be explanation enough for the military disaster that occurred there: "By 1971, a vast gay subculture existed within the American military stationed in Vietnam. Six years of intense U.S. presence had been time enough to establish huge networks of gay servicemen throughout Southeast Asia. . . . Libidinous GIs hardly had to leave the base for their adventures. The swimming pool at Pan Son Nhut, for example, had a reputation as one of the most active gay cruising areas that side of Fire Island" (p. 149).

Of this giddy portrait—painted by one of the gay rights movement's most talented propagandists—John Lehman, former Secretary of the Navy, writes: "Mr. Shilts is not reluctant to accept exaggerated stories in his mission to inflate the homosexual presence in the military. He accepts as fact one mythologist's story about gay discos on board aircraft carriers (I somehow missed these in 25 years of service on carriers)" (*Wall Street Journal,* May 18, 1993).

Whether Schmitt and Shilts are deliberately exaggerating to make a point or whether they are the wide-eyed victims of tall tales, their ultimate strategy is clear. They want to convince supporters of the ban that their cause is hopeless, that homosexuals have already taken the high ground.

THE CONSERVATIVE RESPONSE

As the debate got under way, the conservative community as a whole was either unwilling or unable to come to grips with the initiative to abolish the ban. The military, in particular, remained unaware of the true danger or else, like Scarlett O'Hara, said: "I'll worry about that tomorrow." I had been in contact with various military officers about the possibility of the lifting of the ban since 1983 when Family Research Institute was in the midst of drawing our first national sample. I met with representatives of the Army Litigation Division for their input on what kinds of questions they wanted us to ask when we took our sampling to Dallas, Texas in 1984. We modified and added questions as they suggested. Although they were personally enthusiastic about our effort, they could not locate funding within their division for it. Likewise, our formal request for funding from the Army was also turned down. So, on a smaller scale than we would have liked, we did what we could afford to do without government assistance. The issue continued to simmer. From time to time the Army would send me transcripts of affidavits and the like, but I and the data we had collected at Family Research Institute were being held in reserve for the time when the case "got to the merits." Up until then, all the cases the military had prevailed in the courts by using the argument that the armed forces exist to defend the country and must be permitted to carry out their mission without interference. No case had ever gone to trial where a judge demanded that the military present a "rational basis" for discriminating against homosexuals. I believed that such a demand would soon be issued, while the folks in Army Litigation thought that it would happen in the distant future— if ever. As it turns out, they were right: A "show rational basis" order didn't come from a federal court until 1993. From 1987—when Family Research Institute moved its offices from Lincoln, Nebraska to Washington, D. C.—through 1992, I met off and on with Army Litigation personnel. I also sought to meet with officials at the Pentagon from late 1988 when our first professional publication on the issue came out. Although our results received some attention from *Navy Times* and other military magazines and newspapers, and although the findings spoke directly to military concerns, no meeting with Pentagon officials took place.

In early 1990, when it had become obvious that the gay rights movement meant business in its confrontation with the miliary, a number of other attempts were made to get the research wheels moving. Some got closer than I did. For instance, Paul Mero of Congressman Dannemeyer's office set up at appointment with service representatives at the Pentagon to discuss the issue and to offer significant support. He and another Dannemeyer staff member were ushered into a conference room where five or six middle-echelon officers and civilian bureaucrats were waiting. Mero and his associate quickly laid out the problem. "You're in greater trouble than you think," they said. "These people have no intention of giving up. They are as persistent as any political group in history and have as little regard for the truth. They will make up statistics, manufacture studies, distort and misrepresent opposing arguments, and work Capitol Hill until they get what they want. In the final analysis, virtually all the genuine science available supports the continued imposition of the ban; but the general public will never know the truth unless some effort is made to counteract the current trend. The media have heard only one side of this issue, a side they are temperamentally inclined to support. Until exposed to alternative sources of information, they will continue to beat the drums for the gay activist agenda. We have a network of scientists and scholars who are doing work in this field. We can put together a report for you that will counter what's out there now and give you something substantial with which to defend the status quo. It won't cost a whole bunch of money. We can get it done for pennies—maybe for nothing. All you have to do is say the word."

The Pentagon representatives listened with stony faces, occasionally nodding. They asked few questions; and while they seemed friendly, they were hardly enthusiastic. On the way back, Mero and his fellow staff member speculated on the likely outcome of the meeting. They agreed that the poker faces were necessary, given the fact that all those present were probably sitting in for higher authorities. No one was in a position to make a commitment. "The question is: Are the people up top in favor of dropping the ban or opposed to it? If they're opposed then they have to give serious consideration to such a study. We should hear something in a couple of weeks. If they don't get back to us in a month, then we'll know the guys in the Department of Defense are either chicken or else they're actively supporting the elimination of the ban."

Congressman Dannemeyer's office waited for a call from the Pentagon, but two weeks passed and no one called. Then a month. Then six weeks. That was almost three years ago. Dannemeyer has left Congress, and still the Department of Defense has not asked for help.

Of course, everybody in D.C. already knew that Pete Williams, the Defense Department's Assistant Secretary for Public Affairs, had been "outed" by Washington ACT-UP members frustrated with the Pentagon's failure to drop the ban of its own accord.

All this was known by the national press but given little attention. Secretary of Defense Dick Cheney retained Williams and eventually the hullabaloo died down. Still, Mero and his network of researchers and scientists couldn't help but speculate that Williams, or someone like him, had been responsible for the fact that no telephone call had been forth-coming.

Because Williams wasn't the only high Department of Defense official who was outed. Cheney had also hired Steve Herbits to recruit personnel from the Department, and Herbits was named as an open homosexual by no less a publication than *Fortune* (December 16, 1991). If Herbits had been chiefly responsible for Cheney's hiring policies, then how many of the middle echelon people he'd brought aboard were of the same sexual persuasion? It was a question that gay activists would have immediately termed "homophobic," yet there is strong anecdotal evidence that homosexuals tend to "nest" (i.e., hire their own).

When Cheney was quoted as saying the ban was "an old chestnut," the gay activists were jubilant, and Mero and friends were even more suspicious—not that Cheney was himself a homosexual but that he was sympathetic to gay rights. Their fears were not alleviated by Cheney's constant equivocation on the ban issue. At that point it appeared likely that Cheney himself was willing to allow the exclusion policy to be swept aside without resistance.

However, in early 1992, the political picture altered drastically. George Bush suddenly found himself in trouble. His standing in the polls fell below 50 percent, and it became increasingly obvious that he had lost considerable support in the conservative community. Some of the pro-family leaders made their chief complaint abundantly clear: They were unhappy with the Bush Administration's courting of the gay rights movement.

George Bush, who had invited gay rights leaders to the White House with little regard for conservative sensibilities, awoke to the fact that he might lose his base among evangelical Christians; so the Administration began to back-peddle just a little. General Colin Powell was allowed to say publicly that he opposed the dropping of the ban, and that statement served as a signal to the pro-family, pro-military crowd that Bush was still with them, despite earlier appearances to the contrary.

However, at first Cheney did not chime in. In fact, for a while he remained curiously silent on the subject. His reluctance to speak out made some conservatives believe that Powell might be left twisting in the wind once the election was over. Cheney, who had the reputation of being a conservative, seemed to be flirting with the moderate wing of his own party in his failure to back up Powell. (He was prominently mentioned as a potential candidate for the Republican presidential nomination in 1996.)

Meanwhile as the campaign began to heat up, a full-page ad featuring faked photographs of Clinton and Gore in skimpy beachwear, appeared in more than one homosexual newspaper; and the Democratic campaign organization, after reportedly ordering a hundred copies, quietly spread the word that ending the military ban would be one of Clinton's first acts as President. Instead of challenging Clinton on the gay rights issue, the Republicans allowed the Democratic ticket to have all the advantages of the issue and none of the liabilities.

Immediately after the election, I started lobbying military organizations to hold an academic conference and possibly commission an empirical study before Christmas. It seemed to me that we ought to get in a good shot before Clinton became president. As long as we were a couple of weeks out from Christmas we could get the media attention and perhaps frame the debate. I argued that we should emphasize sexual harassment of heterosexuals and privacy concerns of heterosexuals, thus turning Pat Shroeder's rhetoric against her. On November 19, Admiral Kilkline, head of The Retired Officers Association agreed that we needed a strategy along the lines I had suggested. He got his board's approval and launched the only study that rewarded my efforts. Between November 27 and December 1, Gallup was in the field, interviewing 1,013 TROA members who lived in the continental United States. But, with the exception of this small but decent study, no scientific evidence was collected to combat the almost certain Clinton directive.

THE TROA SAMPLE

The sample was taken from those members who had telephones, and interviewers made up to five call-backs to control for bias in favor of those more easily reached. The first question interviewers asked was: "How familiar are you with the issue of allowing homosexuals in the military?" The response indicated concern among the membership. 58 percent said they were "very familiar," 36 percent said they were "somewhat familiar," and only 4 percent said they were "not too familiar." The second question asked was: "Currently, homosexuals are not allowed to serve in the military and an admission of homosexuality is sufficient evidence for discharge. President-elect Bill Clinton has said that he will lift the ban and open the military ranks to homosexuals. In general, would you say that you favor or oppose allowing homosexuals in the military?" Two percent refused to answer this question. Three percent were "strongly in favor" of lifting the ban. Ten percent "favored" the move. 16 percent said they were "opposed" to lifting the ban. And 67 percent said they were "strongly opposed."

The third question asked: "Did you ever have to deal administratively with a homosexual incident during a tour of duty?" 36 percent said "yes." 63 percent said "no." If you cross sort these answers according to whether or not the respondent favored or opposed lifting the ban, you discover that about one-third of both groups had encountered some incidence of homosexuality—33 percent of those who favored lifting the ban, 38 percent of those in opposition. The fourth question asked: "Would you say that experience, or those experiences, was a major disruption, a minor disruption, or no disruption at all with regard to the normal operation of the command?" The answers to this question reveal a genuine difference in attitude between those who favor and those who oppose lifting the ban. 66 percent of those who favor the change in policy were inclined to dismiss the homosexual in-

cident (or incidents) as a "minor disruption" and 41 percent
said there was no disruption at all. Indeed, only 2 percent of
this group termed the disruption "major." On the other hand,
58 percent of those who support the ban said that the incident
was a "major disruption," 33 percent said it was a "minor disruption," and only ten percent said it was no disruption at all.
To put these answers in perspective, those who reported the
disruption to have been "major" supported the current ban by
a ratio of 180:1. Put another way, the overwhelming proportion of those officers who reported experiencing a major disruption due to homosexuality opposed the lifting of the ban.
On the other hand, those who judged the disruption to be "minor," opposed lifting of the ban by only a 4:1 ratio.

Assuming that the respondents were honest in their answers—and there is no reason to believe otherwise—an objective observer could reach one of two conclusions. First, one
could conclude that those more likely to condone homosexuality would also be more likely to regard incidents as "minor" in
significance rather than "major." Second, one could conclude
that the nature of the homosexual incidents experienced by the
officers had a direct bearing on their attitude toward the ban. If
they encountered major incidents, they were much more likely
to see unacceptable risks in lifting the ban; but if they encountered only minor incidents, they were somewhat more likely to
regard the lifting of the ban as either irrelevant or beneficial to
the service. In order to clarify further the meaning of these responses, Gallup interviewed both groups to ask in a follow-up
question why they took the stance they did. While three percent
of those who favored lifting the ban said they'd had a "good
previous experience working with homosexuals," none reported
a homosexual incident under his command. On the other hand,
among those opposed to admitting homosexuals, twice as many
reported experiencing a "major incident" while in command
(seven percent as opposed to three percent). Clearly, then, experience is a strong factor in determining whether or not to
support the ban. Those commanders who have never had to

deal with homosexual incidents or homosexual advances were much more inclined to favor lifting of the ban. Those who had experienced problems were clearly more inclined to favor the ban. Or to put it in more generalized terms: The more you know about perverse and compulsive behavior, the less inclined you are to tolerate it.

Having confirmed what they already knew about their membership, TROA had no course of action to follow by the New Year. I urged the group to pursue the study so they would have additional data on which to build their case. Once the poll had been run, I advised them to send a fact sheet to their membership, to ask their members to write their local newspapers and their congressmen, and to ensure that the best-known supporters of the ban were enlisted in the fight. "Make certain that high-ranking officers speak out on the question, " I said. "If need be, hire professional writers to help military leaders to write op-ed pieces for the nation's newspapers. Also make certain they are represented on major radio and television discussions of the subject."

Meanwhile, the homosexuals were exulting over the Clinton victory and demanding positions on the new president's transition team. More immediately, they were asking the White House when President Clinton would make good on his promise concerning the military.

However, the President faced significant opposition to any lifting of the ban within his own party. Senator Sam Nunn, Chairman of the Senate Armed Services Committee, a man who had spent many years dealing with military questions at the highest levels of government, stated his opposition to admission of homosexuals to the military, and Nunn came from the wing of the Democratic Party that Clinton was supposed to represent. Nunn's opposition seemed to be based not merely on personal beliefs and attitudes but on a genuine concern for the strength of America's defense capability. He understood how the armed forces operated, knew the top commanders in all branches as well as anyone in government, and was highly regarded in the Senate by members of both parties.

Other supporters of the ban surfaced as well, some of them nationally known commentators on military affairs, some merely people with stories to tell.

Colonel David Hackworth, one of the nation's most decorated veterans, wrote of the Clinton proposal in the *Washington Post* (June 28, 1992, C5):

> I cannot think of a better way to destroy fighting spirit and gut U.S. combat effectiveness. My credentials for saying this are over four decades' experience as a soldier or military reporter.

Instead of arguing from purely a priori principles or offering predictions of things to come, Col. Hackworth gave concrete examples of problems he had actually encountered during his many years of military service:

- He told of a soldier in Italy during the post-World-War-II occupation who "could not keep his hands off other soldiers in my squad." Hackworth said the man "mangled trust among squad members and zeroed out morale."

- In the same unit, he reported, a homosexual personnel major "had affairs with ambitious teenage soldiers in exchange for kicking up their test scores."

- During the Korean War, he went on to say, "a gay commanding officer gave combat awards to his lovers who had never been on the line."

- In Vietnam, he said, a captain in his unit was propositioned by his homosexual commander, an incident which, according to Col. Hackworth "almost destroyed the esprit of a fine parachute unit."

- He said in summary: "These are not isolated incidents: During my Army career I saw countless officers and NCOs who couldn't stop themselves from hitting on soldiers. The absoluteness of their authority, the lack of privacy, enforced intimacy, and a 24-hour duty day made sexual urges difficult to control."

It is important to note that these incidents occurred during a period when homosexuals were barred from the military, when society took a more traditional view of sexual aberration, and when harsh penalties were assigned to anyone who violated the anti-sodomy provisions of the Uniform Code of Military Justice. Indeed, Col. Hackworth reported that "the [homosexual] first sergeant is serving hard time at Ft. Leavenworth. . . ." Certainly there is no reason to believe that such incidents would diminish in number if homosexuals were legally permitted in the Armed Forces.

Writing in the *Wall Street Journal* (December 2, 1992), Kevin McCrane, a retired businessman who served in the Navy in 1945–46, gave an even more detailed account of homosexual behavior in the military, this time on shipboard. He told of his experiences as a sailor just out of boot camp who shipped aboard the *USS Warrick,* an Attack Cargo Auxiliary. The very first night he ran into trouble:

> The awakening was sudden, panic-filled. A hand was caressing my leg, running up the inside of my thigh. A dim figure ducked away as I lashed out, kicking, swinging a fist and striking air. There was no more sleep that night.

McCrane's disturbing experience was by no means the only problem he encountered:

> On the fourth day at sea I visited the ship's post office. The second-class petty officer manning the tiny cubicle greeted me warmly. Grinning broadly, he stepped back from the counter, dropped his dungarees, fondled himself and made an obscene invitation. I walked away.

When McCrane reported the incident to a third-class petty officer on his watch, the man laughed and told him to watch out. "You're on a French cruiser, kid." And McCrane was not the only victim. All the novice seamen were "in the same boat":

> It was in the open now, a subject for discussion among the new recruits. Each of us had been accosted, patted, propositioned. Though we were in different divisions, we flocked together for

meals, averting our eyes when one of "them" leered in our direction. There were five such aggressive homosexuals that we knew
of on board this ship with almost 250 men. They were all petty
officers. Their actions were enough to poison the atmosphere on
the *Warrick*. Meals, showers, attendance at the movies, decisions
about where you went on the ship alone—all became part of a
worried calculation of risk.

If the homosexuals had stopped at no more than overt advances and propositions, the situation would have been bad
enough. But the compulsive sex drives of these petty tyrants
led to something worse:

> After two weeks at sea, I received the whispered news that the
> smallest and most vulnerable of our "team" had been sodomized
> in the paint locker. When I looked at the bearer of this news, I
> saw that there were tears in his eyes. "Why are they doing this to
> us?" he asked.

It was only after the USS Warrick had reached Pearl Harbor
and the five petty officers had debarked on a P-boat that
McCrane went back to his bunk and got rid of the heavy
wrench he had been sleeping with as a weapon to defend himself. His story doesn't tell us what might happen if the military
ban against homosexuals were to be lifted. It tells us what did
happen during a period when, under the Uniform Code of Military Justice, homosexual acts were routinely punished by
prison terms and when such conduct had no apologists among
the press, the clergy, members of the United States Congress,
and the President of the United States. In more recent times,
the punishments have been lighter, but the incidents continue:

- In September of 1992, fourteen soldiers from Ft. Hood were
  discharged from the service after they were videotaped engaging in homosexual acts in a public restroom. Nine were
  separated under "other than honorable conditions." Three received "general discharges," and therefore may receive
  benefits. Two received honorable discharges after a hearing
  revealed "mitigating circumstances." Small wonder that with
  the consequences so light, there should be *fourteen* involved

in this particular incident, which resulted in charges ranging from indecent exposure to sodomy. (*New York Native,* October 12, 1992, p. 14)

- In June of 1993, the press reluctantly and curtly reported the conviction of two sailors in Jacksonville, Florida. Both had raped shipmates, one aboard a U.S. naval vessel, the other while ashore. (*New York Times,* June 7, 1993)

At this stage of the debate, the conservative community fortuitously discovered the work of Major Melissa Wells-Petry. A Dannemeyer staff member, attending a meeting on an entirely different matter, happened to bring up the homosexual ban in casual conversation; and a young woman present mentioned that a friend of hers had written a Masters thesis on the subject at the University of Virginia School of Law. Is it available? the staff member had asked. No, the friend had said, the Army had refused to publish the manuscript and had shipped its author, Major Melissa Wells-Petry to far-off Germany.

That afternoon, Dannemeyer's staff called the Army and asked for a copy of the thesis. It arrived in a few days with a cover letter stating that the work was now being revised and that it was by no means the source of official policy. When staff members began to read the thesis they couldn't believe their eyes. It was 354 pages long, with more than a thousand footnotes and covered every aspect of the subject in clear, logical prose. It was a flawless brief in favor of the ban, so persuasive in its use of legal and medical evidence that no reasonable person could believe any other policy was either wise or judicially sound.

But why had it been repressed? After investigating the matter, they discovered that Wells-Petry's thesis director at the University of Virginia JAG program had previously directed a work attacking the ban and that he who had blocked publication of her response—despite the fact that completed theses from the program were routinely printed in the *Military Law Review.* Unwilling to let the matter rest, Dannemeyer's staff sent the manuscript over to Al Regnery of Regnery-Gateway, a publisher who had previously published manuscripts that were black-balled by the liberal establishment (e.g., *Senatorial Privilege,* an account of the Chappaquiddick affair that had been commissioned by a major publisher and later dropped like a hot potato). Regnery, a lawyer himself, immediately saw the importance of the Wells-Petry work and agreed to publish it as quickly as it could be revised.

The result was a 237-page book, *Exclusion: Homosexuals and the Right to Serve,* Washington:1993. Essentially a legal brief, the book addressed all the arguments used in federal court to challenge the military ban. Having represented the Army in some of these trials, Wells-Petry understood the anatomy of the civil rights position and was able to dissect it with all the skill of a brain surgeon. In the course of three well-documented chapters, she made the following points:

- The American military has historically "discriminated" against a number of groups in its recruitment policy. Among those excluded are: the physically handicapped; women (in combat); the mentally handicapped; certain religious groups (e.g., the Sikhs, who must always wear their turbans); people who are overweight and underweight; the near-sighted and far-sighted; the too-tall and too-short; those who cannot speak English; and those who have not graduated from high school.

- Because of the special mission of the military, there is no "right to serve." Service is either a burden or a privilege, depending on one's point of view; but it is no civil right, otherwise those groups listed above would have to be admitted.

- The courts have ultimately rejected all First Amendment arguments. Refusing to admit homosexuals does not deny their right of free speech or association, nor does it violate any right of privacy. Homosexuals are free to do all of the above outside the confines of military service, so denying them entry does not violate the Constitution of the United States.

- The courts have also rejected the argument that, like Blacks, they are a "suspect class" (i.e. a group subject to persecution because of factors beyond their control) and hence entitled to special protection. Unlike Blacks, the courts have found, homosexuals are not immediately recognizable as members of group, are not provably homosexual as the result of birth, and have not suffered economic deprivation.

In addition to her thorough and convincing exposition of the legal arguments in support of the ban, Major Wells-Petry also supplied additional examples of obsessive sexual behavior on the part of uniformed homosexuals.

After summarizing these examples, Captain Wells-Petry concluded: "Thus, anecdotal evidence suggests [that] homosexuals who enter or remain in the military by evading the homosexual exclusion policy are likely to follow the same patterns of behavior as homosexuals outside the military" (p. 98). She added that this kind of promiscuous behavior, both during off-duty hours and while in engaged in military activities, would only increase were the ban on homosexuals in the military to be dropped. In response, to the argument that heterosexual service members are allowed to pursue active sex lives without interference, Major Wells-Petry devoted an entire chapter to the significant differences between the sexual practices of homosexuals and heterosexuals, differences that are easily discerned after reading the medical evidence on the subject. For example, she pointed out that homosexuals as a whole are much more promiscuous than are heterosexuals, and offered a number of studies to prove her point:

- One study of intravenous drug users revealed that "homosexual men . . . reported a median of 1,160 lifetime sexual partners, compared with . . . 40 for male heterosexual intravenous drug users." (p. 93)
- Another study concluded that "homosexual men had significantly more sexual partners in the preceding one month, six months, and lifetime (median 2, 9, and 200 partners, respectively), than the heterosexual subjects (median 1, 1, and 14 partners)" (p. 93)

- Yet another study stated that while "the median number of lifetime sexual partners of the [more than] 4,000 [homosexual] respondents was 49.5. Many reported ranges of 300–400, and 272 individuals reported 'over 1,000' different lifetime partners." (p. 93)

- A study of AIDS patients yielded the following: "Heterosexual patients from all risk groups reported considerably fewer sexual partners than did homosexual men, both for the year before onset of illness and for lifetime. . . . Homosexuals had a median of 68 partners in the year before entering the study, compared to a median of 2 for heterosexuals. . . . Homosexuals in the study had a median of 1,160 lifetime partners, compared to a median of 41 for heterosexuals in the study." (pp. 93–94)

- A relatively small sample of only 93 homosexuals revealed that the "mean number of estimated lifetime sexual partners was 1,422 (median, 377, range, 15–7,000)." This study also noted that: "Lifetime total partners [may be] more reliably reported than either numbers of partners in the last 6 months or numbers of partners during the high period." (p. 94)

The medical evidence Wells-Petry cited was gathered primarily from medical journals and was overwhelming: Homosexuals were much more likely to engage in promiscuous sexual activities with a variety of partners than were heterosexuals. And she presented conclusive evidence that this kind of activity had dire medical consequences:

- One study of 93 homosexuals revealed the following medical history for the sample:
  - 65.5 percent had contracted gonorrhea,
  - 52.5 percent had contracted hepatitis,
  - 49.5 percent had contracted amebiasis,
  - 40.8 percent had contracted genital warts,
  - 39.7 percent had contracted phthirius pubis,
  - 36.7 percent had contracted syphilis,
  - and a significant portion of the sample reported other afflictions such as nonspecific urethritis (26.8 percent), genital herpes simplex (22.9 percent), shigellosis (16.1 percent),

giardiasis (10.7 percent), nonspecific proctitis (10.7 percent), and scabies (6.4 percent). (pp. 103–4)

- Another study reported: "In addition to high rates of gonorrhea, syphilis, and hepatitis B, gay men have shown to be at high risk for venereal transmission of anorectal venereal warts, hepatitis A, enteric pathogens, and cytomeglavirus infections."

- The recently described immune deficiency syndrome [i.e. AIDS] involving opportunistic infections such as Pneumocystis carinii pneumonia and Kaposi's sarcoma accentuate the public and personal health risk associated with sexually promiscuous gay males. (p. 104)

- According to a study of intestinal spirochetosis—which may result in rectal discharges, bleeding, and diarrhea—"Previous studies have demonstrated intestinal spirochetosis in rectal biopsy specimens from 2 to 7 percent of heterosexual and 36 percent of homosexual patients. . . . We observed intestinal spirochetosis in rectal biopsy specimens from 39 (30 percent) of 130 homosexual men but in none of the control . . . specimens. Among female homosexuals, vaginitis has been cited as the preponderant medical problem." (p. 106–107)

- Because so many homosexuals reported "infection of, or trauma to, the rectum or anus" doctors created a phrase to describe the condition—"gay bowel syndrome." As one study put it: homosexual men are "predisposed to acquiring organisms that are sexually transmitted during rectal intercourse." (p. 107)

- A statistically significant number of homosexuals also engage in anilingus, oral-anal contact, commonly called "rimming." According to one study, "92 percent of these men reported that they practiced receptive anal intercourse, and 63 percent practiced anilingus" (p. 100). Such practices expose them to diseases such as hepatitis A and hepatitis B, which, as noted above, are disturbingly common among homosexuals. As one study concluded: "Homosexual males are at a high risk for acquiring hepatitis A as a consequence of promiscuity and the practice of oral-anal sex." The same study also reported: "Risk factors for [hepatitis B] infection in homosexual males include . . . oral-anal sex." And a case history of a lesbian with hepatitis A revealed that "[patient 2 was] a lesbian with a history of oral-genital and oral-anal sex with patient one . . . [patient 3 also] had regular-genital and oral-anal sex with patient 1." (p. 101)

- In addition to these exotic and dangerous diseases, studies indicate that those who engage in anal sodomy are much more likely to be stricken with anal cancer: "82 percent of homosexual patients and 72 percent of homosexual control subjects reported [practicing anal intercourse]. . . . anal cancer risk for men who expressed a homosexual preference [was] more than 12 times that for heterosexual men." (p. 106)

- Disease is not the only medical catastrophe to which homosexuals are susceptible as a consequence of their aberrant behavior. Anal sodomy and anal-fist contact ("fisting"), common among many homosexuals, may result in trauma and other complications, such as prolapsed hemorrhoids, nonspecific proctitis, perirectal abscesses, penile edema, and anal fistulas and fissures.

- One study noted: "[i]mpalement injuries from penile and fist anal fornication, resulting in mucosal hematoma, laceration, and perforation have been reported" (p. 106). Complications, such as "[a]nal fissure, [are] seen in . . . male and female homosexuals engaging in anal sex" (p. 106). They are frequently the victims of injury and trauma. Another study reported: "A series of 101 patients with trauma of the rectum, secondary to homosexual practices, presenting at this hospital is reviewed. Two patients were injured twice. Thirty-six patients had retained foreign bodies in the rectum, 55 had lacerations of the mucosa, two had disruptions of the anal sphincter and ten had perforations of the rectosigmoid. . . . [There was one mortality]. (p. 107)

- Wells-Petry quoted from a medical report describing a fatality which resulted from the practice of "fisting": "One of these patients died. He was a 23 year old man who presented in a state of septic shock 12 hours after fist intercourse. In this patient, Fournier's gangrene developed which resulted in necrosis of the rectum and perineum, in spite of having fecal diversion performed. Multiple organ failure developed, and he did not respond to treatment." (p. 106)

In a summary both authoritative and eloquent, she concluded that the military was ill-equipped to deal with medical problems of this dimension and that the free access of homosexuals to the armed forces would not only raise costs, but also pose insurmountable problems in the deliverance of health care services, particularly in time of war. She also dealt extensively with questions of privacy, morale, and public confidence, concluding that the abandonment of the current exclusion policy would significant limit the ability of the military to carry out its major responsibility—to fight the nation's wars.

When word got out in Washington of the existence of Wells-Petry's thesis, the whole complexion of the debate began to change. Mischief was afoot. A publication announcement appeared in a column in the *Washington Times,* and the brass at the Pentagon took note. When Wells-Petry made a trip to Washington during the Christmas season, she was summoned by the Secretary of the Army, who spent a great deal of time picking her brain. Then she spoke with other high Army officials who for the first time understood the nature of the exclusion policy and the strength of their case in retaining it.

When the Clinton team came to Washington to assume the reins of power, they found that the Army was prepared to argue this issue. Suddenly a promise that was easily given and seemed easily redeemed began to pose formidable problems. At first these problems were a cloud no bigger than a man's hand. By late January the cloud had spread across the sky and you could hear the roll of thunder way back in the hinterlands. The military had found their legal weapon, as had the conservative activists in Washington. Even before publication, the Wells-Petry thesis was being reproduced on copying machines and sent out all over the country.

Since the debate was now being joined on "rational basis" grounds as well as legal grounds, the questionnaire and interview studies that Family Research Institute was performing all around the United States figured to play a significant role in what was to come.

5

AN EMPIRICAL VIEW
OF GAYS IN THE
MILITARY

Working assiduously in Congress to overturn the ban was Rep. Gerry Studds, who used his office and staff to push the issue. Later on, one project he personally promoted was a book—*My Country, My Right to Serve*[1]—a collection of testimonials by homosexuals who had served in the military. It was edited by Mary Ann Humphrey, a captain in the Army Reserves who was forced to resign because of her lesbianism.

Congressman Studds wrote (or signed) a "Foreword," and he also supplied the author with a Congressional aide, who worked on preparing the manuscript for publication. So in part, *My Country, My Right to Serve* was funded by U.S. tax dollars. (Studds, an openly homosexual Congressman, was once reprimanded by his fellow House Members for having sex with a teenaged male page.)

Both Ms. Humphrey and Congressman Studds were strong supporters of "gay rights" and leading advocates of eliminating the ban on homosexuals in the military. Indeed, Humphrey wrote in her introduction: *"The oral histories in this book pro-*

vide more personal evidence that gays are good workers in the military. We do a good job, we are not security risks, and there is no reason to kick us out." (p. xvii). So the case histories offered in this book provided the "best possible scenario" for homosexual service in the Armed Forces. 130 homosexuals were interviewed. Only 42 were chosen—28 men and 14 women. Make no mistake about it: this was a book with an agenda. Yet to many normal, objective readers, the 42 interviews provided dramatic and conclusive proof that homosexuality and military service are incompatible. Consider the following:

- Of the 28 males interviewed, 21 (75 percent) admitted that they had engaged in sex with other men while in the service, a felony under the Uniform Code of Military Justice.

- Ten of the 28 (36 percent) admitted to participating in sex between officers and enlisted men.

- Of 14 lesbians interviewed, 79 percent admitted that they engaged in sex with other women while in the military.

Unfortunately, those interviewed were not closely questioned about whether or not they had lied to gain admittance to the Armed Forces; but 21 percent of the men and women volunteered the information that they had indeed sworn falsely that they were not homosexuals when, in fact, they were. Here are some quotations and anecdotes gleaned from the published interviews:

- A 52-year-old male said that he had always fantasized about enlisting in the Army in order to engage in homosexual acts and lied about his predilections in order to gain entry. About American society he is quoted as saying: "From what I have ascertained, our culture says you can do anything you like as long as you don't get caught." (p. 7) (He subsequently died of AIDS.)

- A male, 56, reported that he had lots of homosexual experiences while in the Navy, both on-board ship and on leave: "We had 'gang dates'; things like that were going on. But I gave no names. However, they certainly didn't make any mistakes in the people that left. We were all gay" (pp. 8–9).

- A female, 57 years of age, lied about her lesbianism in order to enlist: "But, by God, when I got into basic, I thought I had been transferred to hog heaven! No damn kidding! Lordy!" (p. 11).

- A 65-year-old male reported that he had engaged in homosexual acts both on and off duty: "The smoke stacks on the destroyers were hollow, and there is a platform on top of them, perfect security [for sex]." He also said: "One of the techniques, which I outrageously developed, was merely crawling in with somebody and engaging them in sex and leaving them as if nothing had ever happened. You don't say anything; you pretend it never happened. And so long as you never discussed it, it never happened" (p. 22). His homosexuality produced in him a hostile and rebellious spirit, the antithesis of esprit de corps: "The rebellion that I did was to take the system and use it against them, consciously. I was what they called a sea lawyer—it's a term they used. I knew the rules and used them" (p. 26).

- A 56-year-old male reminisced about his voyeurism: "Ship life had its advantages, too. They had dividers between the individual showers, but there were no shower curtains or anything and the sinks were right in front, so it was rather cruisy" (p. 29). An enlisted man, he goes on to tell of his love affair with a Naval officer: "While based in Norfolk, I met a lieutenant junior grade in the Naval Reserve who subsequently became my lover. . . . It was a real good situation—until he was murdered [in New York by a hitchhiker whom he had picked up and taken to his home]!" (p. 30).

- A 75-year-old male told of his homosexual adventures during World War II: "My problems all started when I was reported for patting a sailor on the shoulder and telling him he was good-looking. That was all, period. He prematurely yelled rape and got the military police. . . . A lousy MP forced me to have relations with him in a solitary-confinement cell. Another MP came in at midnight for the same reason, but he was unsuccessful" (p. 33).

- A midshipman at the Naval Academy, discharged before graduation, made this statement when his case was reviewed by the performance board: "I've been a good midshipman. I haven't done anything wrong. It's true that I'm gay, but I wasn't involved with anybody, nor has it affected my performance, as validated by the documentation you have before you" (p. 240). However, he was lying to the board. In his interview for the Humphrey book he admitted that he "did have a few experiences, but they were few and far between and very, very secretive. . . . the situations I did encounter tended to be with other midshipmen in non-Academy surroundings" (p. 237).

- A female, currently a military recruiter, "sidestepped that god-awful question about homosexuality. I said, 'no.' I lied." (p. 243) In fact, she got married to cover up her lesbianism, saying of her husband: "He was a good friend and knew I was gay. We were really best friends, and we had gotten married as a cover for me. He really didn't need it and shortly afterward, left for a different base. Nevertheless, we were still legally married." (p. 245) She was artificially inseminated, and she and her lover now live together. She is trying to find a homosexual father to "cover" for her.

- Another enlisted man, 56 years old, joined the Army in 1953 and received an honorable discharge from the service. Of basic training he says: "It was wonderful being surrounded by all those men in basic training, but gee, I didn't quite know how to explain it. It was like having a field day, I suppose" (p. 52). Of his long-time lover, a Marine, he says: "We maintained our relationship during my two years in the Army. And when I was sent to Korea, he came to see me once. . . . [H]e was gallivanting around. He had a lover in Japan and a lover in California. Yeah, all over the place. He said, 'Well, you can love three people at the same time.' You know how those Marines are. Gay or straight, they think they are the horniest and the best" (p. 52,53–4). He also describes a brief encounter with an officer: "Once, while I was on R&R in Japan, I met this full colonel. I was in Tokyo and was walking around the Imperial Hotel, looking in the windows, when I happened to look up, and there was this colonel—who was also looking at me. And before we knew it, we were in bed. What could I do? What could I do? Of course, we were both in uniform at the time. It was as shocking to me as anything else. We went to another place, another hotel. He was married. I mean, he was gay, but he was married" (p. 53).

• An enlisted man, aged 65, reminisces about World War II: "I had a wonderful experience with a married man alongside me on the straw, lying in these boxcars made in World War I. . . . Here we were, together all night, going into Germany, and when we got up in the morning, we had to get back into our pants. It's broad daylight, everybody was dressing, and one guy yelled, 'Hey, those guys don't have any pants on!' The captain said, 'Oh, maybe they were just having fun!' Everybody broke up laughing. . . .Phew, that was close!" (p.56).

He also said of his experiences: "Before my final discharge from Fort Bragg, especially when the war was over, the whole atmosphere was relaxed. In the Enlisted Man's Club, the john was very active and guys would meet in there to have sex. If not right there, out somewhere, out in the fields, in the pitch-dark. You could have a new experience every five minutes. The pace—I'd never seen anything like it before in my life. Maybe it had gone on in other places, but I didn't know it. At Fort Bragg, guys were doing it. And doing it a lot!" Who was involved? His answer is disturbing: "Not all were gay; some were just getting their kicks" (p. 57). He said of homosexuals in the military: "Some of the best soldiers I knew were gay." As for straights, he speaks of them with contempt: "There were some straight guys— spoiled, big, straight guys—getting discharged because they were so emotionally immature. I remember a guy panicking at the gas mask drill. He really started carrying on—sobbing and blubbering. He was about forty and couldn't take it. He got himself discharged because he broke down like a baby. I had so much contempt for him, it made me even tougher" (p. 58). Yet of military service he said: "Overall, I hated it. I really hated it. I was so unhappy the whole time I was in— at least 90 percent of the time" (p. 58).

- An enlisted man from the Vietnam era, currently serving in the Washington state legislature, said of his time at the Naval Justice School: "I mean, it was heaven for a gay person because there were folks from all the services: Marines, Army, Navy, Air Force, Coast Guard. . . . But while I was in school, I was involved with a couple of guys. One was this Navy guy who was married in the straight sense, who definitely liked to play around, but was very, very cautious and very scared" (p. 63).

  Of Vietnam, he said: "We had a game where we'd have four or five gay guys go together, spot somebody in a club, and if you were interested, you would bet on . . . who would get him first. I had the award for getting the highest-ranking officer in bed with me. He has since become a brigadier general! In fact, it was always the ongoing joke that I received my second Bronze Star for landing the general-to-be in bed" (p. 64).

- An officer, dismissed under conditions less than honorable, said, when asked if he was homosexual, said "there was no hesitation—I lied" (p. 108).

  Like most of the 42, he went on to boast of his sexual conquests: "I met this private, E-1, who came from Puerto Rico. This became my first sexual encounter in the military" (p. 109).

  He disliked some of his superiors: "They might have been my superiors in terms of rank, but they were idiots. . . . I was known as a communist outspoken queer . . ." (p. 110). "I had become very sexually active with a number of soldiers on the post" (p. 111). "I was outraged that the military could spring this kind of charge on me four days from being discharged" (p. 112).

  "We called every active officer in Special Forces, Airborne Europe, to testify either on my behalf or against me, and figured that we cost the government over a million dollars. On top of that I got paid for my own court martial, which permitted me to take home over ten thousand dollars" (p. 115). "[A]fter the trial itself I slammed open the door of the adjutant's office and said, 'I'm not leaving until I've had my say. You kicked me out of the service—there's nothing you can do to me, you f___ing a___ole!' I was screaming at him; then I turned, went into the colonel's office, and repeated my act. I said, 'You're a bunch of mother___ers!' I was very angry. I'd done nothing wrong" (p. 116).

- An enlisted female, who received an honorable discharge, said. "I actually became involved with the same sex around age thirteen or so. . . . During my formative years I was a rebel . . ." (p. 123). "[W]e were a hot item for about two months; then she got with someone else. Since she had whet my appetite, the rest of the time seems to be a blur of women. The service became an awakening for my sexuality . . ." (p. 124).

- Another enlisted female, who had received both honorable and undesirable discharges, told of early abuse by her adoptive father, then detailed her sexual adventures in the service. "[M]y first affair occurred in the military, just doing what I was told. She was the leader of our troop" (p. 101).

    "[w]e dated with two men because of appearances. . . . I had several [lesbian] sexual encounters but I wasn't the instigator" (p. 102). Alcohol began to become a problem: "I went into a coma" (p. 103).

    "Most of that action, the attentions were coming from the sports teams that I associated with on my new base . . . had sex with an officer" (p. 104).

- A female officer who received an honorable discharge, recalled: "As the years rolled on, networking worked real well for me. That's right. Networking. I had friends in the Pentagon. If I was going to another assignment, I'd call up one of my friends and say, 'If I go to so-and-so city, who should I be looking for?' And they'd say, 'Colonel So-and-so, Major So-and-so.' They'd give me the names. So I knew. And they would tell them if their friends were there, 'Hey, she's coming here.' So you walked into a place and everybody knew each other. We protected each other. When we needed an escort someplace, gay men and women would escort each other" (pp. 131–32).

"In 1982, my career ended with an honorable discharge and full benefits. I retired as a full colonel, an O-6. I was very pleased by my achievements over those twenty years" (p. 133).

- An enlisted female who received an undesirable discharge reported. "[W]e were too paranoid to do anything on base, so we'd go off base whenever we could, which started the development of a close physical relationship. . . . [We went AWOL] for eight days. . . . our sexual exploits for those eight days were unbelievable . . ." (p. 135).

  "The pressures of my ouster and the bleak outlook for employment caused me to turn to the bottle. . . . I don't even know how I became pregnant. . . . After four years Margo finally left me and got married. . . . knowing I was now the one responsible for a soon-to-be-born infant. If I hadn't conceived and had my child, I probably would have killed myself in a car accident or something like that" (p. 137).

- An enlisted female said. "I joined the U.S. Navy. It was there that I had my first lesbian experience. We met for the first time in boot camp" (p. 144). After a few affairs "I got frightened and decided to cover my tracks. I ran a number on my soon-to-be husband, but he was thrilled when we tied the big knot. . . . It shouldn't come as a great shock that our marriage lasted about six weeks. After that I really started my other lesbian relationships" (p. 145).

- A female who served in the ranks and as an officer, was married to a man when she joined the Army, although she had sex almost exclusively with women. She served under Gen. Eisenhower and claimed she told him that she would be next to the top of the list to be discharged if he tried to get rid of lesbians in the WACs [and his secretary at the time would go to the top of the list] (p. 40). She says he relented. She became hooked on drugs, tried suicide. "[Gays] are probably the best soldiers" (p. 42). This good soldier had lesbian sex with a number of fellow service women.

- Another female claimed she was unaware of her homosexual tendencies until she had enlisted and was propositioned. "We would go when her lover wasn't there, but when she did find out, she came back and threatened to kill me. But I felt so strongly about the one I was seeing, that wow, this was it, this was love, it didn't matter" (p. 223). "I started coming on to this lieutenant" (p. 224). "Although I didn't like sneaking around, that was the fun of it. . . . I was one of the best soldiers they had" (p. 226).

These narratives, gleaned from the most moderate and respectable homosexuals discharged from the military, revealed more than Congressman Studds and Ms. Humphrey had intended. In addition to the problems cited above (lying at induction, sex with other military personnel, sex between officers and enlisted personnel) objective readers saw several other problems emerging.

First, there was the attitude toward the military itself. To be sure, a certain amount of bitterness was understandable among people who were dishonorably discharged—and some of those interviewed fell into this category. But it was clear from their own accounts that a significant proportion of those included in this volume were bitter, cynical, and disruptive during their service—quite apart from their predictable resentment of the Uniform Code of Military Justice.

The reader found "sea lawyers," wise guys, defiers of regulations, cynics, and malcontents. Indeed, this collection of narratives—gathered to illustrate the best of the lot—would have provided ample subject matter for a recurring nightmare to any company commander attempting to prepare men for battle or any naval officer who watched them being piped aboard a destroyer. It was obvious from these accounts that homosexuals, rebels by definition, find themselves doubly challenged in the Armed Forces. The rules and constraints they so despise are infinitely more authoritarian in the military than in civilian life and the consequences of disobeying them far more devastating. If homosexuals hate our society—and it is clear that many of them do—then their hatred of the uniform, with all that it represents, is more intense, their rebellion more focused.

A second problem revealed in the Humphrey book was to be found in the compulsive sexuality of homosexuals. It is abundantly clear from these narratives that the great majority of homosexuals find abstinence impossible. Indeed, many obviously seek military service because of the sexual opportunities it affords. These people have no intention of obeying the Uniform Code of Military Justice, or else they soon discover that obedience is impossible or too difficult to consider seriously. They seem driven to engage in illicit conduct despite the severe penalties imposed. They neither respect the privacy of others nor the chain of command that makes the military a coherent and effective force in time of war. They place their own sexual drives above the good of the military—a clear indicator of their hierarchy of values.

A third problem revealed by Humphrey is the essential dishonesty of homosexual service members. Many undoubtedly entered military service by lying about their sexual proclivities, so their very careers are based on deceit. After they were inducted, they continued to live a lie. They were "aliens" within their own military units, subversives by temperament, cheats by definition. Since the large majority involved themselves in illicit sexual activity, they were also criminals, violators of the law who knew they would commit the same crime again and again. Thus they tended to have an outlaw mentality that was difficult to isolate from their ordinary duties and obligations in the military service.

It must be difficult, if not impossible, to compartmentalize dishonesty—to keep it in strict rein except when sexual behavior is at stake. Certainly life in the military for homosexuals mandates secrecy and deceit and does nothing to promote truthfulness and openness—two important traits in the cohesiveness of a fighting force. Of course, there are those who argue that with the dropping of the ban, there will be no further need for lies and dissembling; but the history of the question, particularly in recent years, seems to indicate that homosexuals will still remain in the closet, even after they no longer risk expulsion from the Armed Forces, if only because too many of their comrades will continue to regard them as perverse, less than manly, and hence contemptible.

So *My Country, My Right to Serve,* written and published as a weapon in the battle for gay rights, instead served as a strong argument in opposition to dropping the ban. Like many documents cited by gay rights activists in support of their agenda, it told an entirely different story when viewed through the eyes of a clear-headed and responsible "straight" society.

FAMILY RESEARCH INSTITUTE REPORT ON GAYS IN THE MILITARY

Late in 1992, after the election of President Clinton, I was certain that lifting of the military ban would be a high priority with the new Administration. Bill Clinton had said so during the campaign. I had no reason to doubt his word. And I was convinced that the debate would turn on current data relevant to homosexual performance in the military. The politically correct crowd was already arguing that homosexuals were not a disruptive force in the military. For example, nationally syndicated columnist, Ellen Goodman[2] asserted that "between 5 percent and 10 percent of the military is estimated to be gay right now" so "if showers are such a charged venue, barracks such a threatening situation, how come the problem hasn't already wrecked morale and created dissention in the ranks? How come it's come up so rarely?"

The *Los Angeles Times* published an opinion poll tha painted a somewhat more complicated picture (February 28, 1993). This poll of 2,346 currently serving members of the military reported that only 16 percent of men approved and 76 percent of men disapproved of dropping the ban (i.e., a 1:5 ratio), 35 percent of women approved and 55 percent disapproved (not quite a 1:2 ratio). Was Ellen Goodman's sweeping statement compatible with this apparent discontent among current service members? The Humphrey book provided no real answer to this question. Though unintentionally useful to supporters of the ban, it was clearly designed to reinforce the homosexual argument that they had served honorably and well. We needed an objective survey of homosexual experience in the military—not one that had discarded more than two-thirds of the anecdotal data. When it seemed that no one else intended to conduct such a survey, Family Research Institute took up the task.

Generally, past performance is the best predictor of future success. We considered it likely that past interactions with homosexuals in the military would provide useful information about how the presence of open homosexuals would affect the military in the future. To address this issue, we performed a systematic national random phone questionnaire survey involving 654 respondents who had served in the military or were currently serving; two random mail questionnaire surveys, the first a sample of 5,000, the second a sample of 20,000; and a hand-delivered, anonymous questionnaire survey of 83 officers and enlisted personnel currently serving at accessible bases. These three surveys, though different in methodology and size of sample, yielded 2,457 respondents with remarkably similar attitudes and experiences. Here is what we found.

Those with military experience opposed lifting the ban by a ratio of about 4 to 1. At least an eighth of those who served reported being sexually approached, molested, or raped by a homosexual on their tour of duty. At least 20 percent experienced a homosexual incident. Most of these incidents disrupted the command or unit. Almost a third of these incidents involved homosexual advances, molestations, or rapes, and a significant number of the instigators were beaten—some were killed.

We also discovered an even more disturbing aspect of homosexual life—one discussed in both the Humphrey book and the later Shilts book. Evidence pointed to a "shadow homosexual network" within the military, a clique operating to circumvent military law and promote the careers of fellow homosexuals, a dark countercurrent to the mainstream of military life. This network had significantly disrupted the military mission in the past.

Finally, we found an extraordinary amount of violence surrounding homosexual activity in the military. Wherever these people served, there were altercations, fights, beatings, rapes, suicides, and even murders. While the largest portion of this violence occurred in response to aggressive homosexual behavior—propositions, physical molestation—a significant number of reported incidents involved homosexuals as instigators of violence.

Consider the following analysis of 245 reported incidents:

- Respondents reported three murders, two of them "fraggings."
- Fifty-three incidents (or 22 percent) inc uded beatings.
- Nineteen incidents (or 8 percent) involved homosexual rape.
- Fifty-six (or 23 percent) involved molesting a sleeping or drunken comrade.
- Fifty-four (or 22 percent) involved "fraternization"—that is, a superior engaging in sexual relations with a subordinate.
- Fifty-one (or 21 percent) involved a "pass"—i.e., a sexual approach, either verbal or physical.
- Nine (or four percent) involved children.
- Six of the incidents (or two percent) took place in showers.
- Two of the incidents involved transvestites.
- One service member was knifed, another was pushed in front of a car, two were thrown out of windows, and yet another was hurled down a flight of stairs.

In addition to examining the number of homosexual incidents reported, the influence of the homosexual network in the military, and the violence surrounding the presence of homosexuals, we also considered two secondary questions.

- Since an Administration spokesman charged that conservative, evangelical Christians were the major force driving the opposition to homosexuals in the military, we set out to answer the question: "Do evangelical Christians who served in the military have a different opinion of homosexuality and report different experiences with homosexuals?"

- Since women are disproportionately prosecuted for sodomy in the armed forces as compared to men, we asked: "Is this reflective of greater proportions of lesbians than gays in the military?"

DISCUSSION

Is homosexuality a problem in today's U.S. military?

To those like Ellen Goodman,[3] who argue that homosexuality doesn't really affect the functioning of the military today, and it won't when accepted, it is noteworthy that 16 percent to 24 percent of male respondents encountered some kind of homosexual incident during their service and between 12 percent and 16 percent of men reported that homosexuals approached them. The results for women were similar. Over half of these incidents were of considerable significance for a fighting force since they involved serious breaches of military authority and chain of command—homosexual superiors taking sexual advantage of subordinates, superiors rewarding subordinates for sexual favors, abandonment of strategic combat posts to engage in sexual activity, and the arbitrary imposition or withholding of discipline. (It is perhaps significant to note that no official action was taken in 37 percent of all reported homosexual incidents.) Such breaches of good order and discipline suggest that opposition to the lifting of the ban is not based merely upon "ignorance" and "bigotry" but on experience and objective evaluation of empirical evidence. It is one thing for people like President Clinton and Ellen Goodman, who have never served in the military, to build theoretical arguments about the behavior of homosexuals in the service. It is quite another to render judgment after serving in the military and bearing witness to the disruption and misconduct characteristic of units troubled by the presence of homosexuals. In this regard, it is interesting to note that the anecdotal materials in the Family Research Institute's study bear a striking resemblance to the incidents related in the Humphrey book. Both present a chilling view of the influence of homosexuals on the military. In fact, the two sets of reports are opposite sides of the same coin. In the Humphrey volume, homosexuals report their sexual activities as rollicking adventures, by turns nostalgic and humorous. The FRI survey found that heterosexual service members—and particularly those approached—found these same kinds of incidents distressing and revolting.

Here are some of the testimonies:

- 1938: "I was with a S/Sgt [staff sergeant]. He said he had to pee so we stopped and I started to join him. Immediately he clamped his mouth on my penis and told me that he would bite it off unless I discharged into him. I was afraid and 18 and just avoided him from then on."

- 1940: "I was a 20 year old S/Sgt with my own private room. At the time we were requested to allow new S/Sgts to share our rooms. I drew a new S/Sgt who was transferred from the field artillery. The night of the incident, he entered my room while I was asleep in my bunk and started to put his hands on my legs and lower body. I awoke with a start, immediately jumped up and ordered him to stay in his bunk. He made another attempt to grab me and I tossed him to the floor. I picked up a service shoe and told him not to dare get out of his bunk. He told me that he shaved with a straight razor and he was going to cut my throat while I slept. Since he was a much larger and older man, I never slept that night."

- 1944: In a latrine, "pvt tried to seduce 1st Sgt. First Sgt beat pvt nearly to death. It was reported that the pvt 'fell down a flight of stairs.'"

- 1961: (near San Francisco) "A very young WAF (in her late teens) was assigned to my Squadron. She was fresh, exuberant and full of enthusiasm, so I was somewhat surprised to discover she had gone AWOL for two days. She was apprehended in the vicinity of the Base and although she offered no explanation, I merely administered a verbal reprimand and returned her to duty. A short time thereafter, she again went AWOL. After about three weeks, she was located in her parent's home. This time on the advice of her family lawyer, she returned to the Base to tell the sordid story of having been propositioned, harassed, threatened, and in the present day vernacular: "hit on." She identified a couple of WAF NCOs from the Squadron as her lesbian tormentors. The OSI quickly moved in and a lesbian network was badly shattered as other WAFs came forward to testify to the OSI. "In the future, however, emboldened by an acceptance label, the greatest punishment will more likely be meted out to the 'straights' who forcibly resist unwelcome advances made by those who are protected."

- 1955: "A major picked up two lumberjacks—went to a motel—and they beat the hell out of him."

- 1942: (Guadalcanal Invasion) "Japanese fleet was coming in and shelling us. A large number of casualties was expected. I had to call back to Div. Hdqts to get a relief for the homo that was missing, who I was informed, was with his 'boyfriend.' I was chief of the 1st Pioneer battalion and doing field duty and I had *no* help."

- 1957: "I noticed my clerk (a blue-eyed blonde) began to smell rank of sweat and seemed nervous and inattentive after 3 days on the job after transfer in. . . . I had another female clerk who I knew talk to her—but it took her 5 weeks on the job to [tell me] of her 1st day at Barlsdale female barracks and being raped in the shower. Yes, I helped her and worked with base authorities to trap her lesbian barracks chief and female officers to be put out of service . . . many others came forward after we caught them."

- 1969: (Hunter's Point) "Said he was going crazy, felt like a 'rapist in a girl's dorm' having to watch all the nude guys."

- 1982: (Ft. Carson) "Steady stream of men [to this cross-dresser's room], no one would go within 20 ft. of him. Shunned. Busted after pass at Col.'s driver."

- 1975: (Barracks, Goppingen, Germany) "Too many lesbian incidents to describe. Involved fraternization. . . . Good soldiers had to be disciplined because of retaliation against homosexuals. My integrity was stretched!"

- 1951: (Korea, front line) "Oral sex between EM, jeopardized security of their unit if enemy had infiltrated their area."

- 1985: "An E-7 cook was giving preferential treatment to two male subordinates in the mess hall, and then coercing them to go to hotel rooms with him."

- 1956: "An E was approached by another E. It was not reported. They had a blanket party for him [threw a blanket on him and beat him] and that ended anymore incidents to my knowledge."

- 1963: "An E made a pass to another E and the homo was thrown off the balcony. Homo was hospitalized for a long time. The E received punishment for actions."

- 1972 (Iwakuni, Japan) "A sailor approached me as I left the mess hall and said he wanted to do some disgusting things. I hit him in the mouth. He fell down. End of incident."

- 1943: "Two were approached by fellow cadet—[they] beat him to a bloody pulp."

- 1964: Gay Tokyo Commander? "Reports to IG were fed back to commander. The whole situation smacked of a circle of homosexuals protecting each other. The IG took *no* action. One captain, naval academy grad, eventually left the service in disgust. One captain threatened the commander with real harm. A major went psychotic out of pure frustration. It was a disaster. *I believe the greatest danger is the tight allegiance homosexuals have to each other. It will transcend the chain-of-command, will negate promotion-on-merit, etc.*"

- 1940: "I threw the gay over the railing and into the lake 16 feet below. I was not charged with anything."

- 1954 to 1957: (Ft. Hood) "A ring of homos who assembled a service club. An officer was assigned to the 1st Armored division, reported in one day, went AWOL the next to meet his 18-yr-old lover in D.C. Both apprehended by MPs. The resulting investigation resulted in one officer committing suicide, several court martials."

- 1949: (WAC training center, Ft Lee, VA) "Three lesbians trying to recruit another WAC who rejected their advances, [she] was badly injured by the lesbians." "Practically all our cases involved homosexuals and their passive partners. The passive partners were all in their late teens. From this experience, *I learned that homosexuals are very disturbed people, often bordering on the fringe of mental instability.* In each case, the active homosexual wrote detailed accounts of their involvement in homosexual conduct, and *each indicated that their homosexuality was a learned social/sexual behavior taught by family members at a very early age. The passive member usually indicated they were seeking an added sexual experience.*"

- "A young sailor committed suicide, and the subsequent investigation by the NIS revealed that my medical Department was made up mostly of homosexuals. Because of a recent change in policy by the Bureau of Naval Personnel, young recruits were assigned to shore duty before going to sea. I had over 150 young sailors in their late teens. They presented a very fertile field for homosexual conduct. The NIS investigation found out that the assignment desk at Norfolk, VA was occupied by a homosexual and he was loading my command."

- "Throughout my career as an AF Nurse I watched young talented women leave the service because of these *homosexuals who have their own society within the corps. As they get higher in rank they become more dangerous,* giving good assignments and OER's [i.e., performance report] to only their own kind. Spouses cannot write one anothers' OER but these lovers do it constantly. . . . Much talent has been lost to the service through young potentials leaving to avoid being molested. Homosexuality is recruited not created! I have refused assignments rather than be rated by a gay member."

- 1951: (AG Div, Hq TRUST, Trieste, Italy) "Some homosexuals managed to get into position in the TRUST personnel Division where assignments, promotions, exam questions, etc. were meted out to their favored few at the expense of others."

- 1946: (Ft. Sam Houston) "One man murdered his lover when he learned he was leaving the service. He then committed suicide."

- 1953: (Ft. Bliss, TX) "During the night one E slipped over to another sleeping soldier's bunk and started massaging his privates. The sleeping soldier had been drinking pretty heavily on the weekend, awoke finally and when he realized another man was massaging his penis, he reacted violently. The homo had been approaching several other enlisted men in the company and had been warned to stay away. When the fighting awoke several sleeping soldiers and they found out what had happened, several men threw the homo enlisted man through the window and window-frame of a 2nd floor window. The H was treated at the hospital for multiple bruises and a broken nose and broken collar-bone. All were punished for the incident. . . . homosexual behavior will take priority over a man's required disciplined behavior . . . and *he will split the cohesiveness and fighting camaraderie of any military unit to which he is assigned."*

- 1928: (7th Observation Sqd, France) "The squad threw the homosexual offender out of a window which resulted in bodily injury requiring hospitalization and rehabilitation. The squad had to pay the property damage of the window of the building."

- 1973: "Whenever gay personnel were processed for discharge, they had to be given temporary assignments or work outside their units. As an Adjutant General Officer, I was the one who had to find the interim assignment or job. Nobody wanted them; they disrupted the whole assignment process. They ruined morale in their new, temp assignments.

Knowing they were leaving the Army, they didn't give their best efforts. They took up 'space' but didn't produce."

- 1955: (Tripler Army Hospital, Honolulu) "Gay hospitalman, in a ring including ships cook on my ship, took a 10 year old sick male child and performed oral sex on him. This was the same ward our children would be patients in while we were at sea with no communications (I was a submariner)."

- 1965: (Storeroom aboard ship) "One E, was unable to extract a bottle from his rectum, which led to a medical evacuation problem."

- 1943 (USS San Juan in the Pacific) "A chief gunners mate attempted to get into the bunk of a young sailor. The entire crew became so angry the chief was confined to the brig for his personal safety."

- 1944: (Greenham Commons, UK) "Barrack residents came in to find a cook and a supply man in bed committing sodomy. They beat them within an inch of their life."

- 1965 (El Toro, CA) "My NCO counter-intelligence chief was found to be a transvestite who had falsified investigations of homosexuals within the command. He was covering the homosexual activities of a woman marine officer. He was allowed to leave the service without prejudice because of his large involvement with classified materials."

- 1988: "Homosexual sailor committed suicide via Russian Roulette."

- 1938: (Presidio, Monterey CA) "It was discovered that a certain troop had a homosexual in its rank. Turned out several more were discovered. Troop morale went down. The other troops looked at that troop as part of outcasts."

- 1943: (Ft. Huachuca, AZ) "A homosexual EM tried to get in the bunk of another. The other EM in the barracks were awakened. The homosexual was badly beaten by a number of my EM. He was hospitalized. I refused to identify or prefer assault or battery charges. . . . command pressure [was] applied to all officers and Non-Coms to disclose identities of those who administered the beating [no one would]."

- 1952: (Dharam, Saudi Arabia) "While anal sodomy was performed the lower individual suffocated (his head being in a pillow)."

- 1942: "Aboard an amphibious assault ship prior to landing on Guadalcanal. Sailor and marine contact. . . . disturbed combat unit just prior to combat operations."

- 1951: (Kwajalein, Is) "An ONI investigator was sent to Kwajalein to conduct an exhaustive investigation. We learned that the group had expanded rather rapidly with people transferred to the island covertly and with individuals (straights) pulled into their ranks by intimidation, drunkenness, etc. We found the group had been operating secretly for several months. They had their 'queens' and operatives who were actively involved in recruiting new members. Some young men stated they had fallen prey to the active participants mostly while drunk."

- 1961: (Sacramento) "OG shot himself after being arrested for cross-dressing. He also had children living with him."

- 1993: "I am a practicing homosexual. . . . Grow up all of you and join the real world. Fight a purposeful cause that will really help people—or are you secretly like me?"

It should be clear from this catalogue of incidents that many of those who experienced homosexual incidents in the service were deeply affected by them. Having noted this factor, we subjected our data to further analysis in order to determine whether or not these experiences influenced the attitude of respondents toward lifting the military ban. The question we wanted to answer: "Was there a relationship between the severity of the incident reported and a respondent's attitude toward the ban?" The clear answer was "Yes." Those who reported less offensive experiences with homosexuals were more inclined to admit homosexuals to the military. And those whose experiences were more offensive strongly opposed homosexual entry into the services. (It is interesting to note that in the 1992 TROA [The Reserve Officers' Association] survey, those who favored or strongly favored admission of homosexuals reported only one major incident, 24 minor incidents, and 18 incidents that were not disruptive. Those who opposed or strongly opposed reported 180 major incidents, 98 minor incidents, and 30 incidents that were not disruptive). Thus, in both studies, those who reported negative experiences with homosexuals were much more likely to support the ban.

Having drawn this conclusion we moved on to the next question: "Are evangelical Christians the major force driving the opposition to homosexuals in the U.S. military?" To answer this question, we examined data from the two mail surveys—of retired military and evangelical Christian retired military personnel. The opinions and experiences of evangelicals who served *vs* those of the general sample were remarkably similar. Indeed, the differences were not statistically significant. On this issue, at least, evangelicals were in the mainstream.

Finally, we addressed the question: "Is lesbianism a greater problem among the females in the services than homosexuality is among men?" In examining the data we found that the females in our surveys were more frequently in favor of dropping the ban [women accounted for 3.7 percent of the respondents of our phone survey, 2.5 percent of the mail samples, and 4.8 percent of the active-duty survey]. So examining the reports we got from both men and women, we concluded that homosexuality may be more frequent among female members of the armed services.

HOMOSEXUAL CONVICTIONS IN THE ARMY: THE ARMY STRIKES BACK

In response to the GAO Report (*DOD's Policy on Homosexuality*) and other pro-homosexual propaganda, the U.S. Army decided to conduct a study that would bring into proper perspective the difficulties of absorbing gays into the military. This study would not be an opinion poll or hypothetical speculation on the outcome of dropping the ban, but rather an examination of case histories that resulted in conviction—an anthology of "worst case scenarios" to counterbalance the Humphrey book. Under orders from the Office of the Assistant Secretary of Defense, Col. Richard H. Black compiled a list of 102 punitive separations during fiscal years 1989, 1990, 1991 and 1992—all of those separated from the Army for homosexual acts. In an interview on May 25, Col. Black said that these case histories were obtained via an intensive computer search of official files for those court-martialed and discharged during this period. The 1992 GAO report recorded 200 homosexual discharges from the Army in 1989 and 147 in 1990. The more severe cases—those that involved rape, child molestation, or some serious assault on public decency or military structure—are the ones that appeared on Col. Black's list.

Here it must be noted that most discharges for homosexuality are handled informally at lower levels and do not reach the stage of court martial. In the first place, it takes six months or more to process a discharge if a court martial is involved. In the second place, while awaiting trial, an accused soldier is often non-productive or counter-productive, and his presence poses difficulties for other soldiers. Unless a gross violation of public order has been committed, commanders typically "want the guy out of here." They have little interest in tying up resources in a formal hearing. So most homosexuals are simply dismissed with an honorable or general discharge without specifying homosexual activity as the reason. So the group Colonel Black isolated—those who were punitively separated—comprised about a seventh of males discharged from the Army for homosexual acts (i.e., those listed by the GAO report for 1989–90).

Almost all of the offenders were male (97 percent), and 85 percent of the offenses for which they were tried were molestations or rapes. The following case summaries are instructive in light of: 1) the Humphrey-Studds report and 2) the Family Research Institute national survey of those who had served in the military. The Humphrey-Studds report, detailed earlier, is composed of narratives told from the homosexual viewpoint. With few exceptions homosexuals recounted their sexual exploits in the service in some detail and with pride. These three studies bear a striking resemblance to one another. The situations, the approaches, the outcomes are virtually identical. For example, in all three reports there are accounts of homosexuals invading the bed of a sleeping man with the intent of engaging him in sexual activity. There are also latrine and shower encounters in all three. And there are stories of married men seduced by aggressive homosexuals.

However, the material in the first study differs in two significant respects from the material collected by Col. Black and by Family Research Institute. First, the homosexuals in the Humphrey-Studds book never mentioned sex with children. Second, they never admitted to violent rape. An examination of the following case histories—a selection of those recorded by Col. Black—should be sufficient to explain why the former Army captain and her Congressional patron may have eliminated more than two-thirds of the narratives they gathered.

The summaries that follow are taken from Col. Black's synopses; the specific case number is in parenthesis.

- (57) (child molestation) A private first-class, who was AWOL, kept the two male children of his sister's friend. The boys were 10 and 7. While babysitting, he anally sodomized both boys. He also had both boys put their penises into his anus. Anal sodomy occurred ten times over these months. [2 victims]

- (58) A staff sergeant, divorced from his wife, brought their children to his home on post at Fort Knox, Kentucky. There he took his six-year old son into his bed and had the boy masturbate him to ejaculation. [Guilty, 1 victim]

- (59) (child molestation) A staff sergeant fondled the genitals of his son and placed his penis in his son's mouth while the boy slept. [Guilty, 1 victim]

- (32) (child molestation) A specialist first class admitted that he had engaged in sex with his own sons and had engaged in sex with boys in other countries for money. He also said he had used his rank to gain homosexual favors from junior soldiers. He committed indecent acts with his 13-year-old nephew and had sex with his 14-year-old adopted Korean son. [Guilty, 3 victims]

- (33) (Boy Scout Master) A sergeant, while a Boy Scoutmaster at Fort Hood, Texas, committed oral and anal sodomy on Boy Scouts aged 9 to 12 years. He used leather straps, dog collars, a dildo, and a dildo attached to the end of a policeman's night sick in the performance of these acts. The sergeant videotaped these acts, which lasted between 30 and 50 minutes. Among the acts: anal sodomy of a male child while he screamed: "Oh God, please stop. You're hurting me. Please, please, stop." The sergeant stuck his penis into this boy's rectum six times in a ten minute period, telling the boy to "Relax." [9 victims]

- (34) (child molestation) A specialist seduced a 12-year-old boy who lived just outside the base with his mother and brother. [Guilty, 1 victim]

- (35) (child molestation) An enlisted Military Policeman sexually abused his 3 year old stepson. He also inserted his finger into the vagina of a seven year old female. [Guilty, 2 victims]

- (30) (child molestation) A staff sergeant committed anal sodomy on boys aged 7, 9, and 10, over a five year period. Two were his own sons, and one was a friend of the family, a military dependent. These acts occurred in Giessen, Germany and at Fort Bragg, North Carolina. [Guilty, 3 victims]

- (43) A staff sergeant fellated his adopted son, who was 7 years old. [1 victim]

- (44) (child molestation) A private first class persuaded a seven year old boy to touch his penis. The boy's father caught them. [Guilty, 1 victim]

- (45) A staff sergeant fondled two boys aged 10 and 12. [2 victims]

- (12) (child molestation) A lieutenant colonel repeatedly fondled the penises of the eight and ten year old boys who lived next door. [Guilty, 2 victims]

- (54) (child molestation) A private first class attempted to anally sodomize an eight year old neighbor boy. [Guilty, 1 victim]

- (13) (child molestation) A sergeant rubbed his penis on his six year old son's body on at least five occasions. He also required the son to rub his (the sergeant's) penis and anally sodomized him. In addition, he fondled a seven year old child, a friend of his son who was spending the night, then threatened the boy with a knife if he told. [Guilty, 2 victims]

- (7) A staff sergeant spent the night at a friend's house because he was so drunk. During this stay, the sergeant fellated the friend's sixteen year old son to the point of ejaculation. The son then fellated the sergeant. [1 victim]

- (6) (child molestation) A specialist first class masturbated and fellated his 12-year-old son. Hit another boy who would not participate. [Guilty, 2 victims]

- (4) (child molestation) A sergeant masturbated his stepson. [Guilty, 1 victim]

- (9) (child molestation) A 13-year-old boy spent the night at a staff sergeant's house. Three times the boy awakened to find the sergeant fellating him or trying to sodomize him anally. [Guilty, 1 victim]

- (10) A sergeant invited a ten year old boy to his house to watch a movie. The sergeant stroked the boy's penis and then had the ten year old call a friend to come to the house. The sergeant pulled on boy into his lap and asked the other to take off his clothing. He also approached a boy in the post gym and indecently touched him. [Guilty, 3 victims]

- (19) (Child molestation) A sergeant forced his own son, then eight years old, to engage in oral and anal sex. During anal sex he placed a sock in his son's mouth because the boy was screaming in agony. He also fellated the boy as he was sitting on the toilet. Both the wife and mother required extensive psychological counseling. [Guilty, 1 victim]

- (27) A staff sergeant orally sodomized his 13–14 year old stepson. [1 victim]

- (8) (attempted molestation) A specialist began to masturbate in the presence of a 13-year-old boy. After he had achieved an erection, he asked the boy, "Do you know what I am doing?" He then said, "Do you want a blow job?" The boy ran out of the steam room, very disturbed. . . . The father came and confronted the offender, then called the Military Police. [Guilty, 1 victim]

- (37) A specialist fellated his three year old son. [Guilty, 1 victim]

- (38) A sergeant fellated his adopted 14-year-old son. He also sodomized and copulated with his adopted 12-year-old daughter. [Guilty, 2 victims]

- (52) (child molestation) A specialist fellated four boys ages one to two and inserted his finger in the anuses of some of the boys. [Guilty, 4 victims]

- (40) A specialist first class befriended the parents of his victims. For an 18-month period, he would go to these children's bedrooms or have the children come to his bedroom and commit a variety of perverted sexual acts. He fellated the boys and had them urinate and defecate in his mouth. He also inserted his tongue into the boys' anuses. He committed similar acts, including the urination and defecation, with the female child of his landlords and committed sodomy with two other children from the neighborhood. [6 victims]

- (56) (child molestation) Over a period of three years, a staff sergeant fondled his stepson's penis and fellated him. He also took the stepson and two other boys to the den of the family home, asked them to undress, and then fellated all three. [Guilty, 3 victims]

- (2) A sergeant molested his eight year old stepson. [Guilty, 1 victim]

- (60) (child molestation, Boy Scout leader) A sergeant tried to seduce two members of his troop. [Guilty, 2 victims]

- (62) A specialist committed sodomy with three boys between the ages of seven and eight while his wife was away working at the PX. [Guilty, 3 victims]

- (63) (child molestation) A specialist was caught by his wife in bed with another man. Later, he molested a sleeping 12 year old girl. [Guilty, 1 victim]

- (64) (attempted child molestation) A sergeant tried to persuade his nine year old daughter and a son to fellate him. [Guilty, 2 victims]

- (65) (threatened assault) A private first class was caught trying to sodomize a woman's son and threatened them all with death if she told. [Guilty, 1 victim]

- (78) (child molestation) A first lieutenant exhibited a ten year history of molesting step-children of both sexes. [Guilty, 3 victims]

- (80) (child molestation) A specialist frequented a public park, carrying with him pornography involving boys in homosexual acts. He molested at least three children, including a girl. [Guilty, 3 victims]

- (81) A specialist fondled two young boys in a bowling alley. [Guilty, 2 victims]

- (68) A corporal put his hands and mouth on the penis of his step-son. he also put his finger in the vagina of his step-daughter. [Guilty, 2 victims]

- (69) (child molestation) A military policeman sodomized a 27-month-old male child, causing numerous lacerations, fissures, and bruising of the anus. The child suffered pain for 10 days following this crime and had psychological problems whenever the he came near a man. [Guilty, 1 victim]

- (71) (child molestation) A specialist forced his 5-year-old son to have oral and anal sex with him. he also rubbed his penis on the face of his 18 month old son. [Guilty, 2 victims]

- 83) A specialist committed indecent acts upon son of the woman with whom he was living and also sodomized a female victim. [Guilty, 2 victims]

- (84) A military policeman taught martial arts at Fort Hood Community Recreation Division of Youth Services, where he showed a 13-year-old boy homosexual pornography and asked the child to have sex with him. [1 victim]

- (85) (child molestation) A private first class, a military police investigator, molested at least four boys around the age of seven. [Guilty, 4 victims]

- (86) (Rape) A specialist committed various forms of sodomy, some by force, some while soldiers were asleep. [Guilty, 10 victims]

- (93) A staff sergeant committed sodomy with his natural son from the time the child was in kindergarten until he was nine years of age. [Guilty, 1 victim]

- (90) (child molestation) A sergeant took both a male and female child to bed with him and had sex with them. [Guilty, 2 victims]

- (91) (Child molestation, Assistant Scout Master) A specialist molested two teenage boys on camping trip. [Guilty, 2 victims]

- (95) (child molestation) A private first class fondled his nine year old stepsons's penis when he was asleep. [Guilty, 1 victim]

- (96) (child molestation) A private first class forced his five year old step-son to fellate him. [Guilty, 1 victim]

- 97) (child molestation) A major molested two step-daughters, aged 11 and 12, and a four year old step-son [Guilty, 3 victims]

- (28) (rape) A specialist would wait until his fellow soldiers had fallen asleep in the barracks, then would attempt to masturbate them. Three complained after awaking, and the third struck the offender. [Guilty, 3 victims]

- (31) (rape plus extortion) A private first class was in the barracks room with a soldier newly assigned to the unit as his roommate. The private first class told the new soldier, "Suck my dick." New soldier did so reluctantly out of fear. After the new solder had fellated the private first class for five minutes, the private first class looked at his watch, told victim to stop, and then demanded $150 from the new soldier for "services." The money was extorted from the victim with threats and violence. [Guilty, 1 victim]

- (25) (rape) A private first class anally sodomized another soldier while they were both drunk in the back seat of a car. His fellow soldier had passed out. The private first class was caught in the act by the German police. [1 victim]

- (16) (rape) A private was in his barracks room in Germany, drinking and watching videos with two other privates. A specialist was down the hall in another room watching a pornographic video that showed scenes of anal intercourse. The private continued drinking and fell asleep. The other privates left the room. The specialist returned to the room and began anally sodomizing the unconscious private. The private awoke and "froze" in shock and fear, whereupon the specialist attempted to insert his penis into the private's mouth. The private screamed and then began crying and cowering in the corner of the room. His screams led other soldiers to the room. . . . [Guilty, 1 victim]

- (5) (Rape) A specialist became ill from drinking too much and made several trips to the latrine to vomit. On one such trip, another specialist approached him and attempted to fellate him. [Guilty, 1 victim]

- (3) (Rape, with a knife) A private first class, a boxer, held a knife to a specialist, spit on his own penis for lubrication, and forcibly anally sodomized his fellow soldier. Then he forced the specialist to fellate him. [Guilty, 1 victim]

- (18) [Rape, attempted rape] A specialist first class and an airman went out drinking together. The airman became extremely intoxicated, fell asleep, and awoke to find the specialist first class rubbing his penis against the airman's leg and buttocks. [Guilty, 1 victim]

- (15) (rape) A sergeant found a private drunk, took him to home, and sodomized him. [Guilty, 1 victim]

- (36) (rape) A private first class twice tried to sodomize a specialist while he was asleep. [Guilty, 1 victim]

- (1) (fraternization, maybe rape) After a private first class had become intoxicated, a specialist first class sodomized him and visa versa. [Guilty, 1 victim]

- (41) (rape) A specialist invited a private to a party, then, when he passed out, took off his clothes and fellated him. [Guilty, 1 victim]

- (46) (rape) A staff sergeant attempted to rape a specialist.

- (49) (rape) A specialist asked a private to masturbate. He also stripped another private who was drunk and fellated him. [Guilty, 2 victims]

- (53) (rape) After another soldier had become intoxicated and passed out, a private fellated him. [Guilty, 1 victim]

- (51) (rape) A specialist got drunk and fell asleep. A staff sergeant undressed the specialist, kissed him, fellated him, and attempted to anally sodomize him. When the specialist awoke and resisted, the sergeant took out a knife and forced him to continue. In an ensuing struggle, the sergeant bit his penis. [1 victim]

- (55) (rape, of struggling soldier) After drinking heavily, a sergeant returned to his battalion and told a private first class, a trainee, to accompany him. The sergeant took the private to his Bachelor Enlisted Quarters room and grabbed the private's genital area as soon as they were in the room. He told the trainee to watch television with him and to lie on top of him. The private fled to the bathroom and locked the bathroom door to keep the sergeant out. He even wrote "Help" on the bathroom window. The sergeant told the trainee to come out, that he could leave. When the trainee emerged from the bathroom, the sergeant was standing naked and grabbed the trainee by the neck. The sergeant put his hand down the trainee's pants. The trainee tried to escape through a window, but became stuck in it. He called out for help and was rescued by six other trainees. [Guilty, 1 victim]

- (70) (rape) A second lieutenant would enter barracks in middle of night to fondle sleeping soldiers. [Guilty, many victims]

- (82) (rape) A private first class pulled down a sleeping soldier's trousers and fellated him. The private attempted to put his penis into the sleeping soldier's anus, but the sleeping soldier awoke, jumped out of bed, and picked up a crowbar. The private first class fled. [Guilty, 1 victim]

- 94) (attempted rape upon a subordinate) A chief warrant officer invited his driver to spend the night in the garrison rather than return to a field location. The officer purchased dinner and provided his 23-year old driver as many as a dozen beers. After the driver had passed out, the officer lay on top of him, took hold of the driver's penis, and tried to turn the young soldier over, saying he was going to "mount" him. The driver pretended to be asleep. The driver testified he stayed in the room because he feared the authority of the officer. Later the officer got on top of the driver, kissed him, and moved in a way that suggested oral sodomy. The driver fled to the bathroom and later reported the incident. [Guilty, 1 victim]

- 92) (rape of subordinates) A staff sergeant invited a private first class to his home near Fort Ord. On at least two separate occasions the private slept in the staff sergeant's living room. During the night, the private awoke to find that he had been partially disrobed and that the sergeant was masturbating himself as he fondled the private's genitals. On the first occasion, the private thought the staff sergeant was simply drunk and moved to another couch to sleep. After the second occasion, the private stopped visiting the sergeant's house. The private did not tell his chain of command because he thought it would be his word against that of a noncommissioned officer. The private did tell a corporal, his best friend at Fort Ord. The corporal revealed that the sergeant had also molested him. Later, the corporal told the private that another private had been molested and his First Sergeant wanted statements prepared against the staff sergeant. The private said that if the First Sergeant had not intervened, he would not have made any report of these incidents. [Guilty, 3 victims]

- (98) (rape) A staff sergeant, on three separate occasions asked three different subordinates to "suck your dick." This sergeant also molested sleeping soldiers and exposed himself to civilians. [Guilty, 4 victims]

- (75) (rape of sleeping roommate) Two privates second class were watching pornographic movies. One fell asleep. He awoke to find that he was being fellated by the first private. There was a struggle. [Guilty, 1 victim]

- (72) (rape) A sergeant at various times had sodomized or attempted to sodomize three individuals junior to him. [Guilty, 3 victims]

- (76 and 77) (rape of fellow soldier in showers by 2 homosexuals) Two privates accosted a third in the shower and, after sexual overtures followed by physical abuse, anally sodomized the victim and then forced him to fellate one of his attackers. (Guilty, 1 victim)

- (29) (abuse of authority) A sergeant, a guard at the U.S. Disciplinary Barracks, solicited an inmate suspected of being homosexual to commit oral and anal sodomy. [Guilty, 1 victim]

- (24) (Fraternization) A captain engaged in repeated acts of sodomy with a male noncommissioned officer. [Guilty, Dismissal]

- (73) (Fraternization and rape) A First Sergeant in Korea used his rank to seduce at least five other soldiers junior to him. [Guilty, 5 victims)

- (23) (Rape plus Fraternization) A specialist testified he was unconscious from alcohol when a sergeant anally sodomized him. [Guilty, 1 victim]

- (20) (Fraternization) A sergeant took advantage of a private first class and tried to force him to commit fellatio. Then the sergeant anally sodomized him. . . . [Guilty, 1 victim]

- (17) (Fraternization) A sergeant and a captain had a homosexual affair.

- (11) [HIV+, had sex anyway] An AIDS-positive sergeant had anal and oral sex with 3 soldiers junior in rank and with one civilian. [Guilty, 4 victims]

- (21) (Fraternization, HIV+) An HIV-positive sergeant had oral and anal sex with an officer. He also entered a restroom located on Fort Hood, Texas and masturbated in the presence of another enlisted man, who also masturbated.

- (99) Two lesbians, a specialist and a staff sergeant, were lovers. They lived in government quarters with the staff sergeant's child. The staff sergeant tried to end the relationship, and the specialist knifed the sergeant in the groin. [Guilty, 1 victim]

- (100) The case of Col. Modesto, known as the "tooth fairy," is perhaps the most bizarre and instructive of all those chronicled by Col. Black. Col. Modesto was an oral surgeon at Ft. Carson, Colorado and well-known in the local gay community. In fact, he often performed in drag at area gay bars. He also went about in women's clothing and had even exposed himself to women in a local laundromat. A drug user, he was able to avoid detection through connections with the non-commissioned officer in charge of urinalysis. His activities came to light following a "troubling" security investigation involving Modesto, the non-commissioned officer, two servicemen working in "sensitive positions at NORAD," and an Army counterintelligence agent. After Modesto was convicted of conduct unbecoming an officer, local gay rights activists claimed he was the victim of a "witch hunt."

When I heard about Col. Black's study, I realized that these case histories, which numbered over 100, could supply Army experts with the raw data for a significant analysis of criminal homosexual activity in their midst. When I learned that no such analysis was planned, I urged Col. Black to consider the possibility. I suggested that as a comparison group they use the total set of sex crimes for the same four years—heterosexual as well as homosexual. Unfortunately, it was too late to obtain data for the full four-year period. Consequently, by May 28, 1993, William S. Fulton, Jr., Clerk of the Court, had compiled a list of all the sex offense convictions for the fiscal year 1992. These 365 cases included 22 who were separated for homosexuality.

Of the 111 cases of child molestation, 13 (or 11.7 percent) were committed by homosexuals. Overall, homosexuals made up 22 out of 365 (or 6.0 percent) of all the sex-crime convictions. Col. Black's May 27, 1993 report estimated that about 1 percent of those in the Army were homosexual. It thus appears that homosexuals were disproportionately involved with children—on the face of it, over 12 times more apt to molest them. Also, since they represented 6 percent of the sex-crime cases, it would appear that homosexuals are over 6 times more apt to engage in sexual acts in violation of the UCMJ than are heterosexuals.

In addition, 29 (i.e., 29 percent) of the homosexual events for which court martials were held occurred in the barracks, 6 in the latrine, 3 in the shower. 89 (84 percent) of the cases involved a non-consenting victim. Of those who had homosexual relations with soldiers, 40 out of 50 (or 78 percent) were forcible (i.e., rape), and of those with children, 25 (46 percent) were with their own child or an adopted child, and 29 (54 percent) with a child or children of others.

It is also interesting to note that "fraternization" was a serious issue in 31 of 50 cases involving adults (i.e., 62 percent). This should come as no surprise, since the Army is among the most hierarchical institutions in American society, and therefore more open to the abuse of authority.

This study, which Col. Black released to the press in June of 1993, gave flesh-and-blood reality to the fears that many veterans had expressed about the proposal to lift the ban. Here for the first time was a grim history of the question—names, dates, explicit details, penalties meted out. These cases defined at least three major areas of concern.

First, a large proportion of homosexuals have been unable to control their desires while serving in the military. Despite the severe legal consequences of homosexual activity in the service—dishonorable discharges, prison terms—gay service members have seemed unwilling or unable to discipline themselves when presented with sexual opportunities. Their conduct has been reckless and obsessive. They have displayed little regard either for their own well-being or for the dignity and integrity of others.

Second, their chief victims have tended to be those who were under their authority—their own children, the children of relatives, their subordinates in the service. The Armed Forces have always operated by "chain of command." Both enlisted personnel and officers are taught to obey those above them. In battle, blind obedience is a necessity for survival, and any force or circumstance that introduces doubt or distrust is dangerous to the success of our military and hence to the survival of the nation. Col. Black's anecdotes suggest that with a growing homosexual presence, our Armed Forces are already compromised.

Third, force and violence play a significant role in most of the homosexual activities chronicled above. When physical force is not present in these cases, it is lurking in the shadows, ready to spring. Those who were convicted of homosexual crimes, almost always accomplished their ends by coercion. Most cases involved rape, either statutory or forcible. Small wonder that in the Army, where violence is the business of virtually all its members, sexually obsessive people should accomplish their ends through the exercise of force, either actual or implied. As noted in chapter 1, homosexuals are a violent lot; this tendency is clearly illustrated by Col. Black's detailed report, just as it was in the Family Research Institute study.

CONCLUSION

What can analysts conclude from an examination of these studies? In addition to the points already discussed, there are at least two disturbing trends evident here.

First, in the living memory of those who have served in our Armed Forces, homosexuality has posed significant problems—from World War II to Korea to Vietnam to Operation Desert Storm. The record reveals combat incidents that have compromised security and threatened the survival of our troops in the field—corruptions of the very idea of chain of command, intolerable disruptions of barracks life, graphic incidents of forcible rape, the systematic abuse of subordinates and children, and the destruction of morale in entire military units. This is no hypothetical scenario outlining a potential danger; this is what happened according to the best recollections of those who have actually served. So if in the future our Armed Forces are to be staffed by openly homosexual recruits, then we must be prepared to endure much more of the same.

Second, in recent years homosexuals in the U.S. military service have been more brazen and more organized in their activities. In part, this can be explained in terms of the effect of the gay rights movement on all segments of American society. In recent years, gay rights organizations have begun to focus on the military ban and are urging those already in uniform to assert themselves and to affirm their sexual orientation. The result: a number of court challenges and a great deal more openly homosexual activity among service members, as evidenced by newspaper headlines over the past several years.

However, this increase of activity can also be explained in terms of the establishment and expansion of a homosexual network inside our Armed Forces—an organization within an organization, with its own secret membership, its own goals, its own rules, its own covert strategy. This network is growing in strength as the controversy over the ban reaches a climax. If the ban is dropped, then it is conceivable, even likely, that we will see a huge influx of homosexuals into our service branches and a sudden and dramatic growth of the network. This is the unvoiced fear that many military leaders now entertain.

Well they might. Such a network is not without historical precedent. One of the most durable of these occurred in Egypt

during the 13th century, when the Mamelukes, a mercenary war-
rior class, were imported by the Egyptians to fight their wars.
The Mamelukes, after defeating Egypt's enemies, turned on
the civilian authority and gained control of the nation. They
ruled for 500 years, and were in power when the young
Napolean led a French force into that ancient realm. By the
time he arrived, as J. Christopher Herold[4] reports in *The Age
of Napoleon,* the Mamelukes "down to the last man, practiced
homosexuality" (p. 70) and were unable to replenish their
ranks except by buying or capturing little boys.

The Imperial German Army prior to World War I was severely subverted by a homosexual network. Indeed, there are
those who argue that Germany's defeat at the hands of the
Allies can be traced to that particular weakness in the German
military establishment.

Ironically, the same problem cropped up again in the early
days of the Third Reich, when Ernst Roehm, commander of
the infamous Brown Shirts, gathered around him a large and
militant homosexual cadre. This network soon constituted a
formidable counterforce to civilian authority. Indeed, it was
the predominately homosexual Brown Shirts who provided
Hitler with the brute force necessary to support his rise to
power.

It would be irresponsible to suggest that the growth of a
homosexual network has hopelessly compromised our military
forces. Such is not the case. However, these studies clearly
indicate that the presence of a network designed to circumvent
military law and promote illegal sexual activity has already
damaged morale and efficiency. This fact alone should disturb
those who are concerned for the future safety of our nation,
particularly in view of the policy ultimately adopted by the
Clinton Administration.

That policy was announced on July 19, four days after the
promised date of July 15, and the President looked like a cheater
facing the school honor council as he addressed a grim-lipped
military audience at Fort McNair's National Defense University.

He spent a good deal of time reciting gay-rights clichés belied by the military experiences contained in the studies summarized above. As reported by the *Washington Post:*

> He suggested that if the military leadership know homosexuals personally, their opposition to removing the ban would ease. He cited the honorable service of homosexuals in the U. S. Armed Forces, foreign militaries and other occupations. He noted that the American military had struggled without harm through other momentous changes and made the case that if the services did not act on the gay issue, the courts would.

Had he read any of the careful studies prepared by opponents of lifting the ban, he would have realized how empty and wrong-headed his arguments were.

As for the policy itself, the President did not exactly issue an executive order, but rather "ordered Secretary Aspin to issue a directive." The directive consisted of the following provisions:

> One, service men and women will be judged based on their conduct not their sexual orientation.
>
> Two, therefore, the practice, now six months old, of not asking about sexual orientation in the enlistment procedure will continue.
>
> Three, an open statement by a service member that he or she is a homosexual will recreate [sic] a rebuttable presumption that he or she intends to engage in prohibited conduct, but the service member will be given an opportunity to refute that presumption. In other words, to demonstrate that he or she intends to live by the rules of conduct that apply in the military service.
>
> And four, all provisions of the Uniform Code of Military Justice will be enforced in an even-handed manner as regards both heterosexuals and homosexuals. And, thanks to the policy provisions agreed by the Joint Chiefs, there will be a decent regard to the legitimate privacy and associational rights of all service members. Just as is the case under current policy, unacceptable conduct, either heterosexual or homosexual, will be unacceptable 24 hours a day, seven days a week, from the time a recruit joins the service until the day he or she is discharged, Now, as in the past, every member of our military will be required to comply with the Uni-

form Code of Military Justice, which is federal law and military
regulations, at all time and in all places. (*Washington Post,* July
20, 1993, p. A-12)

Section Three clearly removes the risk to gay service personnel of speaking out about their homosexuality, since now they
are permitted to deny that such an assertion means they intend
to commit sodomy. Section Four allows homosexual service
personnel to frequent gay bars, to move in homosexual circles,
perhaps even to patronize bathhouses, since the Joint Chiefs
have apparently promised not to police any such gatherings.
Together these clauses virtually lift the ban against homosexuality in the military, and make it all but impossible to investigate allegations of misconduct or to prosecute violations.

And dropped from the policy was the statement that homosexuality is incompatible with military service. As soon as the
President read these four points, supporters of the ban knew
that they had lost everything.

The President went on to thank the Joint Chiefs of Staff for
their support in devising this policy, singling out General
Colin Powell by name. Powell certainly deserved the presidential thanks. He was the key figure in the collapse of resistance.
With only a few months to go until retirement—and with his
extraordinary stature as the first Black to chair the Joint
Chiefs—had he wanted to defend the ban, he could have done
so successfully and carried the Congress and the American
people with him. Instead he chose to compromise the strength
of the U. S. fighting force.

The other Joint Chief's of Staff must also share in the
blame. All—with the possible exception of General McPeak
of the Air Force—must have opposed the lifting of the ban.
All looked robotic as they sat alongside General Powell and
listened to the President justify this patent political payoff. All
failed to speak out in opposition or to resign in protest.

These military men are not the only group, however, to allow the prancing, screeching gay rights activists to run rough-
shod over them. The Republican leadership likewise turned

tail and ran. No loud, clear voice was raised in opposition. No presidential hopeful called a news conference to protest and promise a reversal of policy in 1996. Indeed, a few days before the President made his momentous announcement, Haley Barbour, the oily chairman of the Republican National Committee, announced that the homosexual Log Cabin Clubs would be welcomed into the Party with open arms. The battle seemingly had ended, in large measure because no opposing force had even taken the field.

Many Americans, bewildered by the struggle, shrugged their shoulders and turned back to their usual preoccupations—making a buck, television, beer drinking, baseball. "Well, that's the end of that," they said.

But they were wrong. It was only the beginning. Already the homosexual movement was preparing for the next assault. Half-mad with anger that they didn't get everything the President had promised during the election campaign, they were making plans to punish him. There would be wild, orgiastic protests—complete with obscene placards and vulgar posturing. There would also be law suits, challenging the policy. On the weekend before the presidential announcement, one gay rights leader, anticipating the decision, told a radio interrogator: "We'll litigate and litigate and litigate. It will cost the government millions and millions of dollars."

And even as they were promising revenge and a new assault on the military policy (an assault guaranteed to win new concessions), other developments clouded the future:

The Supreme Court of Hawaii handed down a ruling that favored homosexual marriages in that State.

The Supreme Court of Colorado refused to lift a District judge's injunction that prevented that State from implementing Amendment Two, a measure passed by a majority of voters that struck down local gay rights ordinances.

And in Fairfax County, Virginia, distraught guidance counselors reported that it was so chic to be homosexual in the local schools that heterosexual girls were pretending to be bisexual because, as one sixteen-year-old put it: "For people who are heterosexual, it's to protect themselves from just being normal."

So it looks like it's going to be the Gay 90s, whether the rest of us like it or not.

NOTES

Chapter 1: Science, Religion, and Myth

1. Aberle, S. D., Comer G. W. *Twenty-Five Years of Sex Research: History of the National Research Council Committee for Research in Problems of Sex, 1922–1947.* 1953 Philadelphia: Saunders.

2. Kallman, F. J. Comparative twin study on the genetic aspects of male homosexuality. *Journal Nervous; Mental Disorders* 1952;115:283–298.

3. Wardell Pomeroy *Dr. Kinsey and the Institute for Sex Research* New York: 2972

4. Ibid.

5. Simon R From the Editor *Family Therapy Net-worker* 1991;15:2.

6. December 16, 1991, p. 43.

7. November 13, 1991, p. A-1.

8. November 29, 1991, p. A-3

9. The studies on the prevalence of homosexuality are reviewed and detailed in Cameron P. and Cameron K. The prevalence of homosexuality. *Psychological Reports.* (1993, in press). Some that should have been known to Bryant Welch are cited and referenced below.

10. Schofield, M. *The sexual behavior of young people.* 1965 London: Cox and Wyman.

11. Gebhard, P. H. "Incidence of Overt Homosexuality in the United States and Western Europe." *National Institutes of Mental Health Task Force on Homosexuality: Final Report and Background Papers.* 2972 Rockville., MD: NIMH, 22–9.

12. Klassen, A. D., Williams, C. J. and Levitt, E. E. *Sex and morality in the U.S. Middletown,* CT: Wesleyan Univ. Press, 1989.

13. Ubell, E. Sex in America Today. *Parade Magazine* October 28, 1984.

14. Stiffman, A. R. and Earls, F. "Behavior risks for human immunodeficiency virus infection in adolescent medial patients." *Pediatrics* 1990:85:303–310.

15. Gordin, F. M., Gilbert, C., Hawley, H. P., and Willoughby, A. "Prevalence of human immunodeficiency virus in unselected hospital admissions: implications for mandatory testing and universal precautions." *Journal Infectious Diseases* 1990:161: 14–7.

16. Johnson, A. M., Wadsworth, J., Elliott, P., Prior, L., Wallace, P., Blower, S., Webb, N. L., Heald, G. I., Miller, D. L., Adler, M. W., and Anderson, R. M. A pilot study of lifestyle in a random sample of the population of Great Britain. *AIDS* 1989:3;135–41.

17. Forman, D., and Chilvers, C. "Sexual behavior of young and middle aged men in England and Wales" *British Medical Journal* 1989:298:1137–42.

18. Ross, M. W. "Prevalence of risk factors for human immunodeficiency virus infection in the Australian population." *Medical Journal of Australia* 1988:149:362–5.

19. Sundet, J. M., Kvalem, L. L., Magnus, P., and Bakketeig, L. S. Prevalence of risk-prone sexual behavior in the general population of Norway. In *The global impact of AIDS*. NY: Liss, 1990.

20. Schmidt, K. W., Krasnik, A., Brendstrup, E., Zoffman, H., and Larsen, S. O. "Occurrence of sexual behavior related to the risk of HIV-infection" *Danish Medical Bulletin* 1989:36:84–8.

21. Michael, R. T., Laumann, E. O., Gagnon, J. H., and Smith, T. W. "Number of sex partners and potential risk of sexual exposure to human immunodeficiency virus" *Morbidity and Mortality Weekly Report* 1988:37:565–8.

22. Hingson, R. W., Strunin, L., Berlin, B. M., and Heeren, T. "Beliefs about AIDS, use of alcohol and drugs, and unprotected sex among Massachusetts adolescents." *American Journal Public Health* 1990:80:295–9.

23. Forman, D., and Chilvers, C. "Sexual behavior of young and middle aged men in England and Wales" *British Medical Journal* 1989:298:1137–42.

24. Kotloff, K. L., Tacket, C. O., Lemens, J. D., Wasserman, S. S., Cowan, J.E., Bridwell, M. W., and Quinn, T. C. "Assessment of the prevalence and risk factors for human immunodeficiency virus type 1 (HIV-I) infection among college students using three survey methods." *American Journal Epidemiology* 1991:133:2–8.

25. Upchurch, D. M., Brady, W. E., Reichart, C. A., and Hook, E. W. "Behavioral contributions to acquisition of gonorrhea in patients attending an inner city sexually transmitted disease clinic." *Journal of Infectious Diseases* 1990:161:938–41.

26. Smith, T. W. "Adult sexual behavior in 1989: number of partners, frequency of intercourse and risk of AIDS." *Family Planning Perspectives.* 1991:23:202–7.

27. *National household seroprevalence survey feasibility study final report.* RTI/4190–01 April 30, 1990.

28. Dawson, D. A. "AIDS knowledge and attitudes" [various dates] Advance Data, National Center for Health Statistics: DHHS Pub. No. (PHS) 88–1_250, nos. 160, 161, 163, 176, 183, 193.

29. Harry, J. "Sexual orientation as destiny." *Journal of Homosexuality* 1984:10:111–24.

30. Bell, A. P., Weinberg, M. S., and Hammersmith, S. K. *Sexual preference: statistical appendix.* Bloomington: Indiana University press, 1981.

31. Klassen, Williams, and Levitt, *Sex and morality.*

32. Cameron, P. and Ross, K. P. "Social psychological aspects of the Judeo-Christian stance toward homosexuality." *Journal of Psychology and Theology,* 1981:9:40–57.

33. Cameron, P., Cameron, K., and Proctor, K. "Effect of homosexuality upon public health and social order." *Psychological Reports* 1989:64:1167–79.

34. Hooker, E. "The Adjustment of the Male Overt Homosexual," *Journal of Projective Techniques,* 1957:21:18–31; "Male Homosexuality in the Rorschach," *Journal of Projective Techniques,* 1958:22:33–52.

35. "A Preliminary Analysis of Group Behavior of Homosexuals," *Journal of Psychology,* 1956:42: 217–25.

36. "Homosexuality:Compatible with Full Health," *British Medical Journal,* 1988 297:308–9.

37. "Reflections on Homosexuality: Sodom and Begorrah," in *National Review,* April 29,1991, 35–38.

38. Quoted by R. Schoch in "California Q and A," in *California Monthly,* April, 1990, p. 9.

39. Amici curiae brief, in *Bowers v Hardwick,* 1986.

40. Weinberg, G. *Society and the Healthy Homosexual* NY: St Martin's, 1972, preface.

41. *Washington Times,* May 20, 1993, A8.

42. Corey, L. and Holmes, K. K. "Sexual transmission of Hepatitis A in homosexual men" *New England Journal of Medicine* 1980:302:435–38.

43. Bell, A. and Weinberg, M. *Homosexualities* NY: Simon &Schuster 1978. Also see Beral, V. *et al* "Risk of Kaposi's sarcoma and sexual practices associated with faecal contact in homosexual or bisexual men with AIDS" *Lancet* 1992:339:632–35.

44. Cameron, P. *et al* "Sexual orientation and sexually transmitted disease. *Nebraska Med J,* 1985:70:292–99; "Effect of homosexuality upon public health and social order" *Psychol Rpts* 1989, 64, 1167–79.

45. Corey and Holmes, "Sexual transmission of Hepatitis."

46. Ibid.

47. Manligit, G. W., *et al* "Chronic immune stimulation by sperm alloantigens." *J Amer Med Assn* 2984:251:237–38.

48. Cecil Adams, "The Straight Dope," *The Reader* (Chicago) 3/28/86) [Adams writes authoritatively on counter-culture material, his column is carried in many alternative newspapers across the U.S. and Canada]

49. Corey and Holmes, "Sexual transmission of Hepatitis."

50. Elford, J., *et al* "Kaposi's sarcoma and insertive rimming." *Lancet* 1992:339:938.

51. Jay, K., and Young, A. *The gay report* NY: Summit, 1979.

52. Beral, V. *et al* "Risk of Kaposi's sarcoma."

53. McKusick, L., *et al* "AIDS and sexual behaviors reported by gay men in San Francisco" *Amer J Pub Health*1985: 75:493–96.

54. Gebhard, P., and Johnson, A. *The Kinsey data* NY: Saunders,1979.

55. Jay and Young, *The gay report*.

56. Beral, V. *et al* "Risk of Kaposi's sarcoma."

57. Gebhard, P., and Johnson, A. *The Kinsey data*.

58. Jay and Young, *The gay report*.

59. Beral, V. *et al* "Risk of Kaposi's sarcoma."

60. Gebhard and Johnson, *The Kinsey data*.

61. Jaffee, H., *et al* "National case-control study of Kaposi's sarcoma" *Annals Internal Med* 1983:99:145–51.

62. *USA Today* 11/21/84.

63. McKusick, L., *et al* "AIDS and sexual behaviors."

64. Rodriguez-Pichardo, A., *et al* "Sexually transmitted diseases in homosexual males in Seville, Spain" *Genitourin Med* 1990:66;423–427.

65. Dritz, S., and Braff "Sexually transmitted typhoid fever." *New Engl J Med* 1977:296:1359–60.

66. Beral, V. *et al* "Risk of Kaposi's sarcoma."

67. Dritz, S. "Medical aspects of homosexuality." *New Engl J Med* 1980:302:463–4.

68. Ibid.

69. "CDC Hepatitis A among homosexual men—United States, Canada, and Australia". *MMWR* 1992:41:155–64.

70. Christenson, B. *et al*, "An epidemic outbreak of hepatitis A among homosexual men in Stockholm" *Amer J Epidemiology* 1982:116:599–607.

71. Schechter, M. T. *et al* "Changes in sexual behavior and fear of AIDS" *Lancet,* 1984:1:1293.

72. Beral, V. *et al* "Risk of Kaposi's sarcoma." Also see Jay and Young, *The gay report*.

73. Jaffee, H., *et al* "National case-control study of Kaposi's sarcoma"

74. Quinn, T. C., *et al* "The polymicrobial origin of intestinal infection in homosexual men" *New Engl J Med* 1983:309:576–82.

75. Biggar, R. J. "Low T-lymphocyte ratios in homosexual men" *J Amer Med Ass* 1984:251:1441–46; *Wall Street Journal* 7/18/91, B1.

76. "CDC HIV/AIDS" *Surveillance* February 1993.

77. Corey and Holmes "Sexual transmission of Hepatitis A."

78. Biggar "Low T-lymphocyte ratios."

79. Beral, V. *et al* "Risk of Kaposi's sarcoma."

80. "CDC HIV/AIDS" *Surveillance* February 1993.

81. Cameron, P. "Is homosexuality disproportionately associated with murder?" Paper presented at Midwestern Psychological Assn, Chicago, 1983.

82. Swigert, V. L., *et al* "Sexual homicide: social, psychological, and legal aspects" *Archives Sexual Behavior* 1976;3:391–401.

83. Before the Law and Justice Committee of the Washington State Senate (12/15/89).

84. Gebhard, P., and Johnson, A. *The Kinsey data* NY: Saunders, 1979.

85. Jay, K., and Young, A. *The gay report* NY: Summit, 1979. Also see Cameron, P., *et al* "Effect of homosexuality upon public health and social order" *Psychol Rpts* 1989, 64, 1167–79.

86. *Crime and the Human Mind.*Columbia U. Press, 1944 p. 122.

87. Cameron, P., *et al* "Effect of homosexuality upon public health."

88. *Out Front* p. 10 8/5/92.

89. e.g., *Sparticus, Bob Damron's Address Book*

90. Smith, D., and Rodgerson, G. "Free the spanner men" *Gay Times*, April 1993, p. 8.

91. Gebhard and Johnson, *The Kinsey data*. Also see Jay and Young, *The gay report*. Also see Cameron, P., *et al* "Effect of homosexuality upon public health."

92. Cameron, P., *et al* "Sexual orientation and sexually transmitted disease." *Nebraska Medical Journal* 1985:70;292–299.

93. *History of AIDS* Princeton: Princeton Univ. Press, 1990, p. 19.

94. Gebhard and Johnson, *The Kinsey data*. Also see *Out Front* p. 10 8/5/92.

95. *History of AIDS.*

96. Cameron, P., *et al* "Effect of homosexuality upon public health." Also see Cameron, P., *et al* "Sexual orientation."

97. Newell, A., *et al* "Sexually transmitted diseases and anal papillomas" *Brit Medical J* 1992:305:1435-6.

98. Harlow, C. W. "Female victims of violent crime." US Dept Justice January 1991, NCJ-126826. Ronet Bachman, "Crime victimization in city, suburban, and rural areas: A national crime victimization survey report." US Dept Justice 1992 NCJ-135943.

99. Forman, B. "Reported male rape" *Victimology* 1983;7:235-6.

100. Lipscomb, G. H., *et al* "Male victims of sexual assault" *J American Medical Assn,* 1992;267:3064-66.

101. Gebhard and Johnson, *The Kinsey data.* Also see Harlow, "Female victims of violent crime." Also see Forman, "Reported male rape."

102. Harlow, "Female victims of violent crime."

103. Bell, A. P., *et. al. Sexual Preference: Statistical Appendix* Bloomington: IN Univ Press, 1981.

104. Gebhard and Johnson, *The Kinsey data.* Also see e.g., *Sparticus, Bob Damron's Address Book.*

105. Cameron, P. "Homosexual molestation of children/sexual interaction of teacher and pupil." *Psychological Reports* 1985;57:1227-36.

106. Bell, A. P., *et. al. Sexual Preference.*

107. Schwartz, M. F., and Masters, W. H. "The Masters and Johnson treatment program for dissatisfied homosexual men." *Am J Psychiatry* 1984;141:173-182.

108. Goyer, P. F., and Eddleman, H. C. "Same-sex rape of nonincarcerated men." *Am J Psychiatry* 1984:141:576-79.

109. "FBI releases stats on hate crimes." *Washington Blade* 1/1/93, p. 1.

110. Cameron, P., Playfair, W., and Wellum, S. "The lifespan of homosexuals." Paper presented at Eastern Psychological Assn Convention, April 17, 1993.

111. Paul, W., p. 302. In W. Paul, Weinrich, J. D., Gonsiorck, J. C., and Hotvedt, M. E. (Eds) *Homosexuality: Social, Psychological, and Biological Issues.* Sage: Beverly Hills, 1982.

112. *Daily Oklahoman* 10/2/92.

113. Cameron, P., and Cameron, K. "The prevalence of homosexuality." *Psychological Reports,* 1993, in press.

114. Cameron, P., *et al* "Child molestation and homosexuality." *Psychological Reports* 1986:58:327-337.

115. Siegel, J. M., *et al* "The prevalence of childhood sexual assault" *Amer J Epidemiology* 1987; 126: 1141-53.

116. *Los Angeles Times* August 25,26 1985.

117. Schofield, M. *The Sexual Behavior of Young People.* Boston: Little, Brown, 1965.

118. Cameron, P. "Homosexual molestation of children/sexual inter-action of teacher and pupil." *Psychological Reports* 1985;57:1227–36.

119. Freund, K., *et al* "Pedophilia and heterosexuality vs. homosexuality." *J Sex and Marital Therapy* 1984;10:193–200.

120. Quoted by A. Bass, *Boston Globe* 8/8/88.

121. "Child molesting" *Sexual Behavior* 1971;1:16–24.

122. Interview with Dr. Raymond A. Knight at his presentation, "Differential prevalence of personality disorders in rapists and child molesters," at Eastern Psychological Assn Convention, New York 4/12/91.

123. Wasserman, J., *et al* "Adolescent Sex Offenders—Vermont, 1984." *J American Medical Assn*, 1986;255:181–2.

124. Marshall, W. L., *et al* "Early onset and deviant sexuality in child molesters." *J Interpersonal Violence* 1991;6:323–336.

125. Bradford, J. M. W., *et al* "The heterogeneity/homogeneity of pedophilia" *Psychiatr J Univ Ottawa* 1988;13:217–226.

126. Walmsley, R., and White, K. "Sexual offenses, Consent and Sentencing," Home Office Research Study No. 54, HMSO, London, 1979, pp. 30–32.

127. Rees, J. T., and Usill, H. V. *They Stand Apart* 1956 NY: Macmillan, pp. 28–29.

128. Gebhard, P. H., and Johnson, A. B. *The Kinsey Data: Marginal Tabulations of the 1938–1963 Interviews Conducted by the Institute for Sex Research.* NY: Saunders, 1979.

129. Bell, A. P., and Weinberg, M. S. *Homosexualities: A Study of Diversity Among Men and Women.* NY: Simon and Schuster, 1978.

130. Jay, K., and Young, A. *The gay report* NY: Summit, 1979.

131. Dr. Edward Brongersma as quoted by Tom O'Carroll in *Paedophilia: The Radical Case* Boston: Alyson, 1982.

132. Abel, G. G., *et al* "Self-reported sex crimes of nonincarcerated paraphiliacs." *J Interpersonal Violence* 1987:2;3–25.

133. Schofield, M. *Sociological Aspects of Homosexuality* Boston:Little, Brown, 1965.

134. Gebhard and Johnson, *The Kinsey Data.*

135. McGeorge, J. "Sexual assaults on children" *Medical Science and the Law* 1964:4:245–253.

136. Hechinger, G., and Hechinger, F. M. "Should homosexuals be allowed to teach?" *McCalls's* 1978:105(6), 100ft.

137. Paper at the 24th International Congress Psychology, Sydney, Australia, August 1988.

138. Cameron, P., *et al* "Child molestation and homosexuality."

139. Cameron and Cameron, "The prevalence of homosexuality."

140. Interview with New Orleans street-youth worker Paul Henkels January 27, 1993.

141. Bigras, J., *et al* "Severe paternal sexual abuse in early childhood and systematic aggression against the family and the institution" *Canadian J Psychiatry* 1991:36:527–529. Also see Oates, K. R., and Tong, L. "Sexual abuse of children: an area with room for professional reforms." *Medical J Australia* 1987:147;544–548.

142. 1986–7, 13, #2,3, pgs. 89–107. 30. Stonewall Union Reports February 1991.

143. Verified by telephone interview with the Dutch Embassy, August 5, 1993.

144. 1910 letter to Sandor Ferenczi.

145. *Wall Street Journal* 4/21/93 A6.

146. Letter to the New York Times 4/25/93, E16.

147. Bell, A. P., and Weinberg, M. S. *Homosexualities: A Study of Diversity Among Men and Women.* New York: Simon and Schuster, 1978. and Hammersmith, S. K. *Sexual Preference: Its Development in Men and Women.* Bloomington: Indiana University Press, 1981.

148. Letter to the New York Times 4/25/93, E16.

149. Dixon, J. K. "The commencement of bisexual activity in swinging married women over age thirty." *J Sex Research,* 1984, 20, 72–90.

150. Cameron, P., Cameron, K., and Proctor, K. "Homosexuals in the Armed Forces," *Psychological Reports,* 1988, 62, 211–219; "Effect of homosexuality upon public health and social order." *Psychol Rpts,* 1989, 64, 1167–79.

151. Dixon, J. K. "The commencement of bisexual activity in swinging married women over age thirty." *J Sex Research,* 1984, 20, 72–90.

152. Cameron, P., Cameron, K., and Proctor, K. "Homosexuals in the Armed Forces," *Psychological Reports,* 1988, 62, 211–219; "Effect of homosexuality upon public health and social order." *Psychol Rpts,* 1989, 64, 1167–79.

153. For other results of this study, see footnotes 33, 44, 81, 92, and 105.

154. Ibid.

Chapter 3: The Federal Government Joins the Revolution

1. Remafedi, Resnick, Blum, and Harris, "Demography of Sexual Orientation in Adolescents," *Pediatrics,* 89, 1992, 714–721

2. Margaret Fischl, et. al., "Heterosexual Transmission of Human Immunodeficiency virus (HIV): Relationship of Sexual Practices to Seroconversion," *III International Conference on AIDS,* June 1–5, 1987, Abstracts Volume, p. 178.

Chapter 4: Military Retreat

1. Mary Ann Humphrey, *My Country, My Right to Serve* (New York, 1990), p. xxiii)].

Chapter 5: An Empirical View of Gays in the Military

1. Humphrey, M. A. *My Country, My Right to Serve: Experiences of Gay Men and Women in the Military, World War II to the Present.* Harper Collins: NY 1990.

2. Ellen Goodman, "Mail suggests men's biggest concern over gays in military: being ogled" *Omaha World-Herald,* January 25, 1993.

3. Ibid.

4. New York: American Heritage Publishing Co., 1963.